CW01023905

Ian Conrich is Director of the Centre for New Zealand Studies at Birkbeck, University of London. His books include *The Cinema of John Carpenter: The Technique of Terror* (2004), *Film's Musical Moments* (2006), and *Contemporary New Zealand Cinema* (I.B.Tauris, 2008).

Horror Zone

The Cultural Experience of

Contemporary Horror Cinema

Edited by Ian Conrich

I.B. TAURIS
LONDON · NEW YORK

Published in 2010 by I.B.Tauris & Co Ltd
6 Salem Road, London W2 4BU
175 Fifth Avenue, New York NY 10010
www.ibtauris.com

Distributed in the United States and Canada Exclusively by Palgrave Macmillan
175 Fifth Avenue, New York NY 10010

Selection and editorial matter copyright
© 2010 Ian Conrich
Individual chapters copyright © 2010
Stacey Abbott, Linda Badley, Mick Broderick, Brigid Cherry, Ian Conrich, Joan
Hawkins, Matt Hills, Ernest Mathijs, Jay McRoy, Tamao Nakahara, Angela Ndalianis,
Julian Petley, Jeffrey Sconce, Angela Marie Smith, Estella Tincknell

The right of Ian Conrich to be identified as the editor of this work has been asserted by
him in accordance with the Copyright, Designs and Patents Act 1988.

All rights reserved. Except for brief quotations in a review, this book, or any part thereof,
may not be reproduced, stored in or introduced into a retrieval system, or transmitted, in
any form or by any means, electronic, mechanical, photocopying, recording or otherwise,
without the prior written permission of the publisher.

ISBN: 978 1 84885 262 4 (HB)
978 1 84885 151 1 (PB)

A full CIP record for this book is available from the British Library
A full CIP record is available from the Library of Congress

Library of Congress Catalog Card Number: available

Printed and bound in Great Britain by CPI Antony Rowe, Chippenham,
from camera-ready copy edited and supplied by the editor

FSC
Mixed Sources
Product group from well-managed
forests and other controlled sources
Cert no. SGS-COC-2953
www.fsc.org
© 1996 Forest Stewardship Council

Contents

Part 1: Industry, Technology and the New Media

Part 2: Audiences, Fans and Consumption

Part 3: Manufacture and Design

Part 4: Boundaries of Horror

Illustrations

Acknowledgements

I would like to thank the contributors for their continued support and Julian Petley, in particular, who was there in the early stages. This collection benefited immensely from the involvement of Jodie Robson, and Philippa Brewster and Jayne Ansell, at I.B.Tauris, were invaluable in their commitment. Finally, a very big thank you to Tory Straker, for assisting with a crucial part of the book's preparation.

Introduction

Horror Zone
The Cultural Experience of Contemporary Horror Cinema

IAN CONRICH

The horror film is arguably the most robust, pliable, and successful of genres within contemporary cinema. As a popular form, its pervasiveness has seen it succeed as a modern series of blockbusters (*The Mummy* [1999–2008], and *Hellboy* [2004–2008] films), independent breakthroughs (*The Blair Witch Project* [1999], and *The Sixth Sense* [1999]), films for children and young adults (*Coraline* [2009], and *Twilight* [2008]), and innovative international arthouse releases (*El labertino del fauno* [*Pan's Labyrinth*, 2006], and *Låt den rätte komma in* [*Let the Right One In*, 2008]). Horror, like other major genres, works in cycles and there is a definite return within the contemporary form to its modern origins and to the classics of the horror new wave of the 1970s and 1980s, with recent remakes and sequels of *The Texas Chainsaw Massacre* (1974), *It's Alive* (1974), *The Hills Have Eyes* (1977), *Dawn of the Dead* (1978), *Halloween* (1978), *The Amityville Horror* (1979), *Friday the 13th* (1980), and *The Fog* (1980). The American remakes industry has in addition turned to foreign horrors for ideas, with English language versions of *Let the Right One In* and *Martyrs* (2008) scheduled, and Asian films such as *Ringu* (*The Ring*, 1998), *Ju-on* (*The Grudge*, 2002), *Gin gwai* (*The Eye*, 2002), *Geoul sokeuro* (*Into the Mirror*, 2003), and *Shutter* (2004), already reproduced.

Any reflection on the drive of the contemporary horror film for establishing remakes could conclude that the genre is saturated, imitative, and lacking progression. But this would be overlooking the multifarious nature of contemporary horror and the ways in which it has developed over the last thirty years into a global and multimedia phenomenon. Contemporary horror cinema provides a transcultural experience, one that demonstrates the striking presence of the genre globally and the levels of influence and crossovers between different national forms and identities.

The horror film has always had an international dimension, with European examples of production peaking in particular in the 1960s. It is, though, the spread of European countries releasing significant horror films now that is noticeable as well as the emergence of horror new waves from countries such as Spain and France. Vital horror new waves from Japan and South Korea have also emerged, with the burgeoning horror film industry in Asia effectively combining traditional stories and myths with comic book creations and the aesthetics of new media digital technologies.

The dawn of the video age some twenty-five years earlier, which marked a dramatic adjustment in the non-theatrical consumption of films in general, coincided with the early years of the horror new wave. It is not surprising that the horror genre experienced a surge in production and interest, as the video industry sought to establish itself partly through sensational films and lurid video covers. The ability then for video rental shops to frequently bypass the age restrictions set for theatrical releases – in the UK, for instance, videos did not carry certificates and a minimum age for viewers until 1985 – added to the appeal of rental horror as a dicephalous cultural form. In many instances the horror videos were 'for adults only', yet they were everywhere on the urban and suburban high streets, easily reached and borrowed by under-age youths. It is significant for a cyclical genre that many of the auteurs who were most associated with the horror new wave – John Carpenter, David Cronenberg, George A. Romero, and Joe Dante – had been inspired by the films of the Hollywood studios, and post-war B movies and experimental filmmaking. Horror directors of the last ten years – such as Christopher Smith, Neil Marshall, Eli Roth and Rob Zombie – have subsequently been acknowledging their debt to the 1970s and 1980s and the horror films of the new wave and the video age.

In a digital age which fuels a culture of exchange and transfer, horror films have acquired greater ubiquity and are viewed on portable DVD players, on mobile phones, and over the Internet. The latter presents a supporting culture of discussion groups, fan appreciation, bloggers, independent reviewers, and online trailers, that have extended the connections of a horror community that was before most dependent on a print culture of fanzines and specialist magazines. The synergies between the horror film and popular culture can be observed in the post-war boom in horror comics, such as those from EC Comics – *Tales from the Crypt*, *The Haunt of Fear* and *The Vault of Horror* – which inspired the omnibus features of Amicus and the work of Romero and Carpenter. These synergies are enhanced in a contemporary cinema of interconnected multimedia industries, where horror films are developed from theme park rides (*The Haunted Mansion*, 2003) and theme park rides from horror films (*The Mummy* and *Saw* [2004–2009] series). Computer games are reconstructed into live action horror features (*Resident Evil* [2002–2007], *Silent Hill* [2006]), horror films emerge from cult comic books (*From Hell* [2001], and *Constantine* [2005]), from musicals (*Sweeney Todd: The Demon Barber of Fleet Street* [2007], and *Repo! The Genetic Opera* [2008]), and retro television (*The Addams Family*, 1991–1998), and inspire popular merchandise (the *Nightmare on Elm Street* [1984–2010], *Child's Play* [1988–2004], and *Scream* [1996–2000] series).

The experience of contemporary horror cinema is broad and it is the context, the culture and society, in which the films are produced, exhibited and viewed that is the focus of this collection. Horror films are presented and received in a heterogeneous manner, and this is not simply the regional and social differences. The films *My Bloody Valentine* (2009), and *The Final Destination* (2009), were made essentially for screening in 3D, with effects exploiting the extra dimension, but they were also exhibited in neighbouring venues in 2D and without the attraction of lethal objects 'breaking through' the screen and assaulting the audience. A film such as *Antichrist* (2009), has been shown in UK cinemas with – somewhat bizarrely, considering the story – added special 'parent and baby' screenings, a recent development which has also seen special 'autism friendly screenings' for films such as *Igor* (2008). Meanwhile, the development of horror film festivals for premiering and promoting new features to devoted and knowledgeable audiences has seen an explosion in cities and towns hosting gatherings that create a concentrated cultural environment. In the UK alone, there are now annual festivals in London, Edinburgh, Nottingham, Bradford and Aberystwyth (with the suitably named Abertoir festival). Such is the cross appeal of a core of contemporary horror that it can cater for both a subculture and the mainstream.

The strong presence of the horror film in contemporary culture has often been read as a reflection of a crisis in society. The horror film has been seen to peak at times of war, and during periods of economic, political, and moral exigency. And whilst other factors should be considered when contextualising the wave of horror films in the 1930s and 1970s, there is no doubt that some of the films and filmmakers were drawing on contemporary experience and social pressures. There should be some care when approaching texts in this way, but horror films in particular can act as effective cultural and social barometers and with recent productions there is a discernible occurrence of panic narratives, a horror cinema of abandonment, helplessness, and futility, a concentration on torture and extreme distress, and an inescapable, omnipotent force. In a post 9/11 global society, there is an increase within horror films in carnography, an unsettling obsession with assaulting the body in protracted and inventive ways, and an edginess to the depictions of human behaviour, where few can be trusted in a dystopian society. As this book seeks to address the cinema of contemporary horror, moving beyond the common approach of focusing just on the film text, articles within this collection will explore the cultural parameters and, especially in the last section, the boundaries and borders that these horror productions are pushing.

The concept for this book came from realising the need to consider in depth the contexts in which contemporary horror cinema has been operating. There has been a growth within cinema studies to look beyond the traditional approaches to the film text. In particular, within the large community of film researchers focused on the horror genre there has been, alongside the many conventional studies, significant work produced in addressing these new concerns.[1] However, none of the existing publications on the genre had brought together the different areas of this new research, or the prominent researchers who were exploring horror cinema as opposed to the horror film. This collection takes the mid 1970s as the starting point for a contemporary cinema that saw notable changes in both industrial practices and the content of horror films. There are four parts to the book – Industry, Technology and the New Media; Audiences, Fans and Consumption; Manufacture and Design; and Boundaries of Horror. Each section aims to give breadth to the central issues or exposure to the areas that have been absent from consideration within the studies of the horror genre.

The three articles in section one cover theme park rides, blockbusters, and independent video production, and present a wide-ranging consideration of the different experiences and cultural-economic factors – from big budget event movies to low-budget non-theatrical releases – found at contrasting ends of the entertainment industry. The collection opens with an article by Angela Ndalianis, which explores the modern-day renaissance of the theme park horror ride in relation to the historical presence of these attractions and their contemporary appeal. Nowadays, such rides have been in conjunction with major film productions – most noticeably, Universal Studios' *Mummy* horror film franchise, starring Brendan Fraser. For Ndalianis, the aspects of shared identity, image and narrative, that allow theme park rides to abstract or rebuild the original cinematic form for a physical machine-driven experience, demonstrate the cross-over ability of different entertainment structures. Moreover, these 'dark rides' promote an experience which can induce the bodily threat and reactions associated with a good horror film, which makes the genre an effective media for such synergies.

The productions that generate a franchise offer the greatest attraction to creators of theme park rides. Such horror films are predominantly part of the studio-based industry of event movies that have marked contemporary cinema, and been committed to exploiting the most from a concept. In the second contribution to this book, Stacey Abbott sees these horror blockbusters (*Bram Stoker's Dracula* [1992], *The Mummy*, and *Blade* [1998–2004] series of films), which became established in the 1990s, as functioning within a space previously dominated by star-driven action spectacles. Abbott argues that through two key periods in the 1990s, the horror movie moved into the mainstream with productions adapted from classic horror fiction, and from comic books, aimed at maximising appeal with controlled seasonal releases, aggressive marketing campaigns, lower classifications for a younger audience and associated merchandise.

Linda Badley, in her article, considers a different revolution in film culture, with the VCR rush of the 1980s and the ways in which video and then digital technology has affected horror film production and consumption. This has led to the development of a video subculture with obscure films receiving better distribution, the emergence of video auteurs and, since the 1990s, guerrilla-style direct-to-video horrors made by committed amateur and semi-pro filmmakers; a DIY counter-cultural cinema, which was inspired by the success of *The Blair Witch Project*. Like Ndalianis, Badley notes the common functions of different media and recognises, in particular, the technology of the digital versatile disk (DVD) for allowing consumer interaction and manipulation. Contemporary horror films such as *My Little Eye* (2002) and *fear.dot.com* (2002) have foregrounded this position of subjectivity and control, which Badley argues reveals a fear of voyeuristic digital technology in a post 9/11 society.

The opening article of section two, by Brigid Cherry, continues the discussion of technology, horror, and reception, but it is focused on the Internet, and on fan consumption. Cherry is interested in the vast growth in horror fan culture, the online communities, the fan fiction (consumer generated writing inspired by a specific film text), and the use of the Internet by filmmakers for marketing. This situation sees a tension between quite different consumers and producers, and between the private and the public, and reveals that the online horror fan is a sophisticated user who openly differentiates between texts. Matt Hills continues this discussion in his study of horror fan participation at film festivals and conventions. These gatherings interest Hills for the subcultural capital that they provide, a social status acquired through what Hills terms 'liveness'. It is another form of fan ritual, but for Hills it is higher in the horror fan community hierarchy than the online consumers identified by Cherry, as there is a form of authenticity in 'being there' and part of a 'flesh-and-blood' experience – attending perhaps an exclusive preview, or in social proximity to the filmmakers themselves.

The subcultural form of horror is addressed by Jeffrey Sconce, in the final article in section two, in which he explores aesthetic sensibilities and questions of taste. This is an abridged reprinting of Sconce's seminal article, in which he defined the existence of a paracinema, films of a lower budget, lower quality, disreputable or excessive nature, that operate beneath the mainstream level of acceptance. These unconventional films are welcomed and valorised by a paracinematic audience, a dedicated cinephilia, who assert their particular taste for a cinematic style and present a political challenge to dominant aesthetic judgements. In the article by Joan Hawkins, which opens section three, the issue of an aspect of horror cinema presenting a cultural confrontation is continued. Like Sconce, Hawkins identifies questions of taste and a capacity to defy convention, but her focus is on art horror films which have had a troubled reception due to their generic hybridity. Extending her focus from her book *Cutting Edge*, she considers recent art horrors, such as *Bad Boy Bubby* (1993), *Oldboy* (2003), and *The Machinist* (2004), that continue to demonstrate that in certain markets, and the US in particular, the boundary between high culture (arthouse) and paracinema has never been clear. Art cinema can easily transgress and it is the notable mainstream appearance of disreputable or exploitation films, which Sconce also observes, that Hawkins argues is a contemporary development. Echoing the contribution by Badley, Hawkins identifies video/DVD culture as the component in horror cinema that is allowing for the wider circulation of 'obscure' texts, which reach out beyond festivals, where they had previously been inaccessible to a remote audience.

Adding to the discussions of horror form, Tamao Nakahara writes on costume and set design. This is a specific area of cinema studies, which is receiving some attention, but not within research on the horror film. Their significance is argued by Nakahara, as the overdetermined reading of the text, reading meaning into detail, is a practice exhibited by horror fans, who trawl publications for supplementary information, often repeatedly watch a favoured movie, and appreciate DVDs for the paratextual extras. She concentrates on films such as *The Texas Chainsaw Massacre* and *The Silence of the Lambs* (1991), fiction inspired by the true case of Ed Gein, a serial killer with fetishist fixations and who decorated his home and body with parts of his victims. Nakahara is drawn to these texts as striking examples of where the body of the monster, or the central character, is united with the body of the home, the central location and the theatre of horrific play.

Where there has been attention given to the detailed design of the horror film is with the special effects. These design elements have certainly not gone unnoticed within the horror film and are promoted and celebrated within horror fan discourses. The horror new wave is associated with the golden age of special make-up or latex effects (as opposed to the later 'less authentic' digital effects of the 1990s) and, as Ernest Mathijs argues in his article, it was in this period that the effects often became almost as important as the stories. For Mathijs, the rise and importance of horror effects in the 1970s and 1980s needs to be read in the context of the culture in which they were received, which he demonstrates in regards to the fanzines, the effects auteurs and artists, marketing and the media response. Key films have been regarded as most exploitative of this effects technology and in the canon of notorious effects-heavy horrors is the *Friday the 13th* series of slasher films, which Ian Conrich discusses in his article. Part of a successful horror subgenre, which displayed explicit death and mutilation at structured points within the story, the *Friday the 13th* films were more than simple repetitions of a slasher film narrative. Conrich, like Mathijs, is drawn to the reception of these horrors within popular culture, and he argues that the series operates as a modern grand guignol, with the fans of the films elevating them to cult status. Their central selling point is the series of gruesome and inventive deaths controlled by Jason Voorhees, the relentless killer of the series, who functions as an executioner encouraged by devoted grand guignolers, the audience which follows the films.

In the final section of this collection, contributors consider the boundaries, cultural and otherwise, that the horror film pushes against, threatens, and transgresses. Jay McRoy extends the discussion of splatter, and the aesthetics and design of horror, with a consideration of the body-centred violence of horror and its comparison to pornography, another vilified film form, where flesh is the violated boundary. Horror shares with pornography a fragmentation of the body and, importantly, a marked impact on its audience on exposure to corporeal extremes. McRoy is concerned with the body in parts, as opposed to the unified whole, and he concludes that the splattered and pornographic bodies are ever-differentiating and challenge fixed identities. In contrast, Julian Petley's article on Nazi horrors recognises a screen identity that has become clichéd, and repeated around a number of specific themes, with the occult, extreme torture, and the union of sex and horror, or sexploitation, common approaches to popularising and fictionalising the monstrous Third Reich and fantasies of a 'Fourth Reich'. Petley argues that Nazis have become short-hand signifiers for contemporary depictions of inhumanity and depravity, and mythologised as transgressive figures.

The cultural boundary that essentially interests Mick Broderick is the millennium, and the fears that the passing from the year 1999 came to represent in screen fiction. Broderick identifies a subgenre of horror films that depicted fantasies of the apocalypse, Armageddon and the Antichrist.

Within this body of films, Broderick notes an emergent group of biblically influenced conservative dramas, produced mainly for a Christian audience and supported by religious organisations. These independently produced horrors appeared at the same time as studio backed films, but despite their political differences and production origins the motifs and tropes overlapped. As with Petley's article, Broderick concludes that there is a mythic structure underlining cultural expectations of specific horror subjects and figures.

The powerful relationship between film and television is the subject of Estella Tincknell's discussion. These mediums, which also borrow a music video style, have presented over the last ten years a new Gothic horror hybrid associated with feminine identities and adolescence, in productions such as *The Craft* (1996), *Ginger Snaps* (2000), and *Buffy the Vampire Slayer* (1997–2003). Here, there is a liminal boundary between the youthful teenage girl, and adulthood, as well as a line between the female seen as ordinary or possessed with supernatural powers, which has been emphasised through changing cultural identities of adolescence. Angela Marie Smith, in the final article, also observes femininity as a subject associated with boundaries and explores a group of women-in-peril horror films that centralise a blind or near-blind woman as victim. Smith is foremost concerned by depictions of disability within the horror film and what this says about contemporary culture and screen politics. Taking issues of vision and looking as factors linking the disabled on-screen female and the film audience, Smith examines the discrimination and continued stereotypes of blindness or impaired vision in films such as *Jennifer 8* (1992) and *Red Dragon* (2002), where it is employed to emphasise a victim status, whilst functioning as a device to unsettle the viewer. The cultural experiences of horror are many, as this book illustrates and, like other contributors to the collection, Smith shows how in context horror is socially and politically a formidable cultural form.

Notes

1. Valuable monographs include Matt Hills, *The Pleasures of Horror*, London: Continuum, 2005; Joan Hawkins, *Cutting Edge: Art-Horror and the Horrific Avant-Garde*, Minneapolis: University of Minnesota Press, 2000; and Kevin Heffernan, *Ghouls, Gimmicks, and Gold: Horror Films and the American Movie Business, 1953–1968*, Durham: Duke University Press, 2004. Also of note is the collection edited by Steffen Hantke, *Horror Film: Creating and Marketing Fear*, Jackson: University Press of Mississippi, 2004.

Part One

Industry, Technology and the New Media

1

Dark Rides, Hybrid Machines
and the Horror Experience

ANGELA NDALIANIS

"Click here if you dare!" So begins the warning on the website to Universal Studios' *Revenge of the Mummy – the Ride*. It continues:

> It's a psychological adventure that will tap into your most primal fears like . . .
> Lysgophobia . . . Fear of the Dark
> Entomophobia . . . Fear of Insects
> Tachophobia . . . Fear of Speed
> Acrophobia . . . Fear of Heights
> Demonophobia . . . Fear of Evil Spirits
> Necrophobia . . . Fear of Death.[1]

On the back of the success of the films *The Mummy* (1999) and *The Mummy Returns* (2001) the 2004 ride at Universal Studios presents itself as upping the ante on the film horror experience. Participants begin by entering the Museum of Antiquities, which is, in 'actuality' the set location for the next Mummy film sequel. Surrounded by cameras, lights, statues, and scaffolding, video monitors soon inform us that the curse of the Mummy Imhotep may be more than a fabrication. Brendan Fraser, Arnold Vosloo and other actors from the films are interviewed in a mockumentary and express concern about a real curse that has haunted the latest production. To add to the backdrop of the climaxing calamity, the deeper we enter the ride, the more we realise that the set for the new Mummy film is on location. The Museum of Antiquities, in fact, houses the underground catacombs of the Imhotep. Walking through what looks like a temple, we eventually enter the loading bay where ancient Egyptians (ride operators) help participants into a ride buggy. And so it begins. All the classic signs of horror are here: a darkness that harbours the unknown, eerie whispers, passages that appear labyrinthine, stolen souls, blazing fires, and a monstrous Mummy that threatens to bring about our demise. Like the films that influence this ride, the audience shares an experience that is common across horror, regardless of the medium. As Noel Carroll stresses, the horror genre is affect-driven: it seeks to elicit an emotional state from its audience.[2] A shudder, a scream, a feeling of threat or terror – what Carroll calls being "art-horrified".

Horror has made a lucrative market across a variety of media, including films, television shows, computer games, novels, and theme park attractions over the last two decades. Perhaps, the environment in which it has shared one of its strongest and longest connections is as part of the amusement park and fairground. The ghost trains, magic phantasmic illusions, tunnels of love, and freak shows that first scared audiences in Exposition midways and fairgrounds have continued to make their presence felt in amusement and theme parks today and, as will be outlined below, were predecessors of contemporary horror rides like *Revenge of the Mummy – the Ride*. Most famously, Coney Island's attractions from the turn of the twentieth-century included the latest in cutting edge examples of horror rides that would persist in inciting the fear factor for decades later: the indoor scenic railway at Luna Park called the Dragon's Gorge (which included a brief trip to Hades and its River Styx), the Ghost House and Tunnel of Laffs at Steeplechase Park, and Dreamland's Haunted House, Haunted Swing, Hellgate and Freak Street with its "40 human monstrosities".[3] Variations of similar rides continued to attract audiences in fun parks throughout the twentieth-century, and many popular seaside and other holiday destinations even developed horror as an attraction theme. In the 1970s, for example, entrepreneurs developed the pier sector in New Jersey to include a series of popular 'haunted attractions' that included Castle Dracula, Brigantine Castle, and the Haunted Mansion.[4] The attractions tended towards the hokey and corny – an aesthetic that did not necessarily reduce the scares and frights that were on offer. As William Paul has so convincingly argued in relation to horror films of the 1970s and 1980s, the carnival origins of such experiences are concerned with a playful theatricality that generates the affective state of "laughing screaming".[5]

Over the last two decades horror rides have undergone a renaissance, returning to the hi-tech and grand scale attractions of the earlier amusement park tradition, but this time within the context of the theme park: *Scooby Doo and the Haunted Mansion* opened at Paramount's King's Dominion in Doswell Virginia; new versions of Disney's *Haunted Mansion* have opened in the Paris and Tokyo Disneylands, and in the Orlando parks visitors can experience the *Twilight Zone, Tower of Terror Ride*; *Revenge of the Mummy, Van Helsing: Fortress Dracula,* and *Terminator 2: 3D* scare audiences at Universal Studios in Los Angeles, Orlando and Osaka; and *The Labyrinth of the Minotaur* and *Pyramid of Terror* rides attract

DRAGON'S GORGE, LUNA PARK, BY NIGHT
CONEY ISLAND, N. Y.
©1920 The American Art Publishing Co

1. The horror ride as amusement park attraction: A postcard promoting the Dragon's Gorge at New York's Coney Island

crowds at Paramount's Terra Mitica park at Benidorm, Spain. The horror ride business has become so lucrative that it has sprouted a booming special effects rides industry, one of the most successful being the Sally Corporation which specialises in horror rides such as the *Challenge of Tutankhamen* (Six Flags, Belgium), *Zombie Paradise* (Geopolis, Tokyo), *Mine of Lost Souls* (Canobie Lake Park, Salem), *Haunted Hotel* (Pavilion Amusement Park Myrtle Beach, South Carolina), *Frankenstein's Castle* (Indiana Beach, Monticello, Indiana) and *Ghost Blasters* (Knott's Camp Snoopy, Mall of America, Minnesota; Castle Park, Riverside, California; Santa Cruz Beach Boardwalk).[6]

Since the 1950s, the themes and experiences offered by horror rides most often draw upon a consciousness that horror films have burned into audience's minds over the last century. Increasingly, the exchange of character types, settings, sound effects, stories, and themes that are present across a variety of horror media reveals the complex interchange that occurs between contemporary entertainment industries. At first glance, this exchange seems to involve the simple transfer of codes and conventions from one medium to the next, but on closer analysis it becomes evident that each medium adapts common generic conventions to create experiences required of their own form.[7] In an era when mainstream films are being described as being more like roller coasters and roller coasters as being closer to films, it comes as no surprise to discover that the overlaps between the two media are deeply connected on a systemic level. Today, film production is only one component of the economic drive behind the conglomerates that run the industry. As a result, the aesthetics that emerge support an industry that has multiple media investment interests. Some of these economic strategies and the ways they affect horror media will be the focus of this essay. In addition to exploring the financial benefits of media crossovers, attention will be given to the formal overlaps found between the horror ride of the theme and amusement park industry and horror cinema. In particular, attention will be drawn to the 'dark ride' – also known as the 'laff-in-the-dark-ride' – which has been common to the amusement park since its beginnings at the turn of the twentieth-century. In dark rides, participants board a buggy, train, or boat and enter a dark, enclosed space. The space is themed – a ghost train, a haunted house, a trip to the moon – and the vehicle on track allows the designers some control over the ways the story unravels.

Returning to the example that I began with, the *Revenge of the Mummy* ride reveals the complex relationships that currently exist between entertainment structures. The cross-over between popular culture forms such as films and theme park rides tests the clear separation between diverse media forms, and this overlap has ramifications for genre analysis, which tends to contain and homogenise an understanding of genre within specific media. A more flexible account of generic development and the production of meaning should acknowledge the dynamic interchange between media. The horror genre is not a closed system that draws solely on examples of its kind within a specific medium. Its 'meaning' also crosses into other media. Clearly, audience familiarity with genres from related media is economically advantageous to entertainment companies. Genre and media hybridisation is crucial to creating a larger cross-over market. The blockbuster *Mummy* films, for example, were produced by Vivendi Universal and have proved especially successful crossover variations. *The Mummy* films – *The Mummy, The Mummy Returns, The Scorpion King* (2002), and *The Mummy: Tomb of the Dragon Emperor* (2008) – have found new media environments, the theme park attractions *Revenge of the Mummy* being only one of them. In an attempt to extend its audience by reaching out to the comic book audience, the release of *The Mummy Returns* was accompanied by a 3-part comic book series called *The Mummy: Valley of the Gods*.[8] The comic book includes the films' main characters, but takes them on different adventures. Chaos Comics, the highly successful horror and fantastic comics publisher, negotiated a licensing deal with Universal in order to make this possible. Also, coinciding with the release of the sequel came *The Mummy Returns* collectible trading cards from Inkworks, a trading card company specializing in entertainment products.[9] This cross-media extension of the Mummy franchise also included computer games: *The Mummy* (PC and Playstation2: Konami, 2001); *The Mummy Returns* (Playstation2: Universal interactive, 2001); *The Scorpion King: Sword of Osiris* (Game Boy Advance: Universal Interactive, 2002); and *The Scorpion King: Rise of the Akkadian* (Playstation2: Universal Interactive, 2003).[10]

When considering the formal and aesthetic properties of genre, it is also crucial to consider the socio-economic context that has informed and nurtured its production. In contemporary culture, the formal properties of entertainment have responded dramatically to the contexts of globalisation, conglomeration and postmodernism. The ailing film industry that emerged in the post-1950s was one that eventually recognised the competitive nature of a new, conglomerate economic infrastructure that increasingly favoured global interests on a mass scale. Entertainment industries – film studios, computer game companies, comic book companies, television studios and theme park industries – expanded their interests by investing in multiple interests, thus combating growing competition more effectively and minimising financial loss or maximising financial gain by dispersing their products across a diversity of media forms. Horizontal integration, therefore, increasingly became one of the successful strategies of the revitalised film industry. To continue with the example of Vivendi Universal – the parent company that owns the Mummy franchise – it is a major leader in media and telecommunications with entertainment interests that cross into film, television and games. Subsidiaries include Universal Music Group, Vivendi Universal Games (studios and publishing labels include Blizzard Entertainment, Fox Interactive, Massive Entertainment, Universal Interactive and Sierra Entertainment),[11] Canal+Group satellite and pay-tv company, and the mobile companies SFR Cegetel Group and Maroc Telecom. In addition, Vivendi Universal is part owner of NBC Universal (the merger occurred in 2004) whose interests lie in television, film and theme park operations.[12] Aside from funding arrangements made with independent specialist companies like Chaos Comics and Inkworks, the diversity of its own subsidiary interests meant that Vivendi Universal was able to distribute the Mummy franchise – as an example of the horror genre – across a range of media. Indeed, it was in their financial interests to do so. Cross-media production allows for the stabilisation and standardisation of some costs: Universal Interactive and NBC Universal, for example, could use sequences from the films in the production of their games and theme park attractions; Decca Records, a subsidiary of the Universal Music Group, benefited from the release of the film soundtracks; and the Canal+Group satellite and pay-tv company had first access to the release of the films to television audiences. While ensuring that profit is distributed across a variety of media, this strategy also operates on the 'don't put all your eggs in one basket' principle. If your film flops, maybe your games and rides will be a success. The key drive behind the diversification of products and company specialisation is to reach as wide an audience as possible.

Justin Wyatt suggests that the "relationship between economics and aesthetics" has become crucial to the formal properties of entertainment media.[13] Of course, the same may be said of the relationship between aesthetics and economics that eventuated during the classical Hollywood era. The Universal Studios that produced the early Mummy films, for example, did so according to the economic logic that drove the industry during the 1930s-1940s. The recent films have successfully regenerated what had been a very successful franchise during the heyday of Universal's horror output with the release of classics like *The Mummy* (1932), *The Mummy's Hand* (1940), *The Mummy's Tomb* (1942), *The Mummy's Ghost* (1944), *The Mummy's Curse* (1944) and, of course, the later example of Universal's foray into the generic hybrid *Abbott and Costello Meet the Mummy* (1955). Extension of the Mummy franchise was contained within the one medium – film. This was typical of a film industry that operated according to the logic of vertical integration:[14] the classical Hollywood studio structure specialised in one medium, and despite venturing into some cross-merchandising, film was the primary business.[15]

Since the 1960s, however, Hollywood progressively changed from a "Fordist mode of production, consisting of the vertical organisation of the assembly line factory of studios", to a post-Fordist mode of production reliant upon horizontal organisation.[16] Early examples of this shift are reflected in attempts made by Universal during the time to extend their products beyond film production. Universal even toyed with attempts at migrating their horror franchises – Dracula, Frankenstein, the Werewolf, the Mummy – into comic book stories. In 1963, for example, Universal Pictures collaborated with Dell Publishing to release *Universal Pictures Presents Dracula - the Mummy and Other Stories* (September-November 1963).[17] The publication was publicity motivated, and the comic book coincided with the popularity of the television show *Shock Theater*, which had appeared in various guises since the late 1950s and which showcased horror movies – including those of Universal – for television audiences. Clearly then, cross-media production and merchandising is definitely not a phenomenon specific to our times, however, horizontal integration has now become integral to the survival of the entertainment industry.

To return to Wyatt's assertion, the economic context that was transformed in the late twentieth-century was also accompanied by transformed formal and stylistic properties. By now, the basic premise of what Jay Bolter and Richard Grusin call *remediation* has been well rehearsed.[18] Remediation involves the refashioning or assimilation of one or more media conventions by another medium. Perhaps more intensely than any other genre, horror possesses a rich and diverse media history that includes an array of sources – films, comic books, computer games, amusement park attractions, paintings, books, television – that survive by succumbing to remediation. The early amusement park ride, for example, drew upon a rich tradition of park and ride cultures and conventions that ranged from eighteenth and nineteenth-century pleasure gardens and rides aimed at the middle classes, the popular rise of the Gothic and horror novel, and magic lanterns and other optical devices that spooked audiences with their phantasmic displays in the nineteenth-century. While borrowing predominantly from the theatre, horror cinema of the pre-1940s also turned to the stories and affective states elicited by horror rides found in amusement parks and fun fairs, pulp and other novels and radio serials.[19] Contemporary horror media are even more excessively engaged in this intertextual and intermedia logic. What is fascinating about the horror rides found in today's theme parks is that this intertextuality and intermedia tendency becomes literal: not only are multiple media referenced or alluded to, they are often literally incorporated into the ride experience. Contemporary horror is marked by an excess of self-referentiality and remediation that is as multifarious as the conglomerate structure that produces it. It gives rise to a hybrid logic that has significant ramifications for genres and the critical models used to analyse them and, in the case of the theme park attractions, this is all the more so because of the excess media hybridity.

In addition to being influenced by the rich history of the recent Mummy horror films that preceded it, especially the more recent blockbuster films, the *Revenge of the Mummy* ride, for example, extends the parameters of the amusement and theme park ride by introducing into its structure a variety of media. The roller coaster is given new life with the incorporation of cutting-edge technology that relies on a magnetic launch system. Single-sided, linear induction motors, or SLIMs, run under the track and magnetically propel the ride buggies during the coaster sections, accelerating riders from 0 to 40mph before they have had time to catch their breath.[20] Reaching zero-gravity has never been easier for ride technology. Furthermore, digital animation and film are called upon to add to the illusion of the horror images that cause such terror in the dark. Images familiar to the Mummy films are strategically projected onto screens and the interior space of the ride. Film projections of the Mummy (including one of Imhotep's digitally animated sand-face with its cavernous mouth as it reaches to swallow the riders) and scarab beetles that emerge from wall cracks in the thousands threaten to invade the space

2. A thrilling welcome: Monstrous guards stand over the entrance to the *Revenge of the Mummy* ride

of the ride participants. Again, when Imhotep rises to draw us into his gaping mouth, the ride buggy follows the path of escape by plummeting what appears to be hundreds of metres downwards. This effect is produced by falling between two screens on which are projected images that create the illusion of movement through space at an extremely high velocity. The advanced robotics that Disney made famous in theme parks in the form of his animatronics again push technological boundaries in the attempt to thrill and frighten. The larger than life animatronic version of the Mummy and the four mummy warriors that lunge at the participants were produced by hi-tech hydraulics that give the impression of greater realism when compared to the electric or pneumatic systems that have been used in theme park animatronics in the past. Add to this theatrical effects such as explosions of fire and sprays of water and the architecture that gives life to the ride, interior and exterior, and it can be said that the *Revenge of the Mummy* ride (like *The Amazing Adventures of Spider-Man* ride at Universal's Islands of Adventure theme park in Orlando)[21] is emblematic of the hybrid and multi-remediated theme park attractions of recent years.

One of the strongest influences on *Revenge of the Mummy* is that of the 'dark ride'. Within the ride, participants journey in darkness only to then be exposed to a series of lit 'scenes' that are created through props, figures in costumes, animatronics and sound effects.[22] An early version of the dark ride (possibly the first) was 'A Trip to the Moon', the cyclorama created by Frederick Thompson and his partner Skip Dundy for the Pan-American Exposition held at Buffalo, New York in 1901. Here, viewers were taken on a trip to the moon by a giant ship. As the cyclorama revolved around them revealing images on a painted canvas, the travellers met the moon people before soaring back to earth. The popularity of the ride attracted the attention of George Tilyou, who owned Steeplechase Park at Coney Island, and by 1902 this hugely popular ride was entertaining audiences there before moving to the nearby Luna Park where it also transformed into a roller coaster. It was in the Luna Park version that the horror themes emerged: the moon dwarves (the Senelite), led participants to a dragon's mouth that opened and allowed them to move into its stomach. Navigating the rocking stomach cavity, they made their way to their seats before the ride proceeded.[23]

The transformation of the dark ride experience along the more hybrid lines typical of our era was to come along in the 1960s with the opening of the *Haunted Mansion* at Disneyland in 1969.[24] Originally intended as a walk through attraction in the haunted house amusement/fun park tradition, the ride became a turning point between old and new dark ride technologies. In the Haunted Mansion, the montage of various disjointed horror stories epitomised Walt Disney's lack of interest in narrative development and greater concern with immersing the audience into an experience. Entering the house on foot, a ghost host guides the crowd through a gallery of bizarre portraits that transform – a goddess becomes a Medusa, a woman becomes a hag – in a room where solid walls and a ceiling appear to distort, stretch, and finally disappear. From here, the visitor is guided to the 'Omnimovers' or 'Doom Buggies'. The buggies revise the ghost train tradition but, in addition to the buggies being able to travel on a track, they are also capable of moving forward, tilting in every direction, and performing 360° turns, the range of movements ensuring that the riders' view is controlled by the creators at every point in the ride. From the moment the visitor enters the Haunted Mansion, they are confronted with many remediated media illusions.

In the nineteenth-century John Pepper, a professor of Chemistry from the London Polytechnic, popularised an illusionistic technique involving an image projected onto a piece of glass at a 45-degree angle by presenting it to audiences on a grander scale as public education and amusement. Using a mirror and directed lighting techniques, Pepper's Ghost made objects (most often ghosts) seem to appear or disappear, or to make one image metamorphose into another. While John Pepper was primarily interested in the technique as an experiment in optics and science, it was the entertainment displays of this technology that brought science to the people – as made evident by Pepper's first and most famous public demonstration which occurred during a Christmas performance of Charles Dickens's *Haunted Man* in 1862.[25] While separated by a century, the Pepper's Ghost technique was used for many of the ghost effects in Disney's *Haunted Mansion*. The reflection of the psychic Madame Leota's face in a crystal ball, the appearing and disappearing spooks that float, dance, and hang off chandeliers in the ballroom during a birthday ball, and the hitchhiking ghosts that appear to be sitting with us in the doom buggy as we exit the ride – these illusions are all due to Pepper's Ghost.

This was not the only earlier optical technology that Walt Disney and the Imagineers remediated. Other optical technologies that had been used in the past to conjure horror illusions also resurfaced: one of these was the magic lantern. Its origins hark back at least to the late sixteenth-century, but it was in the nineteenth-century that the magic lantern became one of the essential tools of the magician and was used primarily in the ghost or apparition shows that involved phantoms suddenly appearing 'out of nowhere'. Unlike Pepper's Ghost, which required the physical presence of the illusion off stage, the magic lantern conjured its illusions by projecting images onto screens. The most famous and most duplicated was the *Fantasmagorie* by Étienne Gaspard Robert (known as Robertson). Robertson was a Belgian inventor, physicist and student of optics who improved the technology of the magic lantern, including its capacity to enlarge and decrease images. In 1797, Robertson performed a live horror theatre in a Paris cemetery. Crowds flocked to the dimly lit tombs to see magic lantern effects that included skulls, atmospheric lighting, sound effects, and the appearance of ghostly apparitions in an effects display concerned with an "optical explosion of the senses".[26] Similar illusions are present in the Haunted Mansion: the disappearing ceiling at the beginning of the ride was created by projecting then no longer projecting a painted ceiling onto a translucent screen – as were the bicycling and flying ghosts in the cemetery. These past inventions, however, are transformed into new experiences by also being combined with radically new technologies, both in the inclusion of the hi-tech Omnimovers, which Disney Imagineers had designed for the *It's a Small World* and *Carousel of Progress* rides at the New York World's Fair of 1964, and in the way the ride relied on a multitude of ghost performers who were animatronic in nature.[27] Disney's *Haunted Mansion* was, therefore, an important turning point for the horror ride: the attraction paid homage to past visual traditions and illusions but transformed them by placing them within the context of the theme park. The Imagineers remediated multiple media experiences – phantasmagoria and magic lanterns, Pepper's ghost, automata, film, the haunted houses and ghost trains of amusement parks – and refashioned them into the kind of hybridised, hi-tech spectacle that would come to typify the theme park of more recent times.

Universal's website states that *Revenge of the Mummy* cross-pollinates elements of past rides into a new theme park hybrid, which the Universal marketing department has dubbed a "psychological thrill ride". Taking its cue from the hybrid heritage popularised by Disney, next generation dark rides like *Jurassic Park* (Universal), *The Amazing Adventures of Spider-Man* (Universal), the *Indiana Jones Adventure* (Disneyland) and *Revenge of the Mummy* typically rely on an excessive remediation of media old and the new and, as mentioned above, often literally engage in an intermedia approach. Dark ride, roller coaster, film, television, theatre, architecture, music – all vie for the attention of the participant and seek to make the experience an intensely emotive and sensorial one. While the horror theme is not a prerequisite of the dark ride (for example, Disneyland's *Peter Pan, Pirates of the Caribbean* and *It's a Small World* are fantasy rather than horror stories) it is understandable why the majority of dark rides have primarily been horror dark rides. Like most horror films they involve an entry into an enclosed space – a journey into the dark that places the viewer in the passive role over the narrative that then unfolds. Interestingly, dark ride aficionados have not missed the horror associations that typify the dark ride. In the special issue on dark rides, the online journal *Skew* published an essay titled 'An Age-Old Terror: The spirit of the Dark Ride has been around for centuries'. Here, the author Brandon Kwiatek suggests that the "dark ride is a ride-through Halloween" that shares a great deal with the "Western imagination of death, the devil and hell . . . [and] Christian beliefs with symbols of heaven and hell, good and evil". Like the famed heroic journeys by Gilgamesh, Odysseus and Orpheus into the underworld or the many biblical stories that depict "hell as, respectively, a pit, a gate and a mouth", the ride participant boards a buggy to partake in a descent journey, opening the way to the horrors that lie therein. [28]

Ronald Simons argues that being startled is one of the experiences audiences desire of horror films; furthermore, the startle impulse is common to many species: "The essence of startle is that it is the mechanism designed to ensure that the startled organism responds to a potential danger as rapidly as possible, even before the eliciting stimulus is consciously classified and evaluated".[29] Startling is a reflexive response that protects the individual from possible danger. It is an "induced emotional state" that is "like the pleasurable arousal sought from roller-coaster rides".[30] There are a great amount of startles to be had when the visitor enters the labyrinth interior of the dark ride. The startles of horror are responses to the unknown that the world of horror opens up: death and the dead, phobias, and moral decay. In horror films our responses are generated via the intermediary main characters and it is through them that we empathise with the threat posed to their moral universe and their material presence. In the horror rides, however, we lose this intermediary and it is we, the ride participants who become the protagonist. For the horror rider, the fear of death and bodily destruction is one step closer to being a real threat. Yes, the participant knows that the technology that drives the rides is supposed to be safe (even though numerous ride-related deaths occur annually) but it does not feel safe when, in the *Revenge of the Mummy* ride, the dread of being swallowed by an enormous vision of Imhotep is replaced by a new horror: the ride buggy plummeting backwards and downwards at full speed.

For horror critics like Carol J. Clover, Linda Williams, and R.H.W. Dillard vision in the horror film unveils a moral commitment. The stories these films have to tell address themselves to the construction of individual and social identity and to the collapse or threat to that identity as symbolically embodied by the monstrous. While horror cinema's desire is to extract affective responses from its audience, its form is also conducive to interpretation. George A. Romero's *Living Dead* films, for example, may make our skin crawl as a result of the overt presence of decaying, rotting dead bodies that refuse to stay dead, but they also have much to say about the state of contemporary society and the way it produces alienation and dehumanisation. Horror rides focus less on the narrative dimensions and the critical and moral interpretations that can emerge from them and more on the affective assault on the participant. Carroll suggests that in horror films, via the character's responses, the spectator is often "counselled" to "the appropriate reactions to the monsters", which usually comprise "shuddering, nausea, shrinking, paralysis, screaming, and revulsion. Our responses are meant, ideally, to parallel those of characters. Our responses are supposed to converge (but not exactly duplicate) those of the characters".[31] In rides, however, there is no need for these parallels to invoke such affective responses. Leaving the story behind, dark rides that incorporate wild roller coasters, for example, have no problem in causing many riders to shudder, feel nausea and scream.

In horror rides, more is invested in what is seen and felt. Vision and all other senses have a far greater role to play in the experience extracted from a ride. When, for instance, the buggy plunged backwards at high velocity in *Return of the Mummy*, I felt the air as it pushed my body back and made my hair whip across my face; I felt, smelt and even tasted the heat of fire on my skin, nose and mouth as it erupted in the Egyptian temple above me; and I felt like I could touch the hundreds of scarab beetles as they ran across my hands, legs and throat (a simple yet clever effect actually conjured by fine sprays of water) while I hyperventilated in anticipation of what 'effect' would confront me next. For Carroll, the monster of horror cinema is a violation of nature.[32] It could be argued that, regardless of the 'story' content of the horror ride, the highly sophisticated, hybrid machines that make rides like *Revenge of the Mummy, The Curse of Tutankhamen*, and *Jurassic Park* possible can also be understood as violations of nature – violations that make monstrous mummies and tyrannosauruses occupy space alongside the visitor and appear to threaten the individual's existence. The hybrid machines of the dark ride are also monsters of sorts. Steffen Hantke has stated that "we are not supposed to understand horror, to comprehend it as the critical discourse lays it out for us; we are supposed to experience it. We are supposed to experience it as a loud, crass, and almost instinctual sensation, rather than as a gray sense of dread…Horror, here, means bodily exertion: to shudder, to sweat, to squirm in our seats".[33] As has been established, many of the recent dark rides favour a hybrid structure that not only draws upon other media beyond the theme park (film, television, comic books) but also from within it. Expanding the boundaries of what constitutes the dark ride by introducing engineering feats like the roller coaster, these rides introduce the horror genre's fear of bodily threat into the experience and, along with it, bodily responses such as sweating, screaming, or cowering. While from a film genre viewpoint rides like *The Amazing Adventures of Spider-Man* and *Indiana Jones Adventure* are not horror, from the perspective of a body's reaction to being hunted, haunted and terrorised by the horror machine that drives the ride technology, such attractions come very close to being horror experiences. Perhaps the parameters that contain the term 'horror' need to be expanded to account for the hybrid nature of the dark ride.

Notes

1. The *Revenge of the Mummy* ride site is available at <http://www.revengeofthemummy.com/>.
2. Noel Carroll, *The philosophy of horror, or Paradox of the Heart*, New York and London: Routledge, 1990, p. 19.
3. For a detailed listing of all the Coney Island rides and attractions, see the Coney Island Project at <http://naid.sppsr.ucla.edu/coneyisland/index.html>.
4. For further information see Rob MacRea, 'The Boo Business', *Haunted Attraction Magazine*, vol. 39, 2005. Available at <http://www.hauntedattraction.com/39/currentissue_boobbiz.shtml>; and Hal B. Rappaport, 'The Legend of Castle Dracula', *Haunted Attraction Magazine*,

vol. 29. Available at <http://www.hauntedattraction.com/29/spotlight1. htm>.

5. See William Paul, *Laughing Screaming: Modern Hollywood Horror and Comedy*, New York: Columbia University Press, 1994. Like much of the original Coney Island, many of these locations have since met their demise in blazing fires. For information about horror attractions past and present, see *The Haunted Attraction Magazine* available online at <http://www.hauntedattraction. com/>.

6. The Sally Corporation site is accessible at <http://www.sallycorp.com/>. Other theme park ride companies include International Theme Park Services Inc. <http://www.interthemepark.com/>, Rhythm & Hues <http://www. rhythm.com> and, one of the most successful, the Landmark Entertainment Group <http://landmarkusa.com/>.

7. For an analysis of the interchange of horror codes between films and computer games, see Angela Ndalianis, 'The Rules of the Game: *Evil Dead II* . . . Meet thy *Doom*', in Henry Jenkins, Tara McPherson, Jane Shattuc, eds, *Hop on Pop: the Politics and Pleasures of Popular Cultures*, Durham, NC: Duke University Press, 2003; and Angela Ndalianis, '"Evil Will Walk Once More": *Phantasmagoria* ~ the Stalker Film as Interactive Movie?', in Greg Smith, ed., *On a Silver Platter: CD-Roms and the Promises of a New Technology*, New York: New York University Press, 1999.

8. Written by Marv Wolfman, the release date was 9 May 2001. Chaos Comics' website is available at <http://www.chaoscomics.com/>.

9. Inkworks' website is available at <http://www.inkworks.com/>.

10. The ride has itself generated its own crossover market, as evident in the toys, t-shirts, hats, action figures and other merchandise, as well as a multi-million dollar deal with Coca Cola and Burger King for advertising tie-in promotions.

11. See <http://www.vugames.com>.

12. See <http://www.vivendiuniversal.com/>.

13. Justin Wyatt, *High Concept: Movies and Marketing in Hollywood*, Austin: University of Texas Press, 1994, p. 160.

14. For more information about the economic structure of the classical studio structure as compared to the contemporary Hollywood system, see Wyatt, ch. 3.

15. In the 1940s and 1950s, for example, comic books that featured famous movie stars were extremely popular. For example, John Wayne, Alan Ladd, Buster Crabbe, Dorothy Lamour and Dick Powell all had comic book series named after them. See Denis Gifford, *The International Book of Comics*, London: Hamlyn, 1984, pp. 224–5. Other cross-media merchandise was also available, including the very popular Shirley Temple dolls, which were marketed from the 1930s, see <http://www.shirleytempledolls.com/dolls. html>.

16. Joseba Gabilondo, *Cinematic Hyperspace. New Hollywood Cinema and Science Fiction Film: Image Commodification in Late Capitalism*, Ann Arbor: UMI, 1991, p. 128.

17. Each of the stories in this compilation had been released as separate comic books in 1962.

18. Jay David Bolter and Richard Grusin, *Remediation: Understanding New Media*, Massachusetts: Cambridge, 1999.

19. I thank Ian Conrich for pointing out that pre-1940s horror films were predominantly stage adaptations. The film *Dracula* (1931), for example, was based on the popular Broadway play of the same title, which was, in turn, based on Bram Stoker's novel. Starring in the play was Bela Lugosi who would also star as Dracula on the silver screen. Similarly, the film *Frankenstein* (1931) was adapted from the 1927 play written by Peggy Webling – *Frankenstein: an Adventure into the Macabre*. See Joseph Maddrey, *Nightmares in Red, White and Blue: the Evolution of the American Horror Film*, Jefferson and London, pp. 12–13.

20. See John Calhoun, 'Mummy Dearest', *Entertainment Design*, 1 August 2004. Available at <http://entertainmentdesignmag.com/mag/show_business_ mummy_dearest/index.html>.

21. For a detailed account of the hybrid media structure of *The Amazing Adventures of Spiderman*, see Angela Ndalianis, 'Special Effects Magic and the Spiritual Presence of the Technological', *Neo-Baroque Aesthetics and Contemporary Entertainment*, Massachusetts: MIT Press, 2004, ch. 5.

22. Even before films were presented to a mass audience, George Hale anticipated the dark rides of the twentieth-century by devising his 'Hale's Tours and Scenes of the World'. Constructing a theatre whose interior looked like a railway car, the audience would participate in a ride that took them to filmed locations from all over the world. Showing Hale's Tours for the first time at the St. Louis World's Fair of 1903, these film 'rides' proved to be so successful that Hale began syndication, and his Hale's Tours became the concept behind and content of Adolph Zukor's first motion picture theatre. See James Forsher, *The Community of Cinema – How Cinema and Spectacle Transformed the American downtown*, Westport: Praeger Publishers, 2003, pp. 11–12.

23. This extremely popular ride would have drawn inspiration from the classic science-fiction novel *From the Earth to the Moon* (1865) by Jules Verne. Interestingly, in the same year that the ride *A Trip to the Moon* appeared at the Exposition, H.G. Wells also published his *First Men in the Moon* (1901). A year later Georges Méliès would release his film of the same title. Given its popularity, it seems likely that Méliès would have at least heard of the Thompson and Dundy ride for the Pan-American Exposition in Buffalo, New York in 1901. For a detailed account of the rides at Coney Island in the early twentieth-century, see Edo McCullough, *Good Old Coney Island: a Sentimental Journey Into the Past*, New York: Fordham University Press, 2000 (originally published in 1957), and the Coney Island Project at <http://naid. sppsr.ucla.edu/coneyisland/index.html>.

24. The Orlando version opened in 1971 and the one in Disneyland Paris (which is called the Phantom Manor) opened in 1992. For a detailed analysis and overview of the *Haunted Mansion* ride, its influences and its various locations,

see Karal Ann Marling, *Designing Disney's Theme Parks: the Architecture of Reassurance*, New York: Flammarion, 1997, and the exhaustive website devoted to the ride available at <http://www.Doombuggies.com>.

25. As Secord explains: "Announced by the Liverpool engineer Henry Dircks at a British Association for the Advancement of Science meeting in 1858 and developed by Pepper for practical use, the technique involved placing a huge sheet of plate glass on stage at a 45° angle, together with screens and special lighting". Secord continues, "Pepper took the spectacle as an opportunity to explain some of the underlying principles of optics . . . Skeptics used Pepper's highly public stage ghosts to argue that mediums claiming to raise the spirits of the dead were fakes. The famous 'Ghost Show', then, was an integral part of a wider attempt by Pepper to inculcate a sense of rational wonder by bringing the public's fascination with spirits, alchemy, and magic to the service of science". J.A. Secord, 'Portraits Of Science: Quick And Magical Shaper Of Science', *Science Magazine*, vol. 297, no. 5587, 6 September 2002, pp. 1648–9.

26. Terry Castle, 'Phantasmagoria: Spectral Technology and the Metaphorics of Modern Reverie', *Critical Inquiry*, vol. 15, Autumn, 1988, pp. 26–61. On the magic lantern, also see Roberta McGrath, 'Natural Magic and Science Fiction: Instruction, Amusement and the Popular Show, 1795–1895', in Christopher Williams, ed., *Cinema: the Beginnings and the Future*, London: University of Westminster Press, 1996, pp. 13–23.

27. General Electric sponsored the *Carousel of Progress*. This ride and *It's a Small World* were to enter the Disney parks after the Fair came to an end. For both rides, Disney Imagineered a hi-tech variation of the mobile seating that had been a part of amusement parks for decades. On Disney's involvement with the New York Fair of 1964 and the impact this had on rides like the *Haunted Mansion*, see Marling, pp. 114–32.

28. Brandon Kwiatek, 'An Age-Old Terror: The spirit of the Dark Ride has been around for centuries', *Skew*, vol. 11, October 1995, n.p. Available at <http://skew.ot.com/eleven/dark.html>.

29. Ronald C. Simons, *Boo!: Culture, Experience, and the Startle Reflex*, Oxford and New York: Oxford University Press, 1996, p. 8.

30. Simons, p. 82.

31. Carroll, p. 18.

32. Ibid., p. 22.

33. Steffen Hantke, 'Shudder As We Think: Reflections on Horror and/or Criticism', *Paradoxa*, (Special Horror Issue), no. 17, 2002 , p. 2.

2

High Concept Thrills and Chills
The Horror Blockbuster

Stacey Abbott

From *The Godfather* to *Jaws* to *Star Wars*, we see films that are increasingly plot-driven, increasingly visceral, kinetic, and fast-paced, increasingly reliant on special effects, increasingly 'fantastic' (and thus apolitical), and increasingly targeted at younger audiences.[1]

The Hollywood blockbuster is defined by Richard Maltby as a filmmaking practice that emerged in the 1950s and 1960s and which produced "lavish and spectacular features" that "were expected to perform equally spectacularly at the box-office".[2] The blockbuster has since evolved into the "event movie" where "merchandising of ancillary goods – toys, games, books, clothing, bubble-gum" are as important to the film's financial success as the box office.[3] The term high concept emerged in the 1970s when television producers were looking for programme ideas that could be conveyed in thirty-second television spots. As a result they would approve ideas that could be summarised in one sentence. This method of pitching and green-lighting new projects was adopted by Hollywood. A high concept film, therefore "has a straight forward, easily pitched and easily comprehended story".[4]

Justin Wyatt argues, however, that there is more to the high concept film than the simplicity of its narrative. A high concept film must be easily summarised but it must also be marketable.[5] In contemporary Hollywood where a wide release of a film is the standard and a film is expected to earn 90 per cent of its box office gross by its fifth week in the cinemas, the opening weekend of an event film is the most significant period in its release.[6] Studios need to flood the media with a marketing campaign that will guarantee the largest possible audiences in those first few weeks. The concept for the film must, therefore, possess a hook that can be used to draw audiences. The familiarity of a successful formula in the form of pre-sold premises, such as remakes or adaptations of bestselling novels, serves as one of the most effective hooks.[7]

The horror genre has not generally been the genre of choice for the blockbuster event film largely due to the perception that it appeals to a restricted audience. The films are usually given an NC-17 or R rating in the US, or an 18 or 15 in the UK, which immediately reduces the potential audience. Furthermore, contemporary horror films have most often been independent productions on a relatively small budget, and featuring a cast of genre regulars who are otherwise largely unknown to a wider audience. Certain films, however, have broken with this tradition and demonstrated that horror has mass appeal. Two notable examples of blockbuster horror films from the 1970s are *The Exorcist* (1973) and *Jaws* (1975). Both were adaptations of bestselling novels, optioned by the studios before the books were published. *The Exorcist*, with its graphic depictions of the possession of a thirteen-year-old girl, was released to controversy and was a striking commercial success. The film earned $86 million at the US/Canada box office.[8] Similarly, Steven Spielberg's shark movie *Jaws* is the film that marks the beginnings of the New Hollywood approach to the blockbuster as it demonstrated the potential financial success of frontloading a release. *Jaws* opened nationwide in 464 cinemas (substantially more than the average in 1975) and $2.5 million was spent on promoting the film in order to guarantee massive audiences in those first few, highly significant weeks of its release.

Since these films, other horrors have been conceived, produced and marketed as blockbusters. These include films in the *A Nightmare on Elm Street* series (1984–91) and *The Silence of the Lambs* (1991). *A Nightmare on Elm Street* is notable for how the popularity of its special effects, wise-cracking humour and, most importantly, its iconic main character Freddy Krueger led to the development of one of the most successful horror franchises. The first five films of the *Nightmare on Elm Street* series earned "over $400 million from the domestic and foreign box office, video cassette sales, television and merchandising".[9] Ian Conrich has demonstrated that while some of these productions were given an R Rating in the US and an 18 in the UK, the producers managed to develop an impressive consumer market that went beyond the films by targeting an extensive amount of merchandise at children. The marketing of such products as a children's storybook, board games, video games, bubblegum cards, yo-yos, watches and most surprising of all a replica of Freddy Krueger's infamous glove were used to encourage children "to develop an active interest in the films".[10]

While eventually becoming a franchise with the production of *Hannibal* (2001)[11] and *Red Dragon* (2002), Jonathan Demme's *The Silence of the Lambs* (1991), produced with the medium-size budget of £22 million, became one of the highest grossing individual horror films, earning $130 million worldwide.[12] In contrast to the *Nightmare on Elm Street* films, this was a prestige picture based upon the bestselling Thomas Harris novel and starring classically trained Anthony Hopkins and Academy Award winner Jodie Foster. It achieved its success by marketing itself as a psychological horror film/detective drama, specifically targeting adult rather than teen audiences and, while it offers the graphic and creatively produced gore indicative of most slasher films, particularly in the form of Hannibal Lecter's violent attack on Lieutenant Boyle and Sergeant Pembry, it is, as Yvonne Tasker argues, "arty-slasher . . . Boyle is transfigured into an angel, fixed to the bars of Lecter's former prison, his body opened up for our inspection".[13] The film's style and sophistication led to industry recognition usually withheld from horror movies with *The Silence of the Lambs* winning each of the top categories – including Best Picture, Best Director, Best Actor and Best Actress – at the 1992 Academy Awards.

It was the success of *The Silence of the Lambs* that specifically renewed Hollywood's interest in the horror genre in the 1990s, with the main studios returning to classic horror tales taken from literature, comics, folklore and film history, but now reinvented through the lens of the high concept movie. This chapter will explore the impact of such high concept approaches to film production, distribution and exhibition upon these pre-existing horror texts in order to ascertain how the 'horror' in the 'horror genre' survives amidst the demands and expectations of the Hollywood blockbuster.

Prestige Horror

Hollywood's next attempt at a big budget, prestige horror release began with Francis Ford Coppola's plans to adapt *Dracula* as *Bram Stoker's Dracula* (1992) to the big screen. While the novel had been the subject of numerous big and small screen adaptations, this version was hailed as the first that was truly faithful to the novel, based upon a screenplay written by James V. Hart. Rather than seeing the R rating as limiting its audience, Coppola's production company Zoetrope, working with Columbia Studios, saw this project as a potential big release for adult viewers. The novel was perceived as a classic that could extend well beyond the traditional audiences for horror and so they set to market the project to as wide an adult viewership as possible. This was not a unique case for, according to Rhona J. Berenstein, it was common practice for classic horror movies of the 1930s to be marketed to general audiences by playing upon the diverse characteristics of each film, particularly romance, drama, mystery and adventure.[14] The first American film version of *Dracula*, made by Tod Browning in 1931, was, like Coppola's film, largely aimed at a mixed audience and featured the tag line – "the Strangest Love the World has Ever Known". To further encourage the romance angle of the film, *Dracula* was released on Valentine's Day.

The promotional material for Coppola's film, like Browning's film before it, does not deny its horror origins but does consistently emphasise that *Bram Stoker's Dracula* is so much more. The production notes for the film describe Dracula as being "as appealing as he is repulsive, seductive as he is terrifying, the only demon who can take truly human form, allowing for the most complex metaphor and allegory".[15] This was not going to be a conventional horror film but "one of the greatest Gothic epics of all time".[16] The marketing campaign was built around this premise. Initial billboards were issued that simply said "Beware" to garner public interest and were eventually followed by a billboard and poster campaign featuring a Gothic gargoyle, framed by the words Love Never Dies. The romance of this line echoes the tag line for Browning's *Dracula* and captures Coppola's and the screenwriter James V. Hart's conception for the film. In interviews Coppola has consistently addressed the film's romantic angle, saying that "the film is as much about the romantic affliction of Count Dracula as it is about the horror!",[17] while Hart described the film as "'Gone with the Wind' with sex and violence".[18]

The tag line Love Never Dies was, however, one of the first public indications that the marketing and conceptual approach to this film was to draw upon the romantic associations with vampirism. The primary target audience for Coppola's film were late teenagers and young adults between the ages of seventeen and twenty-five but Columbia's marketing team were also looking for a strong female audience given the film's emphasis upon Gothic romance within a lushly designed period setting.[19] The casting of the film supports this strategy as its American stars Winona Ryder and Keanu Reeves were popular with young audiences, while Gary Oldman brought sex appeal to the role of the romantic Count as well as an association with independent cinema and quality British film productions. Like Oldman, the Oscar-winning Anthony Hopkins brought the respectability of a tradition of classical acting with the added value of fame for his performance as Hannibal Lecter in *The Silence of the Lambs*. Coupled with the casting was the reputation of the director himself, which lent the film critical prestige.

To maximise audience awareness, the release of Coppola's film on the 13 November 1992 was accompanied by a flood of related merchandise, such as new editions of the original novel, graphic novels, comic book adaptations, and glossy coffee table books about the making of the film. Other related items included coffin-shaped handbags, leather jackets embroidered with the film's logo, gargoyle earrings, t-shirts and Bloody Mary mixes. To cross-promote the film through other media, a video game, designed by Sega, was produced in consultation with Coppola to replicate the look and design of the film.[20]

What is particularly significant about the merchandising for the film was that the marketing team focused their attention on the world of fashion. A line of fashion specific to the film was designed for sale in the US and Canada, while international designers were invited to produce their own lines inspired by the film's distinctive costumes.[21] Fashion journalists were invited to the film's press junket, which included a fashion show. Lester Borden, the Vice-President of Merchandising for Sony Pictures explains that they wanted "to present something that was very much romantic, mysterious but also very saleable – something that really captured the essence of the film".[22]

The release of the film was carefully planned to dominate the US domestic market, which includes the US and Canada, over Christmas, and then move immediately to a broad international release in the new year. The film opened on 2,491 screens to a significant opening weekend gross of $30,521,679, demonstrating the success of its marketing campaign.[23] The film came in at number twelve of the top releases at the US and Canada's box office in 1992 with a box office gross of $81.4 million.[24]

The success of Coppola's film demonstrated the blockbuster potential for classic horror narratives, and so, in true high concept form, *Dracula* was followed by plans for the adaptation of two more nineteenth-century horror novels, Mary Shelley's *Frankenstein* (1818) and Robert Louis Stevenson's *Dr. Jekyll and Mr. Hyde* (1886). *Mary Shelley's Frankenstein* (1994), produced by Coppola and directed by the British actor Kenneth Branagh, followed in the tradition of *Bram Stoker's Dracula* by promising a faithful and epic adaptation. Taking a different approach, the new production of *Dr. Jekyll and Mr. Hyde* was based upon the best selling novel, *Mary Reilly: The Untold Story of Dr. Jekyll and Mr. Hyde* (1990), a contemporary reworking of the Stevenson story told from the point of view of Jekyll's maid. Both films, like *Dracula*, advanced the love story element of the original narrative. Columbia also returned to another classic horror monster, the Wolfman. The film was called *Wolf* (1994), and sets the werewolf myth within the contemporary world of office politics.

What each of these films has in common is its casting of major Hollywood stars not usually associated with the genre. Stars are one of the key selling points for a blockbuster and in the case of *Mary Shelley's Frankenstein*, the casting of the renowned method actor Robert De Niro as the monster was a marketing coup. While a degree of prestige and

3. A-list appeal: Jack Nicholson and Michele Pfeiffer, the stars of the prestige horror *Wolf*

success was brought to *Mary Reilly* (1996) through the reunion of the Oscar-winning team who made *Dangerous Liaisons* (1988), actor John Malkovich, director Stephen Frears, screenwriter Christopher Hampton and producer Norma Heyman, the major marketing attraction was the casting of Julia Roberts as the title character. This project was presented as Roberts's opportunity to break away from light genre movies and showcase her true acting ability by starring in a serious dramatic production. Finally, *Wolf* starred Jack Nicholson, extending his memorable and hyperbolic performances in *The Shining* (1980), *The Witches of Eastwick* (1987) and *Batman* (1989) into the wolfman role.

As with *Bram Stoker's Dracula*, the studio sought to distance each of these films from the specificity of the horror genre in order to draw in larger audiences. The production notes from *Wolf* specifically describe the film as "transcending the horror genre". Mike Nichols explained that he "thinks of it more as an adventure picture . . . It's the adventure of becoming something else and being empowered at first by all sorts of sensory increases and gifts and abilities you didn't have before . . . I think that certainly some of it is horror, but I hope more of it is adventure, and a journey into fantasy that may have a corollary in real life".[25] Similarly, the production notes for *Mary Shelley's Frankenstein* describe the film as a "great horror tale, a rip-roaring yarn, but within it is a wonderfully moving account of human relationships and an epic, full-blooded love story".[26]

Branagh argued that he saw the story as "less a horror film than a larger-than-life Gothic fairy tale. It's full of real psychological insights about family".[27] The production notes for *Mary Reilly* make a claim for the film's feminist stance by suggesting that while the story is one of a "woman in jeopardy, she ultimately takes charge of her own life".[28]

Unlike *Bram Stoker's Dracula*, this approach seemed to backfire as the reviews of *Wolf* demonstrate. Critics responded negatively to the film's attempt to make horror mainstream. For instance, Anne Billson replied to Nichols's comments on horror with the observation, "Can anyone tell me why the horror genre *needs* [her emphasis] to be transcended? . . . Horror is by its very nature tasteless, so when 'respectable' directors like Nichols decide to show the schlockmeisters how it should be done, their literal-minded approach spells disaster".[29]

With this less than successful summer release, Columbia put all of their effort into their next major event movie, *Mary Shelley's Frankenstein*, which was released simultaneously in the US and the UK on 4 November 1994. The studio launched an aggressive campaign to maximise the release of the film but it failed even worse than *Wolf*, with a domestic box office intake of only $11,212,889 in its first weekend.[30] By the time it had entered its fifth week at the US/Canada box office it had earned less than $22 million, a paltry domestic revenue considering the film's $45 million budget.[31] This failure was made all the more pronounced by the release of the long awaited adaptation of *Interview with the Vampire* (1994), as industry headlines such as "Vampire Steals Limelight from Frankenstein" demonstrate.[32] As if to prove that, despite *Mary Shelley's Frankenstein*'s failure, horror still had box office clout, the film opened on 2,604 screens and brought in a domestic income of $36,389,705 in its first weekend.[33] This high concept project featured a bestselling novel finally making it to the screen after approximately seventeen years of discussions and potential adaptations. The film starred an impressive cast of Tom Cruise, Brad Pitt, Antonio Banderas and Christian Slater, and was made by Neil Jordan and Stephen Woolley, who had produced the box office success *The Crying Game* (1992). This combination of factors made *Interview with the Vampire* a success for Warner Brothers.

As for *Mary Reilly*, problems on the set and with the script led to massive production delays and the film was finally released in March 1996 to a lacklustre response at the box office and with the critics.[34] While *Bram Stoker's Dracula* and *Interview with the Vampire* had both demonstrated the blockbuster potential of horror, they had not delivered a repeatable formula. The only one of the classic horror monsters of the 1930s and 1940s not revisited in this period was *The Mummy* (1932). This monster was to emerge during the next wave of horror blockbusters to hit the box office in the summer of 1999, when the strategy for success seems to have been more clearly developed.

Summer of '99: "Horror takes over US BO"[35]

In the summer of 1999 the horror genre dominated the US/Canada box office. Traditionally horror films are not a major part of the summer release schedule but reserved for the autumn, either around Halloween or as part of the Christmas holiday period. The summer of 1999, however, marked a distinctive change to this release pattern with a number of horror films opening throughout the summer and making a noticeable impact upon the box office, reconceived through the high concept style either in their reworking of the genre or through their marketing. Two of the summer's major releases drew directly from classic horror texts as source material: Stephen Sommers's remake of the Universal horror film *The Mummy* (1932) and Jan de Bont's *The Haunting*, an adaptation of the novel *The Haunting of Hill House* by Shirley Jackson that had been previously made in 1963 by Robert Wise. While Renny Harlin's *Deep Blue Sea* (1999), a film about genetically altered sharks, is not a remake or adaptation, it clearly not only drew upon the cultural memory of *Jaws* but also promised to exceed the thrills and scares of the Spielberg classic with the tagline "Bigger, Smarter, Faster, Meaner". The budgets of these three horror films (*The Mummy* – $76million; *The Haunting* – $80 million; *Deep Blue Sea* – $78 million) demonstrate the escalation of the horror classic to blockbuster status and the expectation that higher investment will bring higher rewards, a promise that to varying degrees paid off.[36]

The blockbuster season began with *The Mummy*. The film was released on 7 May, two weeks prior to the opening of the eagerly awaited *Star Wars 1: The Phantom Menace* (1999), in a carefully calculated manoeuvre to dominate the market for two full weeks. This strategy proved successful when the film went to number one at the box office, with a domestic opening weekend gross of $43,369,635 drawn from 3,209 screens across the US and Canada, and held this place for two weeks until *The Phantom Menace* took over for the summer.[37]

The next big calculated summer release was *The Haunting*, which opened on 23 July. Despite a negative response from the critics, the film, like *The Mummy* before it, leapt to the number one position in the charts with a box office gross of $33,435,140 (on 2,808 screens) in its first weekend.[38] A horror classic with an action and special effects twist, made by the director of *Speed* (1994) and *Twister* (1996), and produced by Spielberg, *The Haunting* was in many ways expected to be the major success of the summer. No one could have anticipated the appearance of *The Blair Witch Project* (1999), a small horror film with a budget of $35,000 that made unprecedented use of the Internet as a marketing tool prior to the film's release. This low budget surprise horror success, which opened the week prior to *The Haunting* on a mere 27 screens across the US and Canada, brought in an initial box office gross of $1,512,054.[39] By the time the film made the leap from 31 to 1,101 screens in its third week, its box office income rose to $36,140,299[40] and by the end of the summer (at the end of its seventh week in the cinema) it had earned $128,076,668.[41]

The summer culminated with *The Sixth Sense* (1999). The film was released on 6 August and, while it entered the box office at number one, it only earned $26,681,262 domestically, which was substantially less than *The Mummy* and *The Haunting* had made on their opening weekends.[42] The word of mouth effect of *The Sixth Sense*, however, led to the film remaining number one at the box office for five weeks, by which time it had earned $176,245,282.[43] This was more than either *The Mummy* and *The Haunting* made in thirteen weeks at the domestic box office.

The result of this amazing summer was that while the science-fiction and fantasy film *Star Wars 1: The Phantom Menace* dominated the box office for 1999, three films in the year's top ten box office grosses were horror films, each with a domestic gross exceeding $100 million: *The Sixth Sense* came in at number two with $277.7m, *The Mummy* was number eight with $155.3m and *The Blair Witch Project*'s $140.5m brought that film in at number ten. Going beyond that and looking at the top 100 films for the year, a further eight horror films can be found.[44] This is a noticeable increase in the box office clout of the horror film over previous, or subsequent, years. For instance, in 1990, thirteen horror films made it into the top 100, but the highest placed film was *Arachnophobia* at number twenty with a box office gross of $52,843,860.[45]

One of the key elements that distinguish many of these summer horror films from others within the genre and which contributed to their success is their PG-13 rating. While *Bram Stoker's Dracula* was designed to reach as broad an audience as possible for its R rating, the makers of *The Mummy*, *The Haunting* and *The Sixth Sense* aimed higher by recognising that the target audiences for summer releases are consistently young people. For instance, the makers of *The Sixth Sense* credit the film's success to the fact that it attracted two usually disparate audience groups, teenage boys drawn to the horror angle and middle-aged women drawn to the film's romantic subplot, an audience combination that was achievable because of its rating.[46] The result of this market shift for the genre is a sanitisation of its more extreme characteristics in order to avoid alienating audiences.[47]

While the makers of *The Mummy* were upfront about their affection for the original, they did seek to extend the narrative's appeal and generic allusions well beyond horror. Stephen Sommers describes his version of the Mummy as a "big roaring romantic adventure set in ancient Egypt",[48] and explains that his intention for the film was not to make a "Gothic horror movie or slasher movie. I wanted to make a film with characters I really cared about. Imhotep, the Mummy, is really romantic. Even in the original, Boris Karloff was a hopeless romantic, too".[49] If these comments seem reminiscent of the conceptual approaches to *Bram Stoker's Dracula*, then what distinguishes *The Mummy* from its more classical predecessors is its association with swashbuckling adventure and comedy. In the production notes for the film, numerous allusions are made to generic predecessors such as the swashbuckling films of Errol Flynn and the comic adventure style of *Raiders of the Lost Ark* (1981),[50] while the film's female lead, Rachel Weisz, compared the romance and comedy of the film to a "Katherine Hepburn/Cary Grant movie".[51] These differing generic references were a significant element of the marketing campaign. Two posters were produced, the first of which emphasised the horror elements of the film by featuring the three pyramids of Giza overshadowed by a monstrous mummified face, emerging from the blustering sands of the desert in mid-scream. In the second poster the mummy is presented in silhouette against the setting sun at the top right of the poster, while the bulk of the image is dominated by a trio of adventurers in the foreground. Brendan Fraser, bearing a large rifle, is the image of the swashbuckling adventurer, while Rachel Weisz's presence at his side confirms that romance will play a role in the film. The film's trailers were similarly designed to appeal to different audiences by presenting the horror elements of the film as part of a broader generic hybrid.

The Haunting, unlike *The Mummy*, went out of its way to embrace its horror origins as the behind-the-scenes featurette "An Inside Look at *The Haunting*" attests. In this documentary, the film is placed within the context of real haunted house stories. This horror heritage is reinforced by the fact that the film's producers, Donna Arkoff Roth and Susan Arnold, are the daughters of veteran horror film directors Sam Arkoff and Jack Arnold, while the discussions of the design of the house, "the real star of the movie", repeatedly point out that the sets were so vast and unsettling that many of the cast and crew were too afraid to stay on set after dark.[52] The trailers paint the film as a traditional haunted house story but this time with an action twist. For instance, the teaser trailer begins with the caption "This is Hill House", before a montage sequence of images of the house, over which a child's nursery rhyme about an evil house is read.[53] The final image is of a long shot of the house and as the rhyme concludes, "Won't you Come in", a male voice takes over the verse for the final two words and the house morphs into a monstrous face. The nursery rhyme is then replaced by the fast cutting of images of people running and screaming, intercut with the captions: "From the Director of *Speed* . . . of *Twister*".

This trailer sets up a range of expectations traditionally associated with the horror genre, such as the evil house, childhood fears and innocence under threat, but accompanied by the promise of high-speed action and cutting edge special effects. While the film's content clearly situates *The Haunting* within the horror genre, its reliance upon these computer special effects mixed with the film's many action pieces, in fact de-emphasises the horror and enabled the film to gain its PG-13 rating. It is this shift in tone that accounts for many of the negative criticisms written about the film. For instance Jonathan Romney wrote, "de Bont's farcical *Haunting* demonstrates the noxious effects of the digital age: there's something inherently unfrightening about pixel generated ectoplasm",[54] and J. Hoberman wrote, "Dreamwork's high powered version of the Shirley Jackson ghost story that was first filmed back in 1963, means to be something more than a loud and gory slimefest. But its anemic chills are only further diminished by the megamillions projected on the screen".[55] In both reviews, the film's lack of thrills is attributed to its multi-million dollar budget, suggesting that the spectacle of the enhanced special effects diffuse the horror appeal and sacrifice the genre's intensity and integrity. This is further supported by the success, both with audiences and many critics, of *The Blair Witch Project*, a film that works as a horror film without the need for special effects.

Sequels and Franchises

From as early as the classic Universal horror films of the 1930s through to the slasher and post-slasher films of the 1980s, Hollywood has maximised a successful horror formula by developing sequels. *The Mummy*, and the 1998 film *Blade*, however, introduced two new franchises to the horror market, structured much like *Nightmare on Elm Street* around New Hollywood synergy in which the films not only led to sequels but are platforms for a series of ancillary products such as movie soundtracks, toys, video games and, in the case of *The Mummy*, theme park rides. *Blade* (1998), a Marvel comic book about a vampire hunter who is himself half-vampire, offers a darker horror narrative with more graphic depictions of violence than other filmed comic book franchises such as *Superman* (1978), the *X-Men* (2000), or *Spider-Man* (2002). The half-vampire Blade, much like other

4. The iconic Blade (Wesley Snipes): The modern vampire as superhero

comic book figures *The Crow* (1994), *Hellboy* (2004), *Constantine* (2005), and *The Dark Knight* (2008), is a tortured hero, in this case torn by his own thirst for blood and his hatred for the vampires who made him a human/vampire hybrid.

The first film in the *Blade* series, starring Wesley Snipes, was made for $45 million.[56] Its large budget, simple premise, popular music soundtrack and special effects make it a clear example of a high concept film as described by Wyatt.[57] Furthermore, the film conforms to Wyatt's argument that style is an intrinsic element of the high concept film as the bold images in the film can be extracted for marketing purposes.[58] The horror genre is usually associated with a strong visual style, creating atmosphere through distinctive mise-en-scène or iconic monsters, but not necessarily with what Wyatt describes as the high concept film's tendency "toward sleek, modern environments mirroring the post-industrial age through austere and reflective surfaces".[59] *Blade* however makes complete use of such a visual design in its presentation of a vampire world made up of gleaming high-rises, modern architecture and impeccable fashion style. Additionally, *Blade's* use of colour, in keeping with high concept's tendency toward a "minimal color scheme", is visually designed around the contrast between black, silver and white (both in clothing and set design).[60] This contrast is of course counterbalanced with regular bursts of bright shiny red blood as in the bloodbath beginning sequence in which an orgiastic vampire rave in a meat factory storeroom, lit with strobe lighting, climaxes in a literal shower of blood over the dance floor. Furthermore, Blade is himself an iconic image, the embodiment of a sleek modern superhero in his black leather trousers, long flowing coat, body artfully designed with tattoos and adorned with his shiny silver weaponry.

Blade opened on 21 August 1998, ending the summer season of releases and earned $17,073,856 domestically in its first weekend, a strong enough opening to immediately green-light plans for a sequel.[61] For this, the film's budget went up by $10 million and was evidenced through more spectacular production design and cutting edge digital effects.[62] There is a shift in the tone of the film away from the self-tortured Blade to a superhero who enjoys the action but, unlike most horror blockbusters, the aim of the sequel, according to scriptwriter David Goyer, was to play up the horror angle.[63] To achieve this they hired Mexican horror filmmaker Guillermo del Toro[64] who confirmed that he "was attracted to the idea of making vampires scary again . . . They have become almost Gothic romance heroes à la Anne Rice. I wanted to find the animal component again: something that just wants to drink your blood and kill you".[65]

Blade 2 was released in March 2002 and earned $32,528,016 in the US and Canada on its opening weekend.[66] This was a substantially higher gross than the first film, demonstrating a much broader awareness of the product. It remained in the top ten at the box office for four weeks but in that time it had earned \$73,873,818,[67] an example of the tendency for contemporary blockbusters to earn the bulk of their income at the front end of their release before moving on to DVD releases.[68]

While *Blade* is a franchise aimed at older viewers, *The Mummy*, as has already been discussed, was designed specifically for the broadest market possible and therefore proved more lucrative as a franchise. Stephen Sommers reports that the morning following the opening of *The Mummy*, he was contacted by the studio heads and invited to direct the sequel to the film. While all of the participants in the first film stressed the importance of quality, their primary aim for the sequel, *The Mummy Returns* (2001), was not to vary from the successful formula but to deliver *more* of what made the first a success. In the film's production notes, Sommers explained that he wanted to not only make the sequel bigger but better; John Berton, the Visual Effects Supervisor from ILM, promised more spectacular special effects, and Oded Fehr claimed the film contains more action then the first.[69] In conceiving this sequel, however, the makers were planning more then just a film. Brendan Fraser described the film as a "ride – it is something you really want to go on and get out the other side . . . and do it again and again and again",[70] which, it turns out, is possible through both the video game and the Universal Studios theme park ride based on the film. Furthermore, the introduction of a new character played by WWF superstar The Rock not only opened the film to a potential new market by drawing in his fans, but also set up the next installment in the franchise, the film *The Scorpion King* (2002). Following the success of *The Mummy* franchise, which later included *The Mummy: Tomb of the Dragon Emperor* (2008), Sommers returned to the classics of Universal horror by making *Van Helsing* (2004), another horror/adventure film hybrid this time based around the Dracula, Frankenstein and Wolfman films of the 1930s, which has also become an attraction at the Universal Studios theme park.

As Thomas Schatz explains, in the new industry ruled by multi-media conglomerates, it is not only possible but preferable for viewers to experience the film across media. "The size, scope, and emotional charge of the movie and its concurrent ad campaign certainly privilege the big screen 'version' of the story, but the movie itself scarcely begins or ends the textual cycle".[71] This multimedia approach continues to influence such contemporary horror films as the video-game-inspired *Resident Evil* (2002), and the sequel to *Interview with the Vampire, Queen of the Damned* (2002), which taps into the music industry not only through the casting of rock star Aaliyah but also through a rock soundtrack written exclusively for the film.

The 1990s produced two key periods in which the horror genre was moved out of niche markets and pushed into the mainstream. These are, of course, not the only examples of horror blockbusters, but their successes and failures are instructive. The adult-oriented literary adaptation was not a formula that could be successfully reproduced, while the teen-targeted comic book adventures were often a success. What both types of high concept horror films demonstrate, however, is that for Hollywood producers to invest in horror in the hopes of manufacturing a blockbuster, horror can only be one of many genre influences. The attempt to appeal to general audiences and to manipulate the genre to suit the demands of other media, results in horror no longer being the priority but simply one way of reading and responding to the experience. Equally, these films also demonstrate that there continues to be a taste for horror within the mainstream and a place for the genre within the top end of the box office and at the multiplexes.

Notes

1. Thomas Schatz, 'New Hollywood', in Jim Collins, Hilary Radner and Ava Preacher Collins, eds, *Film Theory Goes to the Movies*, New York and London: Routledge, 1993, p. 19.
2. Richard Maltby, *Hollywood Cinema*, 2nd edn, Oxford: Blackwell Publishing, 2003, p. 580.
3. Ibid, p. 582.
4. Richard Maltby, '"Nobody Knows Everything": Post-Classical Historiography and Consolidated Entertainment', in Steve Neale and Murray Smith, eds, *Contemporary Hollywood Cinema*, London: New York: Routledge, 1998, p. 37.
5. Justin Wyatt, *High Concept: Movies and Marketing in Hollywood*, Austin: University of Texas Press, 1994, p. 9.
6. Maltby, *Hollywood Cinema*, pp. 200–1.
7. Wyatt, p. 15.
8. Schatz, p. 17. Note that, unless otherwise indicated, all box office figures quoted refer to the US and Canadian box office.
9. Ian Conrich, 'Seducing the Subject: Freddy Krueger, Popular Culture and the *Nightmare on Elm Street* films', in Alain Silver and James Ursini, eds, *Horror Film Reader*, New York: Limelight Editions 2000, p. 223.
10. Ibid., p. 231.
11. For a discussion of *Hannibal* as a horror event movie see Philip L. Simpson, 'The Horror "Event" Movie: *The Mummy*, *Hannibal*, and *Signs*', in Steffen Hantke, ed., *Horror Film: Creating and Marketing Fear*, Jackson: University of Mississippi Press, 2004, pp. 85–98.

12. Yvonne Tasker, *Silence of the Lambs*, London: British Film Institute, 2002, p. 35.
13. Ibid, p. 32.
14. Rhona J. Berenstein, *Attack of the Leading Ladies: Gender, Sexuality and Spectatorship in Classic Horror Cinema*, New York: Columbia University Press, 1996, p. 69.
15. Production Notes for *Bram Stoker's Dracula*, p. 8.
16. Ibid., p. 1.
17. Francis Ford Coppola, quoted by Tom Hutchinson, 'Hot-Blooded Dracula', *Mail on Sunday*, 25 October 1992, p. 3. See also Thomas Austin, '"Gone With the Wings Plus Fangs": Genre, Taste and Distinction in the Assembly, Marketing and Reception of *Bram Stoker's Dracula*', in Steve Neale, ed., *Genre and Contemporary Hollywood*, London: British Film Institute, 2002, pp. 294–308.
18. Jim Hart, quoted by Suzi Feay, 'Staking Reputations', *Time Out*, 28 October 1992, p. 18.
19. Brigid Cherry's research on female fans of horror films has shown that Gothic and historical settings play a significant role in women's preferences within the horror genre. Brigid Cherry, 'Refusing to Refuse to Look: Female Viewers of the Horror Film', in Melvyn Stokes and Richard Maltby, eds, *Identifying Hollywood Audiences: Cultural Identity and the Movies*, London: British Film Institute, 1996, pp. 187–203.
20. Ana Maria Bahiana, 'Tooth and Nail', *Screen International*, no. 883, 13–19 November 1992, p. 12.
21. Brigid Cherry's research around female horror fandom strongly suggests that "dressing up and fashion are the principal form of commodity purchase associated with vampire fan culture". Brigid Cherry, 'Screaming for Release: Femininity and Horror Film Fandom in Britain', in Steve Chibnall and Julian Petley, eds, *British Horror Cinema*, London: Routledge, 2002, p. 52.
22. Lester Border, quoted by Ana Maria Bahiana in 'Tooth and Nail', p. 12.
23. *Screen International*, no. 884, 20–26 November 1992, p. 19.
24. *Screen International*, no. 892, 29 January–4 February 1993, p. 15.
25. Mike Nichols, Production Notes for *Wolf*, p. 2.
26. Kenneth Branagh, Production Notes for *Mary Shelley's Frankenstein*, p. 1.
27. Ibid., p. 3.
28. Ned Tanen, Production Notes for *Mary Reilly*, p. 3.
29. Anne Billson, 'Throwing Jack to the Werewolves', *Sunday Telegraph*, 28 August 1994, p. 4.
30. *Screen International*, no. 983, 11–17 November 1994, p. 21.
31. *Screen International*, no. 987, 9–15 December 1994, p. 37.
32. 'Vampire Steals Limelight from Frankenstein', *Screen International* no. 984, 18–24 November 1994, p. 25.
33. Ibid.
34. Its opening weekend domestic gross totalled $2,812,620. *Screen International*, no. 1047, 1–7 March 1996, p. 25.

35. *Screen International*, no. 1219, 30 July–5 August 1999, p. 1.
36. Budget figures available from <http://www.imdb.com>.
37. *Screen International*, no. 1210, 14–21 May 1999, p. 25.
38. *Screen International*, no. 1219, 30 July–5 August 1999, p. 37.
39. *Screen International*, no. 1218, 23–29 July 1999, p. 21.
40. *Screen International*, no. 1220, 6–12 August 1999, p. 29.
41. *Screen International*, no. 1224, 3–9 September 1999, p. 25.
42. *Screen International*, no. 1221, 13–19 August 1999, p. 25.
43. *Screen International*, no. 1225, 10–16 September 1999, p. 25.
44. #21 *Sleepy Hollow* ($96.7m); #22 *The Haunting* ($91.2m), #26 *Deep Blue Sea* ($73.6m), #47 *Stigmata* ($50m), #48 *House on Haunted Hill* (40.8m), #62 *Lake Placid* ($31.8m), #80 *Stir of Echoes* ($21.1m), #87 *The Rage: Carrie 2* ($17.8m). 'Gross Roots', *Entertainment Weekly*, no. 524, 4 February 2000, pp. 38–9.
45. *Screen International*, no. 789, 11–17 January 1990, p. 12.
45. 'Reaching the Audience'. Additionality on *The Sixth Sense* DVD, Hollywood Pictures, Region 1. Another element that contributed to its success was the casting of Bruce Willis against his action hero type as the soft-spoken, child psychologist, while the film's twist ending encouraged repeat viewing.
47. In 1990, while making *Darkman*, Sam Raimi, director of *The Evil Dead* trilogy (1982–92), confirmed that with a larger Hollywood budget comes the pressure to conform to more cautious demands. Universal Studios were concerned that his traditional style was too wild and "would alienate mainstream audiences". 'A Conversation with Sam Raimi', *Screen International*, no. 786, 8–14 December 1990, p. 9. In 1994, Allan Hunter noted that the shift of horror from the periphery of the industry to the mainstream resulted in the genre becoming sanitised. Allan Hunter, 'Undying Attraction', *Screen International*, no. 979, 14–21 October 1994, p. 16.
48. Stephen Sommers, Production Notes for *The Mummy*, p. 4.
49. Ibid., p. 5.
50. See James Jacks, Production Notes for *The Mummy*, pp. 4–5.
51. Rachel Weisz, Production Notes for *The Mummy*, p. 6.
52. Behind the scenes featurette on *The Haunting* DVD, Dreamworks, Region 2.
53. "There once was a house; A bright happy home; Something bad happened; Now it sits all alone. These are its bones; this is its skin [close up images of the bricks and stones]; These are its eyes [over a long shot of the house with lights in the windows flickering as if the eyes were winking]. "Won't you come in". [Over an image of the house morphing into a face.]
54. Jonathan Romney, 'The Return of the Shadow', *The Guardian*, 22 September 1999, p. 16.
55. J. Hoberman, 'Chills and Spills', *Village Voice*, 3 August 1999, p. 59.
56. Scott Macmillan, 'Case Study: *Blade 2: Bloodhunt*', *Screen International*, no. 1314, 29 June–5 July 2001, p. 19.
57. Wyatt, p. 23.

58. Ibid., p. 17.
59. Ibid., p. 30.
60. Ibid., p. 28.
61. Macmillan, p. 19.
62. Ibid.
63. David Goyer, interview in 'Bloodpack: Behind the Scenes Documentary', *Blade 2* DVD, New Line Cinema Region 2.
64. Director of *Cronos* (1993), *Mimic* (1997), *El Espinazo del diablo* [*The Devil's Backbone*] (2001) and, later, *Hellboy* (2004), *El Laberinto del fauno* [*Pan's Labyrinth*] (2006), and *Hellboy II: The Golden Army* (2008).
65. Guillermo del Toro, quoted by Scott Macmillan, 'Close Up: Guillermo Del Toro', *Screen International*, no. 1314, 29 June–4 July 2001, p. 19.
66. *Screen International*, no. 1350, 29 March–4 April 2002, p. 21.
67. *Screen International*, no. 1353, 19–25 April 2002, p. 21.
68. The franchise was extended to include *Blade: Trinity* (2004).
69. See the production notes for *The Mummy*.
70. Brendan Fraser, Production notes for *The Mummy*, p. 34.
71. Schatz, p. 34.

3

Bringing It All Back Home
Horror Cinema and Video Culture

LINDA BADLEY

Introduction: Home? Video

The word 'home' in 'home video' just does not cut it. The spheres of public and private, of theatrical and domestic exhibition are no more separate than the boundary-effacing terms 'home theatre' and 'home office'. Since the 1960s, as Timothy Corrigan has noted, "the centre of movie viewing has shifted away from the screen and become dispersed in the hands of audiences with more (real and remote) control than possibly ever before".[1] With a smorgasbord of cable/satellite television channels, video rental and retail venues multiplying online, PC-activated DVDs that hotlink to archives or transform into role-playing games (not to mention streaming video and live web casts), domestic viewing is changing the way movies are experienced, distributed and made. Increasingly, a 'film' is experienced as a node in the intermediary universe.

This essay about horror on and as video takes four interlocking perspectives. The first surveys production and consumption of horror throughout our ongoing video revolution, beginning with the VCR rush of the early 1980s and moving to the increasingly digitalised present. The second moves to consider how video technology has enabled a new era of *homemade* horror video as guerrilla 'do-it-yourself' filmmakers, amateur to semi-pro, using consumer-level digital cameras and desktop movie shakers, do their part in a war against corporate Hollywood. Moving from production to reception, section three focuses on a video-enabled cycle through which horror auteurs have been and continue to be consumed and reproduced. A conclusion briefly examines the darker side of video culture, finding that the horror *of* video is a concept informing millennial and post-9/11 'film'.

Documentary Featurette: Horror and the Video Revolution

The neo-horror renaissance celebrated by Robin Wood in *American Nightmare* (1979) was over by the 1980s, some histories tell us, and one culprit was the video culture that the horror boom had helped create.[2] As video (so the argument went), horror had invaded rental stores and children's minds with slasher, splatter and teen pics and made obsolete the film communities that had supported the repertories, drive-ins and art-houses. Once out of the theatres, horror was virulent and uncontrollable. Video activated and spread whatever plague the genre was born from, detractors and censors warned, encouraging its impulse to return to the wound site, replay the 'nasty bits', and copy itself in remakes and sequels whose purpose was to top the previous one in shock and gore.[3]

There was a counterargument, of course: If this repetition compulsion resulted in the bloody monotony of *Friday the 13th* (1980), it also produced the brilliant horror-comedy mutation of *The Evil Dead* (1982) and the philosophical, prophetic body horror of David Cronenberg. A different account might claim that video culture provoked horror's second rebirth, one that Philip Brophy announced in 1983 in terms of horror's "violent awareness of itself as a saturated genre".[4] On (and as) video, which rendered it re-viewable and renewable, the genre reinvented itself as metahorror. It became its own cultural critic and historian, producing a wave of hip, self-aware, postmodern splatterpunk – as in George A. Romero's *Dawn of the Dead* (1978) and *Day of the Dead* (1985), Cronenberg's *Scanners* (1980), *Videodrome* (1983), and *The Fly* (1986), John Carpenter's *The Thing* (1982), Wes Craven's *A Nightmare on Elm Street* (1984), Brian De Palma's *Body Double* (1984), and Sam Raimi's *Evil Dead 2* (1987). The wave peaked, subsided and peaked again with the *Scream* cycle of the late 1990s, followed by a recent surge in low-budget, independent, often direct-to-video (DTV) films, all of which have the latest, digital, phase of the video revolution to thank. The current resurgence of interest in cult, horror, and campy B-cinema, director Philippe Mora theorises in the May 2003 issue of *DVD ETC.*, results from "new generations of viewers discovering these films on cable and DVD. Collaterally, new writers in media also discover these movies and explore these waters".[5] In the most exciting trend, international (especially Asian) horror has become newly accessible and wildly popular throughout the Western world, thanks to the globe-sweeping ubiquity of video/DVD.[6]

For people born in the US in the second half of the last century, a sense of cinema begins at home. Here, viewers most likely discovered the public domain of genre, weird, and cult movies through early 1980s cable television and video or perhaps earlier, through *Shock Theater*, the late night horror slot available on network or local television in most North American cities from the 1950s to the present. As Bryant Frazer explains, 1980s American cable television had a "healthy eclecticism" – "you could catch up with Bergman, Buñuel, and Fellini (not to mention Cronenberg and Carpenter) late at night on Cinemax, in between screenings of *Bilitis* . . . and *Emmanuelle in Bangkok*".[7]

This eclecticism was equally a characteristic of the videotape and rental industries in the VCR rush of the early 1980s, when many cheap video labels (such as Intervision in the UK) and independent rental outlets emerged and, for the few short years before Blockbuster, thrived. Ian Conrich notes how UK video companies seeking quick profits acquired "many, often obscure films of a violent and carnal nature" for distribution, packaging them with provocative covers.[8] As videotape prices fell and home video libraries expanded, horror fans became collectors, and were imprinted with a heritage unique in cultural depth and range. One vestige of the era Murfreesboro, Tennessee's, Video Culture, specialises in rare, cult, and hard-to-find videos. Born in 1995 to support the owners' personal collection, the store rents out more than 8,000 videos and DVDs, sells posters and paraphernalia, and functions as an alternative community centre. Video Culture does not advertise other than by word-of-mouth, encourages smoking, and features Buddy, a walking archive with an encyclopaedic knowledge of Italian zombie pictures.[9]

Between the mid-1980s and the early 1990s, as the rental chains drove out the independents, the heydays' eclectic, independent spirit was sustained within the back pages of fan publications (*Fangoria, Gorezone, Cinefantastique, Video Watchdog,* and *Asian Cult Cinema*) and mail-order catalogues (Sinister Cinema, European Trash Cinema, Something Weird Video, Scorched Earth Productions, and Facets Multimedia), from which the fans stocked their collections. That spirit has been reborn in virtual space, thanks to the video/DVD trade on eBay, Buy.com, Amazon.com, and hundreds of independent websites, which make it possible for nearly anyone in the Western world to obtain hard-to-find video titles almost overnight. Even more recently, web-based rental venues such as Neflix, GreenCine, and DVDs on Tap are now making international cult, horror, and exploitation DVDs available and in demand as never before. The Independent Film and Sundance Channels often sponsor international and independent horror, providing loud, unregenerate voices from the margin. Horror flourishes, like the alternative music scene, via the cinematic equivalent of garage bands and MP3, as direct-to-video auteurs distribute their work via the Internet.

A fascinating politics of taste has directed this video revolution. As Joan Hawkins, invoking Pierre Bourdieu, has argued, both avant-garde and 'low'/body cultures have "traditionally had [a stake] in challenging the formally constructed notion of mainstream good taste".[10] As any comprehensive collection demonstrates, horror's paracinematic heritage is eclectic – spanning Euroschlock, George A. Romero and the avant-garde, underground and Mario Bava, *Bloodsucking Freaks* (1976) and *Les Yeux sans visage (Eyes Without a Face*, 1960), and Roger Corman.[11] More to the point is how video, especially DVD, has made horror's international and cultural diversity accessible and hip. On 27–28 September 2002, for example, the Independent Film Channel presented The IFC Cult of Criterion Festival celebrating Criterion's release of five digitally-remastered 'cult masterpieces', Benjamin Christensen's *Häxan* (Denmark, 1922), Masaki Kobayashi's *Kwaidan* (Japan, 1964), Brian De Palma's *Sisters* (US, 1973), Lars von Trier's *The Element of Crime* (Denmark, 1984), and George Sluizer's *The Vanishing* (Holland, 1988).

The role of Criterion, whose fine line laser disks were the first source of the director's commentaries and 'making of' featurettes that have now become standard on DVD, cannot be overemphasised. In the late 1990s, Criterion, Anchor Bay and Universal began to offer a high quality DVD product in classic horror and/or edgy genre entertainment. Notable examples are the Kino International and Image Entertainment restorations of silent German Expressionist classics or Criterion's royal treatment of Michael Powell's *Peeping Tom* (1960), which feature international film scholars such as Lokke Heiss or Laura Mulvey providing sophisticated master classes on audio commentary tracks. Recent restorations of silent or non-scored DVDs have also provided alternative sound tracks, such as the specially composed Philip Glass score for the Universal Classic Monster Collection's release of Tod Browning's *Dracula* (1931/2002) or the Silent Orchestra's score for Image Entertainment's Special Edition of F.W. Murnau's *Nosferatu* (1922/2002). These DVDs amount to upscale cinema 'events' and are reviewed in elite journals such as *Sight and Sound* and *Film Comment*.

They are also reviewed in *Video Watchdog*, the magazine for finicky horror, sci-fi, fantasy, and exploitation movie fans. Invented in 1985 by B-film archivist Tim Lucas, *Watchdog* was the first effort to focus on how films were presented in sell-thru packages and represented "the first steps toward a new way of writing about home video", one that assumed that video was "the cinema's own living archive".[12] Taking advantage of how video allowed, even compelled, one to watch a film an indefinite number of times, Lucas viewed videos side by side, noting transfer quality, cuts, and aspect ratios and treated the home viewer as a discriminating collector, scholar, and critic. In applying auteurist standards to international cult and exploitation films maimed by territorial censors and ignored by critics,

Video Watchdog parodied (and complemented) Facets and Criterion and predicted the future of DVD, on which such attention to the 'lowest' films became de rigueur.[13]

Not Coming to a Theatre Near You: DTV and D.I.Y. (the 1990s to the Present)

Unlike kid-friendly summer blockbuster fantasies such as *Spider-Man* (2002), and *The Hulk* (2003), horror films with smaller budgets and "dark or heady messages that studios think audiences can't handle" often find a 'second wind' and better life on video and are moved quickly to that destination.[14] Released in theatres on 16 July 1999, *The Blair Witch Project* (despite its mega box-office success), was one of the fastest turnovers of its time (available on video by 22 October 1999) and became an indicator of things to come. Now that video counts for the largest percentage of a studio's revenues (with VHS having been replaced by vast DVD sales), most movies are "released theatrically only to legitimise their imminent video release", *DVDFILE* editor Peter M. Bracke argues, and poor box-office numbers hardly sentence a film to death.[15]

In the rental and retail arena, word of mouth has time to accumulate real meaning, says media analyst Pat Moran, mentioning *Thir13en Ghosts* (2001), and *Stir of Echoes* (1999), and the thriller *Don't Say a Word* (2001), as films that did exceptionally good business on video.[16] Second-wind films are often made into bigger-budget sequels, a pattern that holds true especially of slightly offbeat films such as *Darkman* (1990) and *From Dusk Till Dawn* (1996). Edgy low-budget horror movies (such as the 2002 releases *The Ring*, *One Hour Photo*, *My Little Eye*, and *28 Days Later*) bank on the video/DVD market, as the quality and quantity of their extras – commentary tracks, featurettes, trailers, storyboards, alternate branched versions and other interactive features – attest.

The other side of this story (and the real subject of this section), direct-to-video (DTV) horror was inaugurated in 1988 by a no-budget slasher film, *The Ripper*. Until recently "the black sheep of the entertainment world", by the late 1990s DTV was what *Screen Review* calls "the industry's fattest cash cow", with children's video, softcore porn, and horror dominating this rung of the market and filling an increasing demand.[17] Direct-to-video has special appeal as new generations recover horror's heritage on video. Elite Entertainment is typical of DTV horror studios in covering their losses by distributing public domain 'classics' in DVD packages designed to recapture the ambience of the past. The Drive-In Discs series recreates not merely the visual experience of the typical double feature (*Screaming*

5. The resourceful Stefan Avalos (left) and Lance Weiler, the team behind the digitally shot, pseudo-documentary *The Last Broadcast*

Skull [1958]/*Attack of the Giant Leeches* [1959], *The Giant Gila Monster* [1959]/*The Wasp Woman* [1960]) but the extras as well: concession stand ads, the countdown clock, cartoons, vintage ads, previews, and 'Distorto' sound. (This makes the film's soundtrack available only through the front left speaker, enhanced by the ambient surround sound of other speakers, crickets, and laughter.)[18] Applying a similar idea in the DTV *Boogeymen* (2001), FlixMix crossed the monster mash with the horror compilation (familiar since the early 1980s) in a way that fully embraced DVD, creating a completely non-linear, interactive product.[19]

Since the impact of *The Blair Witch Project* (1999) re-established the genre's association with independent filmmaking at the turn of the millennium, no-budget, do-it-yourself horror has accumulated cultural capital, paradoxically, *for* its profit margin, counter-cultural cachet, and what used to be called, in the days of William Castle, showmanship. Now, the 'domestication' of cinema extends not only to the exhibition of films at home but to the production end as well, bringing it all back home. In the digital age, as Lars von Trier announced at Cannes in 1995, "a technological storm is raging, the result of which will be the ultimate democratisation of the cinema. For the first time, anyone can make movies".[20] And anyone can make them at 'home', in several senses.

The appetite for low-budget and DTV niche films now fuels creativity in post-punk do-it-yourselfers who, in the tradition of Roger Corman's protégés, often begin with a 'little' horror film.[21] The cost of making a DVD is a fraction of making a 35mm print, much less the expense of a theatrical release. Video is increasingly the indie choice especially where budgets are tight or where digital video's dynamism, intimacy, and in-your-face realism enhances the horror – as in Danny Boyle's (and Dogme cinematographer Anthony Dod Mantle's) apocalyptic zombie plague epic, *28 Days Later*.[22]

But it may have been *Blair Witch*'s less famous precursor *The Last Broadcast* (1998), that truly confirmed von Trier's assertion that anyone could make an effective film. Shot entirely on digital, this smart, layered, self-reflexive pseudo-documentary about two public-access TV-show hosts murdered in the woods was edited and produced with desktop software, and distributed on the Internet, all for about $900. Unable to afford a 35mm print, filmmakers Stefan Avalos and Lance Weiler brought their own digital projectors to film festivals, later setting up a distribution system through which the film was broadcast via satellite to theatres across the country. In 1999, on the same desktop computer they had used to edit the films, Avalos and Weiler produced a DVD that includes, besides a directors' commentary several featurettes explaining how they conceived, made, and distributed "the first international all-digital release". In contrast to the mystifying and shifting layers of *The Blair Witch Project* DVD (and website), *The Last Broadcast* DVD is a workshop. Demonstrating how the filmmakers used consumer programmes like PhotoShop to manipulate, create, and edit their images, it encourages the home video consumer to do the same.[23]

One thing that brings foreign, horror, trash, and underground cinema together is a combination of communitarianism and also oppositional, 'punk', or do-it-yourself auteurism. Within this context, the underground horror scene in particular is 'oddly popular', comments Sarah Effron: "You don't see fans of underground comedy or drama or action pictures, but homemade horror films always have a following. Fans see the films at special screenings or at specialty video stores. And like most cult hobbies, it flourishes on the Internet".[24] Underground horror appeals to people who want something 'real', raw, or extreme. But horror DTVs produced and distributed internationally by Brain Damage (*Death Factory* [2002], *Hollywood Vampyr* [2003], *Traces of Death Box Set* [2003], *Invitation* [2004]), SubRosa (*Meat Market* [2000], *Meat Market 2* [2001], *Binge & Purge* [2002], *Exhumed* [2003]), Ultragore Underground Horror (*Zombie Gore*, 2003), Badman Productions (*Badman 3: Summer of Love*, 2002), and Nightmare Entertainment (*Goth*, 2003) also make a point of containing

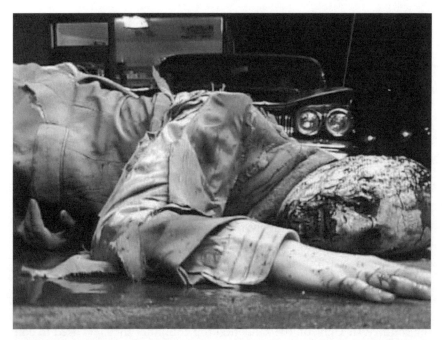

6. Underground horror: *Meat Market*, the low budget tribute to George A. Romero

more and 'better' – more fun and ultimately more instructive – extras than mainstream DVD. Lloyd Kaufman's *Terror Firmer (Unrated Director's Cut DVD)* (1999), the story of a low-budget film crew stalked by a deranged killer, is a two-disc bonanza with 'making of' video, three commentary tracks, and deleted and 'alternate' scenes with commentary, 'Kaufman family secrets', and a video game DVD-ROM.

Frontline's *Meat Market*, made for less than $2,000 and distributed online, was Canadian auteur Brian Clement's neo-splatterpunk tribute to Romero's classic 'Dead' films and appropriately a satire on consumerism, government bureaucracy, and youth culture. With its army of flesh eating zombies, a deranged scientist, a Mexican wrestler, three lesbian vampires, and "enough wit and ingenuity to sink a hundred *Ghost Ships*", according to *Horrorview*'s Head Cheeze, Clement's work "proves that the best horror films are not only being made outside of Hollywood, they are being made for peanuts by people who know what fans of this genre want to see".[25] Another case in point, Mike Mendez' *The Convent* (2000), a furiously energetic, witty variation on the demon-possessed zombie motif, found early fan favour at festivals, but its mix of extreme gore, black humour, and religious satire confused potential distributors. Of this film's many extras, the fan favourite is the interactive 'Gore-On-Demand' feature, which not only allows the spectator to choose 'death' scenes and the order in which they are viewed but also to see them as they were filmed, with the already overt 'special effects' mechanisms (squibs, shunts, masks, flamegear) exposed in slow motion. Instead of the awe-inspiring 'how-they-did-it' documentary one finds on, say *The Planet of the Apes* (2001) DVD, where the anatomy of a scene demonstrates power and capital beyond the capacity of all but a elite few, *The Convent* empowers the would-be horror auteur down to the child improvising a Halloween costume, to make a 'film'.

Independence allowed films like *The Convent* and *Meat Market* to flaunt social satire on overconsumption, eating disorders, religious hypocrisy and corporate power in an iconically arresting style. But the point and perhaps primary pleasure of engaging with horror DTV is envisioning oneself in the role of embattled underground auteur, which *Meat Market* in particular invites. Signed 'A Brian Clement Picture', *Meat Market* pretends to be a 'message' film engaged, like its protagonists, in all-out guerrilla warfare. Pitting its motley street fighters against yuppie zombies who prey on homeless youth, the film is really about Clement's, SubRosa Studios, and the genre's struggle with corporate Hollywood. Before the credits and in place of, say, a sophisticated Dreamworks logo, the familiar 'HOLLYWOOD' sign via searchlights appears on the screen, followed after a beat by 'IS A DISEASE . . .'. and, finally: 'MEET THE CURE'.

But home video has shaped the new D.I.Y. auteurisms of the 1990s through the present in other ways. Supported by a large consumer base and an intensely devoted fan culture, horror auteurs figure prominently in this domestic economy, as fans consume, collect, and canonise directors from James Whale to Romero, Larry Fessenden, and Guillermo del Toro, and aspire to directing horror films themselves. It helps, as in the well-known instances of Francis Ford Coppola, Roman Polanski, De Palma, David Lynch, Sam Raimi, Tim Burton, and Peter Jackson that a horror film is often a director's first 'real' job.[26]

A thoroughly documented example of this cycle of consumption and reproduction is thirty-two-year-old high school dropout Mark Borchardt, the subject of Chris Smith's Sundance Grand Jury Prize-winning documentary *American Movie: The Making of Northwestern* (1999), which became a fan favourite on DVD. Imprinted via VHS by the raw, cinema vérité effects – "gray skies and dead trees and the National Guard and all" – of Romero's *Living Dead* trilogy and Tobe Hooper's *Texas Chain Saw Massacre* (1974), Borchardt dreams of making nothing short of the Great American movie, to wit, *Northwestern*, a dark, psychological drama. The film he actually completes is a 37 minute, direct-to-video 'thriller' *Coven* (1997), which he distributes from his website. The downsizing from *Northwestern* to *Coven* underscores the central point: that the signature film Mark had envisioned and *Coven* are more or less the same film. Another key point is horror video's role in Borchardt's self-education, worldview, auteurial style, and eventual product. Yet another is the extent to which underground filmmaking is a 'home movie' – quite literally a family affair. Borchardt has been making films since he was fourteen, lives in his mother's basement, supports three children by pitching newspapers and working at a cemetery, and makes films in a confessional mode with a cast and crew gleaned from friends and family members.

As Paul Arthur contends, Borchardt's home-schooled auteurism is the new American Dream. The Western once embodied our "cherished cultural myths"; today "as close as we get is the shimmering belief that every one of us, regardless of race, creed, or creative ability, is destined to make a movie – or . . . be endlessly conversant with the intimate details of the moviemaking process".[27] Thanks to DV and DVD (and DTV), and horror, we can.

DVD Master Class: The Consumption and Reproduction of the Horror Auteur

American Movie portrays Borchardt and *Coven* as part of a cycle of domestic/fan consumption, cult formation, canonisation, and reproduction that can be viewed from the other (high) end of the spectrum – in three 'art' films about horror directors and the making of their signature films: Elias Merhige's *Shadow of the Vampire* (2000), about Friedrich Wilhelm Murnau's *Nosferatu* (1922); Bill Condon's *Gods and Monsters* (1999), about James Whale's Frankenstein films, and Tim Burton's *Ed Wood* (1994), about the 'worst' director of all time. Concerned with horror auteurs – or rather, directors who are popularly considered 'masters' of horror in some sense – these 'special' and 'collector's' archival editions are also, in some sense made *by* horror auteurs *for* fans, collectors, and scholars who are armchair, virtual, or would-be auteurs. Adopting the practice of opening credit sequences with auteurial signatures (respectively, 'Saturn Films', 'A Bill Condon Film', 'A Tim Burton Film'), Merhige, Condon, and Burton define their own 'visions' in relation to the already larger-than-life 'originals', reproducing the horror auteur for domestic consumption and further reproduction.

The simultaneous release of restored versions of the originals (in elaborate packages complete with featurettes and full-length documentaries, commentaries, and interviews),[28] puts another spin on the cycle. Condon, Clive Barker, and popular horror film historian David Skal are part of the 'hypertextual' environment not only of the *Gods and Monsters* Collector's Edition DVD but also the Universal Classic Monster Collection editions of *Frankenstein* (1931) and *Bride of Frankenstein* (1935), which all three had a hand in preparing. Burton's film (which many saw on video) invigorated an Ed Wood cult that VHS versions of his once scorned cult masterpieces made possible. In what Gary Morris calls a "happy irony", five Wood "anti-classics" have been restored on "the plushest high-tech video format, DVD" (*Bride of the Monster* [1955], *Plan 9 from Outer Space* [1959], *Glen or Glenda* [1953], *Jail Bait* [1954], and *Pretty Models All in a Row* [1969]) and are now available "to feed the enduring fetish for this [...] model for the indie director with drive, sensibility, and no money".[29] Projects like this create the sense of an ongoing, mythologically complex horror heritage and universe that can be explored across a range of media.[30]

Video, but DVD in particular, appeals to a domestic culture of collectors, students, critics and aspiring filmmakers who find the medium the ideal collectible and archive. Perhaps more important, DVD provides master classes with the film's director, producer or stars and, as David Bohush claims, "has given professional and aspiring filmmakers a look into productions that was rarely available before", providing "a priceless knowledge transfer that costs nothing beyond the normal purchase or rental price".[31] With audio commentary tracks, 'making of' documentaries, biographies, interviews, cast and crew bios, trailers, outtakes, deleted scenes, alternate scenes, multiple camera angles, 'Anatomy of a Scene' features, production notes, interactive games, and hotlinks to sites where, on a DVD-ROM drive, users can read the screenplay while watching the film, engage in role-playing games or enter chat rooms, DVD provides a film school education in a hypertextual environment. With its cultural breadth and historical depth, horror is exceptionally well adapted to the master class form and function, as *E! Online* understood in 1999, launching *Film School*, a series of interactive online 'courses', with 'Horror 101' and the caption, "If only *real* school could be this much fun!".[32]

But 'Horror 101' was inspired primarily by the 'master classes' already embedded within the self-reflexive textures of the genre and particularly the course's capstone text, *Scream* (1996), in which media, horror video in particular, played the leading roles.[33] *Scream* is instructive not only about slasher films but, as Nick Rombes suggests, about how DVD co-opts and even supplants film school education, particularly in articulating filmmaking rules such as continuity editing and genre characteristics.[34] *Scream*'s self-theorising spawned a series of hip, demystifying films, such as *Scream 2* (1997) and *Scream 3* (2000), *Scary Movie* (2000), *Urban Legend* (1998), *Not Another Teen Movie* (2001), *The Faculty* (1998), and *Jeepers Creepers* (2001), that depended upon audiences' "meta-ironic position of superiority" toward the exhausted genre (a position constructed by film theory) and did so by co-opting theory, doing it (for example, Carol J. Clover's 'final girl' doctrine) "better, faster, and more energetically", thus undermining theory's authority.[35]

With their interchangeable, often unknown ensemble casts and masked or dehumanised monsters, slasher films made stars not of their actors but their filmmakers – the writer-directors (Romero, Cronenberg, Carpenter, Lynch, Barker, Craven) and effects wizards (Tom Savini, Rick Baker, Stan Winston). Thanks to *Fangoria*, *Gorezone*, *Video Watchdog* and now horror web zines such as *CHUD.COM*'s *Creature-Corner*, the 'horror auteurs' have been celebrated since the late 1970s as the 'demented minds' from whence the monsters come. DVD extras have enhanced a fan cult of horror filmmakers and a fascination with the horror of filmmaking.[36] And while DVD packages might seem to sell an outmoded (high modernist, auteurist) elitism, they just as often feature alternative commentary tracks that disperse authorisation to producers, cinematographers, special effects technicians, and cast members. In the end, they sell consumers the tools and secrets of the trade, providing inside information on the development of the project and about the shoot, offering deleted or 'alternative' scenes and endings, thereby turning the home theatre consumer into an armchair critic, and more. DVD makes the consumer a virtual 'auteur', compelling him or her to edit the text, select from a plethora of features (multi-angled scene studies that let the spectator view the scene from the director's chair and choose the shot, or that include links or crossovers with video games whose characters seem to 'authorise' reality, as in *Enter the Matrix* (2003), the *Lord of the Rings* games, and the *Resident Evil* and *Van Helsing* (2004) franchises. DVD consumption thus 'reproduces' auteurism, arming consumers with the knowledge and inspiration to pick up a camcorder.[37]

Coda: The Horror of Video

The interactive format encourages spectators to re-search and reauthorise the text, altering not only the consumer's experience of 'film' but also the way films are narrated. Several recent horror 'films' have adapted to the extent that DVD has become perhaps their definitive format, with self-reflexive twists at the end of the surface narrative (*The Sixth Sense* [1999], *Abre los ojos* [*Open Your Eyes*, 1997], *Donnie Darko* [2001]), branched narratives (*Identity*, 2003), or reversed order (*Memento*, 2000). *The Sixth Sense* reinvented the ghost story, narrating it from the uncanny perspective of a subject who has repressed the knowledge that he is dead – that is, until a series of revelations (that return to cues planted carefully in previous scenes) at the end of the film. This structure caused audiences to return to the theatre and/or buy the DVD to research the subtext and to engage in the act of mourning and melancholia the text compelled and celebrated. The authority of the DVD version is suggested in how the film's mega box office was surpassed by a record-breaking $50 million in rentals and sales in its first five days of release,[38] and the issuing, within months, of a second, 'Limited Edition' DVD.

Subsequent thrillers such as *Memento, Donnie Darko,* and *Identity* went further in deconstructing subjectivity, reality, and linear narrative. In these instances, screening demanded a high level of interaction – re-searching and re-shuffling fragments of the story or moving between several threaded narratives – a process that very nearly constituted the film. In *Memento,* the feature film is only one arrangement or reading – a backward reading at that – of an incomplete archive of memory fragments, as both the chapter stops and the Limited Edition DVD's alternative (chronological) version make obvious. The chapter menu of any DVD, this one reminds us, offers the viewer control over what, in a traditional film setting, are flashbacks and flash forwards. Similarly with its Gothic, surreal, and essentially open film 'text', *Donnie Darko* includes twenty deleted or extended scenes with optional commentary, a 'Cunning Visions' infomercial, and the *Philosophy of Time Travel* book. This profusion, along with the conflicting perspectives and alternative realities explored in the film text itself, sets off writer/director Richard Kelly's director's commentary as an idiosyncratic reading (one of several possible) of the film. A competing commentary in which Kelly shares credits with producer/actor Drew Barrymore and most of the cast further disputes his authority.

Justifying the designation *digital versatile disc,* DVD accommodates channel surfing and video gaming. Shifted from home theatre to home office and played in a PC's DVD-ROM drive (there hotlinked to the movie's 'living' website where users can chat with an actor or 'become' a movie character), DVD offers an interface between the 'film'-as-text and the larger mediated world. This techno magic has its darker side, however. The point was made by *The Blair Witch Project* as an intermediary project in which there is no privileged 'film' other than the 'footage' the spectator chooses to focus on. In J.P. Telotte's reading, the promotional and back-story elements rendered the film merely "one more artefact" in an illegible profusion of fragmentary texts, symbols, witnesses, and media. This profusion/confusion of texts terrified audiences by recreating the experience of our postmodern condition of being lost, not in the woods, but in "the mediated contemporary world".[39] Thus, like *Scream,* but with a slightly different twist, *The Blair Witch Project* seems to have predicted the future of horror and home video, DVD in particular. While video game-influenced DVDs grant the consumer the power to choose narrative threads, endings, and universes, an increasingly pervasive theme in self-reflexive horror video explores the unpleasant other side of this illusion of control: as mediation has become ubiquitous, interactive, and invasive, 'home' video (as voyeurism, as surveillance, as lost reality) *is* the bewitchment, the curse, the horror. While this theme goes back to *Videodrome* and even *Peeping Tom* and Hitchcock, continuing a horror tradition concerned with voyeurism as violence and postmodern oversaturation, it comes to have newly threatening meanings in post-9/11 surveillance culture.

Things get scary when, as Nick Rombes points out, cinematic voyeurism has "evolved into extensive technologies of looking and tracking and archiving; the very kind of information management that makes DVDs so popular". This cine-voyeurism leads to a fascination with the secrets, the "captured 'in-between' moments of a film: the multiple takes, the discarded lines, the trimmed scenes that may be more compelling than the film itself".[40] Home theatre is a command centre; it offers an illusion of boundary-sweeping vistas, visionary insight, intimacy, and finely tuned control. Yet its other side is 'Homeland Security', identity theft, and privacy invasion – the surrender of 'home' that participation in the global village now demands. Home video also equals home 'invasion', a theme that resonates, considering horror's profitable association with the video revolution and with direct-to-video and global Internet distribution. Several films have made this point in a particularly up-to-date, self-reflexive mode that means so much more when experienced on video. 2002 films like *The Ring*, *fear.dot.com* and *My Little Eye* are about the present dangers of interactive video, the Internet, and surveillance cameras within video culture.

It is no wonder that in Hideo Nakata's *Ringu* (1998) *and* Gore Verbinski's US adaptation *The Ring*, films about a videotape that causes anyone who watches it to die seven days later, the spectator/user has one loophole: to survive, s/he must become a home video 'filmmaker' too. S/he must copy and distribute the tape – in other words, produce a sequel. The film's last line belongs appropriately to a child: "What about the person we show it to? What happens to them?" Interacting with a 'film' as video makes home video production compulsory and implicates us in the death it causes, a narrative angle explored even more in the DVD version of Welsh filmmaker Marc Evans' *My Little Eye*, which is conceptually one of the more appropriate translations of a movie to DVD to date. Taped with five wall-mounted surveillance cameras as a live reality web cast of five young contestants living for six months in a large isolated house somewhere in North America (as in the survival reality television show *Big Brother*), the 'film' turns on a sadistic twist when we learn we are watching a snuff site beamed to an elite group of subscribers. Viewing the 'film' from the DVD-ROM enhanced 'interactive menu', the user views the web cast as a subscriber and is thus enabled to focus on selected contestants and scenes from different cameras. The panopticon-like web cam 'browser' also offers, in place of the director's commentary track, the voices of the web cast production company and other subscribers as they bet on each contestant's odds. This is video gaming at its most horrific, making the point that in participating in the voyeuristic and exhibitionist culture we take for granted, we have become victims, and worse, like the company-designated executioner who poses as a clean cut young contestant, key players in a lethal game.

These and other recent films are obsessed with the horror potential within our society of the spectacle and epitomised in video as home theatre, posing the question: Whose theatre? The theatre that allows one to watch from home exists only within a larger culture of voyeurism, exhibitionism, and surveillance.

Notes

1. Timothy Corrigan, *A Cinema without Walls* (New Brunswick, New Jersey: Rutgers University Press, 1991), p. 1.
2. Robin Wood and Richard Lippe, ed., *The American Nightmare: Essays on the Horror Film*, Toronto: Festival of Festivals, 1979.
3. Horror video was the central issue in two major debates of the 1980s: the 'video nasties' controversy (the moral panic over video content and regulation in the UK that resulted in the 1984 Video Recordings Act requiring all video tapes to be submitted pre-release to the British Board of Film Classification) and in feminist protests against cinematic eroticised violence in the US. See Martin Barker, *The Video Nasties: Freedom and Censorship in the Media*, London: Pluto, 1984; Linda Williams, *Hardcore: Power, Pleasure, and the 'Frenzy of the Visible'*, London: Pandora Press, 1990; and Kate Egan, *Trash or Treasure? Censorship and the Changing Meanings of the Video Nasties*, Manchester: Manchester University Press, 2007.
4. Philip Brophy, 'Horrality – The Textuality of Contemporary Horror Films', *Screen*, vol. 27, no. 1, 1986, pp. 1–13; reprinted in Ken Gelder, ed., *The Horror Reader*, London and New York: Routledge, 2000, pp. 278–9.
5. Marshal M. Rosenthal, 'Elite Entertainment and Horror/Cult Films: More Gore to Ya!', *DVD ETC.*, May 2003, p. 31.
6. Two books include discussions of this trend: Steven Jay Schneider, ed., *Fear Without Frontiers: Horror Cinema across the Globe*, Guildford: Fab Press, 2003; and Steven Jay Schneider and Tony Williams, ed., *Horror International: World Horror Cinema*, Detroit: Wayne State University Press, 2005.

7. Bryant Frazer, 'Permanent Ghosts: Cinephilia in the Age of the Internet and Video', *Cinephilia Special Feature, Senses of Cinema*, no. 5, April 2000, 28 June 2003, <http://www.sensesofcinema.com/contents/00/5/cine5.html>.

8. Ian Conrich, 'An Aesthetic Sense: Cronenberg and Neo-horror Film Culture', *The Modern Fantastic: The Films of David Cronenberg*, ed. Michael Grant, New York: Praeger, 2000, p. 43.

9. Chad Hindman, 'The Golden Age of Video', *The Sidelines Online*, 28 April 2003, <http://www.mtsusidelines.com/main.cfm?include=detail&storyid=4 07377>.

10. Joan Hawkins, *Cutting Edge: Art-Horror and the Horrific Avant-Garde*, Minneapolis: University of Minnesota Press, 2000, p. 30.

11. As of this writing, horror is the largest genre category (925 titles) excluding 'cult' (998 titles) maintained by highbrow Facets Multimedia, traditionally the best source of international and independent film.

12. Tim Lucas, 'Introduction', *The Video Watchdog Book*, Cincinnati: Video Watchdog, 1992, xvi. Invented as Lucas' column in *Video Times* (1985–86) and *Gorezone* (1988–92), *Video Watchdog* was reborn as a magazine in 1990.

13. The title of a landmark feature, 'The Butchering of Dario Argento', published in *Fangoria*, no. 66, in August 1987, and subsequently as a 'Video Watchdog Special Report' in *Gorezone*, speaks punningly for itself of exploitation robbed of its essence. "Thanks to the scholarly devotion of dedicated archivists like Tim Lucas", writes Joe Dante, "the scales are falling from our eyes to a point where it's even foreseeable that, someday, every Jess Franco movie will be accounted for, in each territorial cut, title and version" ('Foreword', *The Video Watchdog Book*, xiii).

14. Jim Farrelly, quoted in Meriah Doty, 'Film Flops Flourish on DVD, VHS', *CNN.com*, 4 March 2003, <http://www.cnn.com/2003/SHOWBIZ/Movies/03/04/second.wind/>.

15. Peter M. Bracke, editorial, *DVDFILE.com*, 3 December 2002, <http://www.dvdfile.com/news/viewpoints/editors_desk/2002/12_03.html>. Bracke's point was recently reinforced by the $65 million first-week video sales of *Van Helsing* in recouping a relative box office disappointment (Lisa Johnson, '*Van Helsing* Slays Monster DVD Sales', *FilmStew*, 28 October 2004, <http://www.filmstew.com/Content/Article.asp?ContentID=10006&Pg=1>).

16. Doty.

17. Dalle E. Basye, '*Not* Coming to a Theater Near You', *Screen Review, Williamette Week Online*, 3 December 1997, <http://www.wweek.com/html/direct120397.html>.

18. Rosenthal, p. 30.

19. Says FlixMix General Manager Gary Schenk, "Let's give them clips, information, music, fun and games, and allow them to navigate through it in any way they want" ('In the Mix: Feature Story', *DVDFILE.com*, 23 June 2003, <http://www.dvdfile.com/news/special_report/inside_the_disc/flixmix/2.html>). *Boogeymen* is like "load[ing] up a multi-disc DVD player with scary movies and hit[ting] 'shuffle'", says Bryan Tucker in 'Remote Control: How

Interactive DVD will Turn Us All Into Virtual Directors', *USA Weekend*, 21–23 December 2001, p. 12. Horror was the obvious choice in part because collectible horror compilations such as *Terror in the Aisles* (1984), *Stephen King's World of Horror* (1989), *Monster Mania* (1997) and *Bride of Monster Mania* (2000), and clip-heavy documentaries such as *Flesh and Blood: The Hammer Heritage of Horror* (1994) or *The American Nightmare* (2000) were already a subgenre unto themselves, a product of 1980s cable television and VHS. The DVD includes 'Legends of the Boogeymen' (character bios and history), 'FlixFacts Animated Trivia', audio commentary by Robert Englund, an interactive 'Name That Frame' game, and DVD-ROM interactive horror trivia games.

20. 'The Dogme95 Manifesto', *Dogme95*, <http://www.dogme95.dk/menu/menuset.htm>.

21. Thus the current crop of digital filmmaking 'how-to' books advise one to make genre or niche films, with horror as the exemplary model – threaded, for example, throughout several chapters of Gregory Goodel's *Independent Feature Film Production*, New York: St. Martin's Griffin, 1998, pp. 59-72. Claiming DV filmmaking as "the new punk rock, the new medium where anyone can tell his story", Michael Dean's *$30 Film School* (Boston: Premier Press, 2003) is endorsed on the back cover by *The Blair Witch Project* actor/cameraman Joshua Leonard, who hails the book's insight on avoiding "the tired conventions of commercial filmmaking and etch[ing] the subversive onto the screen". Chuck Gloman's *303 Digital Filmmaking Solutions* (New York: McGraw-Hill, 2003) devotes more space to horror and graphic special makeup effects than to action, comedy, and romance combined. It is no surprise when Troma's CEO Lloyd Kaufman's *Make Your Own Damn Movie: Secrets of a Renegade Director* (New York: St. Martin's Griffin, 2003), described on the back cover as "[a] guerrilla film school textbook from America's legendary renegade filmmaker", assumes a cineliterate audience of would-be exploitation/horror fan/auteurs. Troma's shtick involves parodying academic and avant-garde cine-culture while joining it in an all-out war against middle class taste and corporate monopoly. In Kaufman's view, the back pages of *Fangoria*, where "guys who've made a movie . . . are selling it copy by copy to anyone curious enough to shell out $14.95" is merely the other side of Cannes (p. 299). In a similar spirit Kaufman announces 'Dogpile 95', the Troma 'equivalent' of Dogme 95 – remarking that Troma has been practicing von Trier's 'new' D.I.Y. minimalism for thirty years (p. 304).

22. See 'DVD Rentals Top VHS for First Time', *CNN.com. TECHNOLOGY*, 20 June 2003, <http://www.techspot.com/vb/showthread.php?threadid=5988>, and 'DVDs Replacing CDs at Record Stores', *Movie/TV News, IMDB.com*, 7 July 2003, <http://www.imdb.com/news/sb/2003-07-07>.

23. Guido Henkel, 'The Facts About *The Last Broadcast*: An Interview with Lance Weiler', *DVD Review*, 9 December 1999, <http://www.dvdreview.com/html/dvd_review_-_lance_weiler.shtml>.

24. Sarah Effron, 'Independent Horror Film Makers', *CBC Radio, Definitely*

Not at the Opera, transcript, 30 October 2002, <http://www.urbanlegend.ca/horror.htm>.

25. Head Cheeze, 'Meat Market (2001)', *Horrorview: The Last Gasp in Horror Entertainment*, 2001, <http://www.horrorview.com/Meat%20Market.htm>.

26. Francis Ford Coppola famously applied his UCLA film school education working as an assistant in Roger Corman's horror/exploitation factory and debuted with the horror feature *Dementia 13* (1963). Young Spanish director Alejandro Amenabar wrote and directed the snuff-themed *Tesis* (1996) because thrillers were 'easy' and went on to attract Hollywood and Tom Cruise. Marc Evans, whose horror film about surveillance culture, *My Little Eye* (2002) put him on the cover of the October 2002 *Sight and Sound*, followed a slightly different path; he shifted to horror out of desperation when his critically acclaimed dramas, *House of America* (1997) and *Resurrection Man* (1998), bombed at the box office.

27. Paul Arthur, 'Quickies: *American Movie*', *Film Comment*, vol. 35, no. 6, November–December 1999, pp. 78–9.

28. This strategy was shamelessly exploited by Universal Studios Home Video's release, just in time for Halloween, of the three-disc *Van Helsing* Ultimate Collector's Edition DVD (2004) including, in addition to a number of conspicuously interactive features, histories, and a video game, the Universal *Dracula* (1931), *Frankenstein* (1931), and *The Wolf Man* (1940) in their entirety with the package introduced by *Van Helsing* director Stephen Sommers. Thus Universal's Ken Graffeo hopes that the DVD will hook viewers unfamiliar with the originals, and allows them to "stop (the DVD) and dissect (the extras) to learn more about them" ('Van Helsing' Out on DVD', *Guam Pacific Daily News*, 28 October 2004, <http://cityguide.guampdn.com/fe/Movies/20041028-1487875.asp>). What seems clearer is the way *Van Helsing* has cannibalised the classic horror monsters for the current generations of CGI fans and gamers, much as the *Resident Evil* franchise repackages Romero's zombies for a post-9/11 culture of fear.

29. Gary Morris, 'Graverobbers and Drag Queens from Outer Space! Four Ed Wood Greats on DVD', *Bright Lights Film Journal*, no. 28, April 2000, <http://brightlightsfilm.com/28/edwood1.html>.

30. In a *DVD Review* interview, Bill Condon, who has directed a number of television movies, confesses to having made *Gods and Monsters* with the DVD format and video in general in mind. See Guido Henkel, 'Bill Condon: Bringing a Horror Icon Back to Golden Life'. *DVD Review*, 3 June 1999, <http://www.dvdreview.com/html/dvd_review_-_bill_condon.shtml>. Thus the film features two scenes in which characters across classes, generations, genders, and sexual identities view *Bride of Frankenstein* on *Shock Theater* with a range of responses. Such scenes highlight one of the film's themes; they exist as evidence of horror film's history of interfacing across oceans, classes, and generations, suggesting how its intermediary character has made it archetypal.

31. Peter Bohush, 'DVDs: A Master Class in Movie Making', *DVD Master Class*.

WriterDirector.com, 2002, <http://writerdirector.com/articles/dvd_master_class.htm>.

32. 'Horror 101'. *E! Online. Features. Film School*, October–November 1999, <http://www.eonline.com/Features/Live/Filmschool/index.html>.

33. Examples are the video store scene, where the characters discuss probable suspects according to the genre area they are perusing, or in the party scene, in which the rules for slasher films are summarised (as the group watches *Halloween* [1978] on television), enforced at some points only to be upended or turned into grisly jokes at others.

34. Nick Rombes, 'Professor DVD', *CTHEORY*, 21 June 2002, <http://www.ctheory.net/text_file.asp?pick=342>.

35. Ibid.

36. Google's Web Directory lists more horror directors with websites (fourteen) than any other genre category unless one includes 'cult', with twenty-three directors, at least nine of whom are just as often listed as 'horror' directors.

37. Horror-themed video games, which space does not permit me to discuss in this essay, have clearly influenced DVD and vice versa, as games (*Tomb Raider, Mortal Kombat, Resident Evil, Dungeons and Dragons*) are made into high-concept films, lending the games in turn the production values, stars, and big-screen glamour and closure associated with Hollywood. Meanwhile, horror and science-fiction films, particularly when realised on DVD, increasingly imitate video games, with branched narratives and several options for endings and protagonists, representing the player/spectator, who are presented with choices.

38. Emily Farache, "Sixth Sense' Video Scares Up Dollars', *E! Online News*, 6 April 2000, <http://www.eonline.com/News/Items/0,1,6283,00.htm>1. Alejandro Amenabar's supernatural thriller *The Others* (2001) was a sleeper hit and best-renting DVD for similar reasons.

39. '*The Blair Witch Project Project*: Film and the Internet', *Film Quarterly*, vol. 54, no. 3, 2001, pp. 38, 35. The DVD replenished and extended that bewitched/witch hunting experience in its design and contents. The user screened the 'film' within a replication of the shifting surfaces of the website, which s/he could access by playing the DVD in a PC DVD-ROM drive, allowing him/her to sift through maps and excerpts from the *Dossier* and link to other sites. S/he could also utilise more conventional DVD features: director and producer commentary, production notes, theatrical trailers, and the *Curse of the Blair Witch* mockumentary first aired on the Sci-Fi Channel. The *Book of Shadows: Blair Witch 2* (2000) DVD is also notable, the first to include (in addition to the feature with commentary track, web link access to 'Never-Before-Seen Footage and Other Extras') a CD-playable music soundtrack on one side. The *Blair Witch Experience: The Collector's Set* (2000) includes both features, most of the extras from previous DVDs, and three interactive PC video games with Internet hotlinks.

40. 'Your Life Is a Movie: The Surveillance Culture as Entertainment', *SolPix: Film and Fiction Fusion*, <http://webdelsol.com/SolPix/sp-nicknew.htm>.

Part Two

Audiences, Fans and Consumption

4

Stalking the Web

Celebration, Chat and Horror Film Marketing on the Internet

BRIGID CHERRY

> What a waste of my time. I can't believe that Clive Barker would attach his name to this underdeveloped piece of cotton-candy fluff . . . I am a big fan of Clive Barker's work, and I tuned in because of that. I hope that what they paid him [was] enough to merit the sacrifice of his reputation. Because that is, in my humble opinion, what he has done.[1]

This fan review of *Clive Barker's Saint Sinner* (2002) on the Sci-Fi Channel's bulletin board clearly demonstrates that the fans of horror cinema, whilst gathering to celebrate the genre, are only too happy to bite the hand that feeds them when their expectations are not fulfilled. *Clive Barker's Saint Sinner* was heavily hyped on the Sci-Fi Channel website and the online pre-publicity emphasised not just the neo-Gothic plot and visuals, but, more crucially, Clive Barker's name which was attached to the title. As a renowned horror author, director, artist and comic book creator, Barker has a keen fan following. It was these fans, their expectations raised rather too highly by the pre-publicity, who felt aggrieved by the end result. The Sci-Fi Channel, which allows the fans to share in their expectations and then share their opinions via its bulletin board, was – on this occasion – host to negative reviews. This illustrates quite succinctly both the power and the pitfalls of such online marketing. Fans, as Henry Jenkins describes, who love the text are not afraid to speak out when it falls short of their own ideals.[2] Where inviting fan contributions works, with *The Blair Witch Project* (1999) for example (and I discuss this further below), it works exceedingly well. Where it fails, as here, the fans can make their complaints only too well known in an all too public space.

It is, of course, the fact that the Internet has not only become the home of fan culture but that access is widely available and allows any user to freely publish anything they wish (even if they do not have their

7. Raising Expectations: Clive Barker's heavily hyped film

own website) that creates such situations.[3] Since its inception, fans, who are often geographically and socially isolated and yet crave association with others of a like mind, have congregated on the Internet. Online fan culture has thus flourished and fan communities have multiplied. Horror fans have been active users of this online environment since the early days of the technology. The Internet, however, is also exploited as a marketing and publicity tool within the film industry. It is in the areas where these two groups meet, as illustrated by the example above, that the tensions between producer and consumer become apparent. However, in such instances – and in counterpoint to John Fiske's cultural economy of fandom or Jenkins' model of fan textual poaching,[4] these tensions may now populate the border between public and private. The online bulletin board, as well as weblogs and sites such as *Ain't It Cool News*, can render the press preview redundant, word-of-mouth becomes the new billboard and every fan appears to be a film critic. Private opinion has become public cultural criticism. Filmmakers, producers and distributors need no longer fear the popular critical opinion of journalists and reviewers alone, but the in-depth analysis and dissection of the text that now spreads globally and instantaneously via the Internet.[5] The account of online horror film marketing and fan discourse which follows examines these tensions, as well as looking at the forms of debate that take place amongst various segments of the online horror fan community.

There is a vast quantity of online material dedicated to the horror genre: a Google web search on the term 'horror film' alone offers an astounding 181,000 apparent sites. It is impossible to analyse this material in its entirety, and the account which follows is therefore based upon a representative cross-section of online material by and for fans of the genre.[6] Prior to this analysis below (in the form of a series of case studies of a representative range of different interpretive communities and forms of Internet usage), some idea of the scope of the online horror fan community is presented.[7] The largest archive of Internet discussion lists (closed groups with email distribution and membership only in many cases) is Yahoo!Groups, containing at least 240 lists dedicated to or mentioning the horror genre in their names and descriptions.[8] In addition, there are many other Yahoo!Groups dedicated to specific aspects of horror cinema, subgenres and even individual films or actors. To give an idea of the range of the latter, examples of such groups include those for national horror cinemas (Britain's Hammer studio, Italian horror and German Expressionist films); horror stars, personalities and fictional characters (actor Robert Englund, the aforementioned Clive Barker and *Halloween*'s stalker Michael Myers); and films (*Friday the 13th* [1980], *The Evil Dead* [1982], and *The Blair Witch Project*). Many more groups exist which are dedicated to literary and television forms of the genre, particularly the contemporary series *Buffy the Vampire Slayer* and *Angel* as well as older cult series such as *Dark Shadows*. Of the newsgroups (open bulletin boards with no membership requirements) offered by Google,[9] the main ones of interest to horror fans are rec.arts.horror.movies and alt.horror.

The memberships of the Yahoo!Groups vary tremendously, from less than ten to several hundred members per group, as can the traffic on each group, which may be in inverse ratio to the membership. Small groups with few members may generate large numbers of messages, whereas large groups may generate few messages. The Crypt of Dracula group, dedicated to discussion of classic horror films, generates an average of 250 posts per month from 85 members. In contrast, the Hammer Films Ltd group, with 549 members, has no discussion since its aim is to circulate an official Hammer newsletter. With no membership requirements, the size of the newsgroup communities are unavailable and may well vary from week to week; however, statistics for the alt.horror group give the number of people posting at 344, though this does not take account of 'lurkers' who participate passively without contributing to discussion. A second newsgroup, rec.arts.horror.movies, generated between nine and 46 messages per day during May 2003 and 17,200 different discussion topics (known as threads, each thread may contain multiple replies) in the four and a half years since December 1998. These discussion lists and newsgroups are supplemented online by a large number and wide variety of chat rooms, bulletin boards and weblogs, many associated with the vast array of horror-themed sites on the web, some – as illustrated above – corporately-owned, others parts of fan communities or personal fan sites.

To aid the fan in finding their way around the plethora of horror-related material available online, websites such as *The Dark Side of the Net* provide a map to online horror. The site (tagline "Bringing you into the darkness since 1993!") boasts an archive of over 11,000 working, hand-picked links to horror-related sites and online groups and almost 3,000 archived news items.[10] Following on from the point made above with respect to fan interest in future film projects and the expectations this generates, the news column in particular can help the fan keep up to date with their knowledge of the genre. In its news column for 29 April 2003, for instance, *The Dark Side of the Net* offers links to horror-related news items ranging from author appearances and interviews with cult horror filmmakers to trailers for upcoming films and DVD video releases. Categories under which links are filed include literature, art, entertainment (largely television), movies and music. There are also pages for links to discussion, shopping and computer resources. *The Dark Side of the Net* also includes categories for the Goth subculture, the celebration of Halloween, the occult and the paranormal, and vampires. This demonstrates the diversity of interests within the community and the heterogeneity of horror fan culture, and this raises several important considerations. First, many horror fans are not interested in cinema alone, and the culture takes in horror in many other media. Second, it is impossible to consider horror fandom as having distinct boundaries and there is much overlap with other fan cultures. Vampire fandom is a particularly active area and, this too, has flourished on the Internet, overlapping as it does with horror fandom and the Goth subculture. Nor is horror fandom only linked with the 'dark side'. There is overlap too with other genres, as Jimmie L. Reeves et al. recognise: "horror/dark fantasy fan groups . . . exist on the margins of sci-fi fandom".[11] Science-fiction is a category alongside Ghosts, Graveyards, Haunted Houses, Werewolves and Zombies (among others) on *The Horror Search Engine*; it contains 151 entries, compared to Gothic's 472, Horror Movies' 976 and Horror Stories' 616.[12] Thus, the horror fan community fragments and fans can be both eclectic in their tastes and nomadic.

Like other fan cultures, the horror fan community fragments along lines of gender, nationality and other aspects of identity, as well as taste. In this, factors such as geographical location or membership of face-to-face communities may also play a part. For example, the FrightFest horror film festival which takes place annually in London has its own discussion forum on its website, used by festival goers to discuss the films they have seen at the festival and anticipate face-to-face interaction at upcoming events.[13] Gender is also significant. Larger proportions of active female fans are to be found in the discussion groups dedicated to vampire films (the vampire genre is a particular favourite of female horror fans)[14] and in the email lists (this pattern of masculine newsgroups and feminine email lists was also observed by Susan J. Clerc in the online X-Philes community).[15] For example, 75 per cent of the members of the Yahoo!Group The Lost Boys Cave, dedicated to *The Lost Boys* (1987), are female. Fans, then, tend to gravitate towards communities they find most comfortable and are not intimidated by. The fragmentation of online fan communities around preferences and taste must also be considered. Thus, the case studies chosen look at groups orientated around different interpretive communities which take in, first, demographic groups (women, British fans) and, second, key subgenres (adolescent-aimed slashers, gore films). An associated area which is examined is in respect of fan productivity in the form of fan fiction. One of the longest running horror fan groups is the Horror in Film and Literature email discussion list.[16] The list header describes the ethos of the group, which has been in existence since the early 1990s (initially as a university based email list service), and the website for this list claims that there are 'almost

500 members spread out over five continents, and with that many diverse people the discussion wanders quite a bit'.[17]

Amongst the 'diverse people' on the group, there are a large number of active female fans, many of whom have been members of the list since its early days and, more significantly, a high proportion of posts are from female members and the female fans are particularly influential in this group. Discussion has, for example, centred around gender representations in horror films, the sexist nature of horror and Carol J. Clover's *Men, Women and Chain Saws* (with members being unafraid to criticise Clover's analysis and even disagree with her conclusions about gender and horror).[18]

One of the major features of the horror list is its weekly group view of horror films and monthly group read of horror novels (again demonstrating the cross-media tastes of horror fans). As the guidelines indicate, members view or read the chosen text (taking it in turns to select the film or book) and after a set period of time discuss it:

> Here's how the Group View works, for anyone who's new and wants to try it. As many people as possible go out and find the chosen movie, watch it some time during the weekend and chime in on Monday with your thoughts. There are several things the Group View is supposed to accomplish. One, is to foster discussion. Also, the original idea behind the Group View was that if a lot of people see the movie at roughly the same time, it would cut down on, 'Well, I saw it years ago, and I remember it like this'.

Discussion is thus less likely to be trivial (as it can be on the newsgroups). It is frequently also frank, detailed, sometimes highly analytical and even argumentative. The members do more than simply celebrate horror and are more than prepared to disagree and to critique texts in some depth. During a Group View in May 2003 members discussed *The Lair of the White Worm* (1988), which the list owner introduced as 'a classic' that was 'not for the sexually squeamish'. In the first post after the specified weekend period for viewing, Morgan posted to say she mostly found the film silly, though she enjoyed it in a 'so-bad-its-good' way):

> This is a bad film. Really. That doesn't stop it from being a lot of fun. The plot was thin, the acting was mostly wooden . . . I was ok with most of it until the chase scenes at the end, where I wanted to just throw the tv across the room. Dumb Dumb Dumb.

Several list members then jumped in to disagree or to debate points. David's response was typical of several members:

> I strongly disagree that this is a 'bad' movie. I think when you're evaluating a movie, like any art, you have to look at what the creator was looking to

accomplish. And clearly, to me, Ken Russell is *not* looking to make a serious scary movie. He's looking to make something campy and outrageous, and I think . . . he succeeds admirably. :) I was delighted to find what a fun and goofy horror-comedy this was . . . And I think, for its budget, that the film is not badly made.

In support of David, Matt takes an analytical approach, something that is fairly common on this list:

Of course I can see all the same things in LAIR OF THE WHITE WORM that have led so many to dismiss it as pure trash, nothing but camp, a cheesy bit of nonsense. But I've loved it ever since my first viewing back in the early 1990s, and subsequent viewings have only reinforced my attitude toward it. I've never done an in-depth analysis of the semiotics of the film, either in my head or on paper, but I think such an analysis could be done, and would reveal that Ken Russell really knew what he was doing when he chose to do his own stylish riffs on this aspect of Stoker's source novel.

The discussion throughout is well-mannered and participants recognise that views may differ and give space to other members, sometimes going to great pains to explain their differences of opinion. As David says at the end of his post: "But folks with different expectations may completely disagree. :)".

As can be seen by this discussion, divergence of opinion can occur, but more importantly this interpretive community verges on the academic in its level of debate. As David stated in a personal email: "This is really the only discussion list I'm still on, mostly because I like the people, and it gives me a chance to occasionally flex my analytical muscles on a genre I love (and which isn't taken too seriously in most circles)". In this respect, it must be acknowledged that the horror list membership contains a high number of fans working in libraries and universities and many have studied in higher education.

In contrast, the newsgroups can be rather less polite and do not often aspire to as high a level of intellectual debate in their online chat. This difference is unlikely to be accounted for by gender alone since female fans do participate in these forums. Other factors in the fans' background and social situation may apply, but it seems likely that many female (and some male) fans feel more comfortable in the rather more respectful and intellectual debate of the discussion list than the free-for-all that exists in the newsgroups. This is best illustrated in terms of the competitive behaviour in the alt.horror group. A list of the most frequent contributors to the group is posted monthly and this results in verbal jostling amongst the high-ranking clique. It must be noted, however, that not all discussion-based fan communities fall into either of these categories, the horror list and alt.horror representing the two extremes of a continuum of discursive activity (both forms of social interaction). In all of the groups examined, discussion frequently returns to common topics; these include favourite horror films, scariest or most disgusting horror film ever made, and how the fans acquired their taste for horror. These topics not only allow the fans to share their experiences but contribute to a development of a fan canon for the genre and the construction of fan knowledge and competencies.

It is evident that within the individual communities some active participants take up particular functions. Fans with particular interests or knowledge in specific areas of the genre are on hand to answer questions, whilst others with time to indulge their interest disseminate information that they have acquired during their own web surfing to the rest of the group. For example, on the VEIN list – a Yahoo!Group for members of the various vampire fan groups in the UK – one or two active members frequently post links to sites for upcoming films, news items, interesting horror-related sites, new merchandise available online and a range of other material. Members who then look at these sites may discuss and share opinions on the material, and in the case of upcoming films, this may contribute to the raising (or lowering) of expectations. Fans frequently disagree on promotional material and this may be related to individual taste. For example, in the week beginning 4 May 2003 discussion on vein arose after a fan pointed members towards the promotional material for the modern vampire movie *Underworld* (2003). The resulting discussion ended up comparing the look of the film to *The Matrix* (1999) and members were divided, though not ill-naturedly, in expectations according to whether they had liked the latter. Long-term active fans may be well known within the community and their opinion can provide a yardstick by which members can judge whether they might like the upcoming film (just as film critics might in a daily newspaper or film magazine). In this way, the members of the interpretive community can measure, and add to, their own generic competencies. As in any other community, divisions and arguments can occur and posts can sometimes be discourteous and members can be flamed;[19] however, in general, many online fans are supportive of both established members and newcomers and active fans can be helpful and informative.

Many online horror fan communities also have a presence on the web. Although the horror material on the web, as opposed to email communication, is by its nature less discursive, it is nonetheless illustrative of fan activity and discourse, and demonstrates the specific concerns of different fan demographics. The *Evil Dead* fan community, for example, is interested in specific aspects of horror cinema which centre around special

8. Gore, comedy, and lead actor Bruce Campbell: Key factors in the popularity of *The Evil Dead*

effects and levels of gore, but also demonstrates that the appeal of these films is strongly related to interest in the filmmakers and actors (*The Evil Dead*'s director Sam Raimi and actor Bruce Campbell are both cult icons amongst horror fans). The tone of the *Evil Dead* films is also a key aspect: not just the level of gore, but the black humour of the series. It is the humour which makes the films popular amongst female fans as well as the predicted gorehounds; though female fans in general dislike gore for its own sake, they do enjoy it when it is an integral part of what they deem to be a quality film – and in the case of the *Evil Dead* series, there is an appreciation of the comic tone of the films combined with the appeal of its star Bruce Campbell.[20] Thus websites for 'Deadites' cover the features of fan cultures outlined above. *Deadites Online (the fan's source for Evil Dead)* provides detailed news coverage, trivia and links for the film series, together with forums and chat rooms, catering for the knowledgeable fans and contributing to fan discourse.[21] Face-to-face fan activities are catered for by the *Ladies of the Evil Dead*, a site which showcases the female actors from *The Evil Dead* and advertises their public or convention appearances and news and magazine coverage and interviews.[22] Personal opinions are shared on *Cult Horrors* which features other films enjoyed by the website creator (including *The Texas Chain Saw Massacre* [1974] and *From Dusk Till Dawn* [1996]), showcasing tastes and offering contact with other like-minded fans.[23]

Evil Dead: The Ultimate Experience on Gruelling Online Terror features fan art and as this example shows, online horror fans are active producers of secondary material associated with the cult text, including fan fiction.[24] The quantities of fan fiction associated with horror films, however, are small when compared to that for television series such as *Star Trek*, *The X-Files* and *Buffy the Vampire Slayer*, though fans of horror films are nevertheless creating fan fiction. FanFiction.net is a multimedia archive containing fan fic based on a wide range of cult texts.[25] The web page dedicated to films lists 184 titles in total,[26] 13 per cent of which are relatively unproblematical horror titles (Table 1A).[27] *The Mummy* (1999) and *Hannibal* (2001) are the most popular horror film texts for fan fiction writers in this forum. Predominant subjects of the fiction include the (sexual) relationship between Clarice Starling and Hannibal Lecter in the case of *Hannibal* (also seen in the forty-eight fics dedicated to *The Silence of the Lambs* [1991]) and the ongoing family saga of *The Mummy* and its sequel. It seems in these two cases that relationships, familial, romantic and sexual, form a major concern of the fiction writers.

It is, though, the fan fiction related to *Scream*, which is of greatest interest since it provides an example of the aspects of the horror genre which most concern fans of slasher films. The *Scream* series, and the first *Scream* film in particular, began the resurgence in the teen slasher cycle which formed a revitalising junior branch of the subgenre in the late 1990s. The *Scream*-based fan fiction section on FanFiction.net has 69 stories contributed by 59 writers. Most writers have contributed only one piece of fiction with the most prolific having contributed six. This particular writer has twenty-eight pieces of fiction in other categories, namely *X-Men*, *The Lord of the Rings*, *Harry Potter*, *Pearl Harbour*, *Roswell*, *Cruel Intentions*, *Final Destination*, *Angel* and two Kevin Smith films. Amongst this selection is a clear trend towards films and television programmes aimed at a youthful audience (as are slasher films and teen horrors such as *Final Destination*).

Of the 69 *Scream* fictions, the largest number are categorised as horror stories by the writers (Table 1B), indicating that central aspects of the genre and its modes of emotional affect are of paramount interest, and of rather more importance than character relationships and romance, to these writers. This is born out by the fact that thirty of the stories are sequels to the *Scream* trilogy. With the exception of one fic (a crossover story between *Scream* and *Angel*), the rest are almost evenly split between alternative plot developments or endings, character points of view of events in the films, the filling in of narrative gaps or what happened next, and parodies of *Scream* and the neo-slasher film cycle in general. This illustrates that the concerns and interests of this group of horror fans centre around the desire for narrative continuation and more detailed narrative in some instances. As Will Brooker has stated of science-fiction cinema, cult texts generate fan material which suggests new narrative directions, develops characters or builds on the framework of the films.[28] It is clear from the above survey that this fan culture is a "community of imagination" surrounding a heterogenous genre.[29] Unlike fans of an ongoing television text, horror film fans have no continuous weekly fix of new stories. Accordingly, they are constantly seeking new films, and the various segments within horror fandom (be they oriented around identity or taste) are looking for information which will inform them as to whether a production is likely to be of interest.

Before turning to a specific analysis of fan expectations and discourse linked with the marketing of horror films it is worth considering the official sites, since this provides a context for online fan debate. The Internet can provide an accessible and cheap format for horror film marketing, just as it can for fans themselves. In recent years there has been an increasing web presence for official film sites with large online fan followings, and the associated material can include competitions, games, web-only trailers and other exclusive offerings. The major Hollywood studios and production companies now have a significant Internet presence, using their websites to advertise both new horror films and older titles as they are released on DVD, whilst the web is an important marketing tool for the independents. The website content for a Hollywood-based horror film ranges from a simple showcase for the title to a highly-detailed site with pages rich in graphics and offering a wide range of multimedia features. Such marketing is economically important, especially for low-budget productions, many examples of which are highly interactive in order to draw in fans and build word-of-mouth.

The official sites are important to fans and, as mentioned above in the discussion of the VEIN list, fans pass on web addresses for upcoming horror film titles. On this list, Dave pointed members towards sites for *Van Helsing* (2004), *Blade Trinity* (2004) and the remake of *Dawn of the Dead* (2004).[30] These sites demonstrate the range of features which contribute different levels to fans' celebration of the genre. Universal's site for *Van Helsing*, for example, is fairly basic, offering little more than straightforward information and visual material about the film, the trailer and adverts for other Universal products including DVD releases of the classic Universal horror films and the *Van Helsing* theme park experience at Universal Studios, California. Interactivity is at a minimum, though feedback on the VEIN list suggests that the photographic material raised expectations for the look of the film, though not the plot (the synopsis of which was brief). This does suggest that websites can serve their a purpose as adverts. At the other extreme, the website for Universal's *Dawn of the Dead* presents rather more opportunities to celebrate the genre. This site contains multiple movie sequences and richly textured backgrounds, offering a choice of a timeline providing details of zombie novels and films since the 1920s, and several interviews with the filmmakers and the cast. This provides the kind of information fans are likely to be looking for, adding to fan knowledge and competencies. There are also interactive features such as a code-breaking sequence and a game where the fan can shoot zombies. More importantly, the site offers the opportunity to become a member of the Zombie Army, join in discussion and, through points awarded for various activities, rise up the list of top ten fans. The site claims 12,700 members and the discussion board lists over 6,600 posts on the film, zombies in general, fan fiction and social chat, as well as over 100 convention photographs and 400 photographs of fans in zombie costumes. New Line's official website for *Blade Trinity*, though not as interactive, is typical of official sites. In addition to a range of character animations, production notes and downloads, this site also contains a message board where fans can interact and discuss the film. In this case, the fans have generated over 30,000 posts on the mythology of Blade, the weapons and gear seen in the film, vampires in general and other media such as the comic books and games, as well as social chat, and over 1,600 have signed up as members (though the board is also open to guests). These examples illustrate the levels of fan interest, but also demonstrate that through their active participation and celebration of the films fans can achieve an official presence, albeit one which might also be seen as a form of exploitation. This is a successful approach for the film companies, generating fan loyalty and income where official merchandising is sold (though, of course, this may collapse if the film is not a success with the fans). Overall, however, it is evident that marketing and fan activities can co-exist on official sites.

This is also demonstrated in the presence on the web of official sites for older horror films; among these are sites for *The Exorcist* (1973), the *A Nightmare on Elm Street* series (1984–2010) and Hammer Studios.[31] These sites offer historical overviews of the films, other archive material including interviews and critical reactions, and a range of photo galleries, screensavers and games with which the fans can personalise their experience. The *Exorcist* site, for example, contains material on possession and aspects of the real life case on which the film was based, the Hammer site offers a history of the studio and archival material on every Hammer film, and *A Nightmare on Elm Street*'s site contains coroner's reports on the deaths in each of the films. Again, these features allow fans to build on their knowledge and competencies, and also to purchase merchandise, predominantly DVDs. It is not only the mainstream Hollywood studios who exploit the Internet in this way, since the accessible and, more importantly, low-cost space provided by the Internet can play a major part in the success of low-budget productions. The case studies which follow – the online campaigns for the British zombie-plague film *28 Days Later* (2002) and the American 'mockumentary' horror film *The Blair Witch Project* – look at how independent producers have profitably employed online publicity and co-opted fan activity.

The website for the low-budget British film *28 Days Later* illustrates how online campaigns are now a major focus of film marketing.[32] It represents the kind of interactive site which offers a range of exclusive publicity which might appeal to active online fans looking for 'value-added' material. The *28 Days Later* site offered the fan a taster of the film that was atmospheric in both sound (an echoing 'hello' and the hymn that formed the centrepiece of the incidental music) and visuals (throbbing veins and blood red logos) – all strong elements of horror iconography. As well as the film trailer, the music video, interviews with Danny Boyle and other members of the cast and crew, a featurette on the making of the film and a range of film posters and publicity stills which could be downloaded to be used as desktop wallpaper, the fan was offered a range of other 'bonus' material to pique their interest.[33] This material included a short animated film filling in the narrative gap between the opening of the film and the hero's reawakening after the outbreak of contagion. This, as well as a 'Find Jim' animated postcard, could be sent via email to other users. The fan could also subscribe their email address to receive news bulletins on the film. In combination, these 'personal' features serve to initiate and escalate an electronic word-of-mouth campaign, as well as adding to the illusion that the fan is a member of a *28 Days Later* community.

Whilst it is true that by necessity independent filmmakers exploit the cheapest means of publicity available, they may well be aware of the online fan community and exploit the ways in which the Internet is used. Independent filmmakers use the Internet to disseminate information about projects and initiate interest; several low-budget production companies have associated Yahoo!Groups (see Shattered Mirror Productions or Midnight Pictures, for example). As Reel Source President Robert Bucksbaum is quoted as saying of *The Blair Witch Project*, "Artisan didn't have the marketing budget to do a big push on television, so they aimed their campaign at 17- to 28-year-olds who stay at home and surf the Net. If you're getting 3 million hits on your site per day from that, who needs television?".[34]

Despite this, the relationship between producers and consumers remains a fraught one,[35] but horror fans seeking out and disseminating information can be of benefit to filmmakers who may recognise and reward such interest. Whilst this should not be taken as suggesting a lessening of any power imbalance between producer and consumer, it does have certain mutually advantageous features. Fans are brought together around their communal expectations, while the word-of-mouth that frequently boosts box office, particularly for low budget independent and exploitation cinema, becomes a 'global' online phenomenon. As the quote from Bucksbaum suggests, the now famous Internet campaign for *The Blair Witch Project* is the best illustration of this. The fan-base for the film, even before the film was completed, was especially active. In keeping with the constructed actuality of the 'events' depicted in the film, the official film site (which was part of the film experience itself) was designed around the 'historical' documents on the Blair Witch and the police 'evidence' of the disappearance of the filmmakers featured in the film.[36] It was not this site alone, though, which was the focus in the pre-publicity for the film. In the 11-month run-up to the film's release at least twenty fan sites, a web ring, an email discussion list and a newsgroup were established.[37] Ostensibly, this comprised a grass-roots interest in the film widely reported on MTV (which also carried heavy advertising for the film) and other areas of the media consumed by youth audiences. Fans who heard about the film through early television previews and sought out more information online admit that they were fascinated enough to set up their own sites. They were encouraged in this by the filmmakers; Jeff Johnsen, who claims to have set up the first Blair Witch website[38] said, "[d]irectors Ed Sanchez and Dan Myrick have been very accessible to all of us; that made us want to spread the word about the film".[39] Among the other early Blair Witch fan websites was A&e's *The Blair Witch Project Fanatic's Guide*.[40] The creators of this site, Abigail Marceluk and Eric Alan, came to the attention of the filmmakers of *The Blair Witch Project* and worked with them on associated merchandise; in return the fans were rewarded by being linked to the mythology of the film themselves (they are the anthropology students who 'discovered' the lost footage shot by the missing film crew and they appear in the Sci-Fi Channel's *Curse of the Blair Witch* documentary). Their website contains details of their activities.

The early fan base for *The Blair Witch Project* was interpreted as a form of hype in certain quarters of the media, with an unnamed 'industry executive' quoted in Salon as saying: "*The Blair Witch Project* filmmakers are using their friends to generate their fan sites. That was an organised effort . . . They tricked the press".[41] The fans themselves have denied that they were exploited in this way, and given the levels of fan interest in projects at all stages of production in other fan communities, it is only too plausible that filmmakers do not need to resort to recruiting fans or faking a fan base. Equally, the Internet offers low- to no-budget filmmakers the chance to kick-start an online fan base as a way of generating an audience – two other examples being *Cabin Fever* (2002) and *Wrong Turn* (2003).

The hype and hyperbole which campaigns can generate illustrate the fact that the Internet allows the accumulation and spread of information all too well, and that fans no longer have to rely solely on specialist film magazines and the general media as sources of (delayed) information. In their celebration of the genre, then, the relative ease with which they can create online 'shrines' to their favourite texts, whether they be classic, current or highly anticipated upcoming films, must be seen as a key factor in the fan culture.

It is in this environment – where everyone can have their say and anyone can be a critic – that conflict arises within the relationship between producers and consumers. And so, a return to *Clive Barker's Saint Sinner*. The Sci-Fi Channel bulletin board invites visitors to comment with: 'Here's where you can repent your sins, invent new ones, and talk about the Sci Fi Pictures Original Movie *Clive Barker's Saint Sinner*'. The message board for *Clive Barker's Saint Sinner* collected over 77 topics, many with multiple replies, between 21 September 2002 and 5 November 2002 (within two weeks of transmission). Of the 102 posts which discussed the film itself (others were concerned with a competition on the site, various actors in the film or the musical score which was also being hyped on the website), there were 41 posted before transmission all of which were eagerly anticipating the film, despite some reservations about whether and to what extent the film was based on Barker's comic book of the same title. Almost 74 per cent of the 61 posts which gave an opinion after transmission were either highly negative (33) or guarded in their judgements, many because they were confused or annoyed by the plot holes (12). Thirteen posts were positive, the remaining three simply dealt with recounts of the plot without critical comment. There are a few fans, then, who enjoyed *Clive Barker's Saint Sinner* and argued their case on the bulletin board. Several of these were female fans and it may have been that they were responding to specifically gendered aspects of the texts; one fan writes about her mixed, but in balance positive, responses:

I too liked how it didn't turn out to be a quickie romance between the cop and monk, and thought it was sad when he died. Loved the tombstone too. Very nice.

I guess it was watchable, but could have been done much better with a little more thought. It definitely didn't live up to my expectations, but it was much better than MODERN VAMPIRES!! LOL!!

Ok . . . he was a hot monk! 0:)

This is indicative of patterns of feminine readings in its references to the appeal of the hero and what could be interpreted as a feminist response to the absence of the stereotypical romance arc of mainstream narrative. Her third point relates to personal taste within the genre and indicates perhaps that this particular fan has been disappointed in the past with similarly themed narratives. Opinions such as the one that opens this chapter, however, formed the predominant fan response. Negative criticism tended to apportion blame to the Sci-Fi Channel and the makers of the film rather than Barker, although some posters were cynical about Barker 'taking the money and running' but, in the main, it was the failures of the plot that were the concern. Horror film fans such as these, it seems, are sophisticated consumers and expect multi-layered, yet well-constructed narratives. Ironically, the fans were unrepentant in their dislike of the film, and unashamed of the opinions they held. Their only 'new sin' was to speak their minds in an unconstrained manner.[42]

In conclusion then, celebration of the horror genre in its various forms across the Internet is marked by the following features: that tastes are diverse and reflect preferences for many different types of horror films and personalities; that fans establish their own set of canonical texts and competencies; that rituals are established within a range of differently focused communities; that taste is often recognised and respected as personal, but that fans seek out their like-minded fellows; and that fans will often criticise texts which do not meet their expectations. It is this last point which highlights the risk that official online marketing takes when attempting to raise fan expectations and co-opt fans for word-of-mouth campaigns. What is clear, finally, is that fans do celebrate the horror genre, but they do not do this indiscriminately.

Table 1

A: Frequency of fan fic for horror film titles on FanFiction.net

FILM	NO. OF FICS
The Mummy	827
Hannibal	494
The Crow	74
Scream	69
The Faculty	66
Halloween	61
The Evil Dead	60
Th13teen Ghosts	57
Blade	54
The Children of the Corn	53
Dracula	48
The Silence of the Lambs	48
A Nightmare on Elm Street	35
Final Destination	30
The Blair Witch Project	24
The Craft	12
Child's Play	10
House on Haunted Hill	9
Darkman	7
Stigmata	7
It	6
From Dusk Till Dawn	5

B: Genre labels for Scream-based fan fic on FanFiction.net (each story is placed in up to two genre categories)

GENRE LABEL	OCCURRENCES
General	16
Romance	5
Humour	13
Drama	4
Poetry	3
Action/Adventure	3
Mystery	11
Horror	35
Parody	9
Angst	3
Supernatural	1
Suspense	7

Notes

1. 'Katgirl', post to the Sci-Fi Channel bulletin board, <http://bboard.scifi.com/bboard/browse.cgi/1/5/2921/59>, 27 October 2002.
2. Henry Jenkins, *Textual Poachers: Television Fans and Participatory Culture*, London: Routledge, 1992, p. 82.
3. See, for example, Kristen Pullen, 'I-love-Xena.com: Creating On-line Fan Communities', in David Gauntlett, ed., *web.studies: Rewiring Media Studies For the Digital Age*, London: Arnold, 2000, pp. 52–61.
4. See John Fiske, 'The Cultural Economy of Fandom', in Lisa A. Lewis, ed., *The Adoring Audience: Fan Culture and Popular Media*, London: Routledge, 1992, pp. 30–49; and Jenkins, *Textual Poachers*.
5. See Matt Hills, 'Virtually Out There: Strategies, Tactics and Affective Spaces in On-line Fandom', in Sally R. Munt, ed., *Technospaces: Inside the New Media*, London: Continuum, 2001, pp. 147–60.
6. This has been identified through participant observation during previous research into horror fandom. For a partial summary of this work see Brigid Cherry, 'Refusing to Refuse to Look: Female Viewers of the Horror Film', in Richard Maltby and Melvin Stokes, eds, *Identifying Hollywood Audiences*, London: BFI, 1999, pp 187–203.
7. It is, of course, impossible to ascertain the population size.
8. Yahoo!Groups, <http://groups.yahoo.com/>.
9. Google Groups, <http://groups.google.com/>.
10. *The Dark Side of the Net*, <http://www.darklinks.com/>.
11. Jimmie L. Reeves, Mark C. Rogers and Michael Epstein, 'Rewriting Popularity: The Cult Files', in David Lavery, Angela Hague and Marla Cartwright, eds, *Deny All Knowledge: Reading the X-Files*, London: Faber and Faber, 1996, p. 32.
12. *The Horror Search Engine*, <http://www.horrorfind.com/>.
13. *Fright Fest*, <http://www.frightfest.co.uk/>.
14. See Cherry, 'Refusing to Refuse to Look'.
15. Susan J. Clerc, 'DDEB, GATB, MPPB, and Ratboy: The X-Files' Media Fandom, On-line and Off', in Lavery et al., *Deny All Knowledge,* pp. 36–51.
16. L-Soft, <http://www.lsoft.com/scripts/wl.exe?SL2=1879&R=5825&N=HORROR@LISTSERV.INDIANA.EDU>.
17. Horror in Film and Literature, <http://ezinfo.ucs.indiana.edu/~mlperkin/horror.html>.
18. Carol J. Clover, *Men, Women, and Chain Saws: Gender in the Modern Horror Film*, New Jersey: Princeton University Press, 1992.
19. Since the newsgroups are not subject to the control of memberships and list owners, flaming is more likely to occur in these groups.
20. See Cherry, 'Refusing to Refuse to Look'.
21. *Deadites Online*, <http://www.deadites.net/>.
22. *Ladies of the Evil Dead*, <http://www.ladiesoftheevildead.com/>.
23. *Cult Horrors*, <http://members.tripod.com/greg.z/id17.htm>.

24. *Evil Dead: The Ultimate Experience on Gruelling Online Terror*, <http://website.lineone.net/~kyle-p/home.htm>.

25. FanFiction.net, <http://www.fanfiction.net/>.

26. Film titles range from *Gone With the Wind* (79 stories), to *Hedwig and the Angry Inch* (four stories). The films with the highest number of stories are *Star Wars* (7,904 stories) and *X-Men: The Movie* (1,768), whilst the lowest, with one each, include (but are not limited to) *Krull*, *La vita è bella* (*Life is Beautiful*), *Screamers*, *The Deer Hunter* and *Wyatt Earp*.

27. Science-fiction/horror titles such as *Aliens* (there is no Alien-based fan fiction as such, what exists is centred around an Aliens v. Predator crossover) and *Godzilla* have been excluded for clarity, as have fringe titles such as *Signs*, *The Nightmare Before Christmas* and *Heathers*.

28. Will Brooker, 'Internet Fandom and the Continuing Narratives of *Star Wars*, *Blade Runner* and *Alien*', in Annette Kuhn, ed., *Alien Zone II*, London: Verso, 1999, p. 50.

29. Matt Hills, *Fan Cultures*, London: Routledge, 2002, p. 180.

30. See <http://www.vanhelsing.net/>, <http://www.dawnofthedead.net/> and <http://www.bladetrinity.com/>.

31. See *The Exorcist*, <http://theexorcist.warnerbros.com/>, *A Nightmare on Elm Street*, <http://www.nightmareonelmstreet.com>, and *HammerWeb*, <http://www.hammerfilms.com/>.

32. *28 Days Later*, <http://www.28dayslaterthemovie.co.uk/main.html>.

33. Material added for the DVD release also includes a game in which the fan can shoot zombies and, if successful, have their name added to the highest scorer box.

34. Wired News, 'Blair Witch Casts Strong Spell', <http://www.wired.com/news/print/0,1294,21045,00.html>, 2 August 1999.

35. See, for example, Jenkins, *Textual Poachers*, pp.120–51, for an account of *Beauty and the Beast* fan campaigns.

36. *The Blair Witch* Project, <http://www.blairwitch.com/>.

37. For a full account of the *Blair Witch* marketing see J.P. Telotte, '*The Blair Witch Project* Project', *Film Quarterly*, vol. 54, no. 3, 2001, pp. 32–9.

38. *The Blair Witch Project Forum*, <http://www.delphi.com/blairwitch/>.

39. Salon, 'Letters to the editor', <http://www.salon.com/letters/1999/07/23/blair_witch/index.html>, 23 July 1999.

40. *The Blair Witch Project Fanatics Guide*, <http://tbwp.freeservers.com/>.

41. Patrizia DiLucchio, 'Did 'The Blair Witch Project' fake its online fan base,' in Salon Technology, <http://www.salon.com/tech/feature/1999/07/16/blair_marketing/>, 16 July 1999.

42. Whether anyone in any production capacity monitored the negative criticism is another matter.

5

Attending Horror Film Festivals and Conventions
Liveness, Subcultural Capital and 'Flesh-and-Blood Genre Communities'

MATT HILLS

Rick Altman has discussed how communities of consumers gather around specific genres, describing these fans as 'constellated communities'. He notes that:

> while genre fandom sometimes involves . . . actual face to face contact, genre buffs more commonly imagine themselves communing with absent like-minded fans . . . Most of the time, flesh-and-blood genre communities remain beyond reach. Though we may have intermittent contact with others fond of the same genre, we are usually reduced to only imagining their presence and activity.[1]

In this chapter I will follow Altman's account by taking 'flesh-and-blood' or co-present horror fan communities as my focus. Although Altman is quite right in his observation that fan communities are often imagined through texts such as fan magazines, fanzines and via online communities, such an approach underplays the significance of co-present horror fan communities and their events.[2]

Considering horror's "flesh-and-blood genre communities", I will examine how socially-organised fan events work to create and sustain fans' 'subcultural capital':[3] that is, social status in the eyes of other fans. However, in order to address how festivals and conventions allow fans to accrue subcultural social status, it is necessary to consider the ideology of 'liveness' that is thereby valorised by fans of mediated horror texts, as well as highlighting powerfully embedded connections between this ideology – 'liveness' as a source of authenticity – and the very concept of fan 'subcultural capital'. My approach is meant to emphasise that horror fan conventions and horror-themed/related film festivals work, subculturally, in a variety of ways. I will argue that they help to reproduce fan culture's hierarchies by allowing attendees to be more 'in the know' than fellow fans. At the same time, however, festivals and conventions help build and sustain a sense of non-imagined fan community, precisely by virtue of their shared rituals and co-presence.[4] Reinforcing both fan communities *and* hierarchies, festivals/conventions are an intriguing object for study.

Curiously, although conventions have provided a central topic in work on television sci-fi and science-fiction fandom more generally, they have been relatively neglected in work on horror.[5] Ian Conrich mentions the significance of horror fan conventions, collectors' fairs, and horror genre-focused film festivals in passing,[6] and Mark Kermode has likewise referred to the importance of UK horror events such as the London-based Shock Around the Clock (now known as FrightFest), Black Sunday and Fantasm, as well as European and US events. Kermode notes that "[f]or British fans, cut ever deeper by censorious scissors, these festivals are becoming increasingly important".[7]

In order to consider this increasing importance, I will now introduce the concept of 'subcultural capital' in more detail, before relating this to a discussion of festivals/conventions and 'liveness'. The term 'subcultural capital' is used by Sarah Thornton in her development of French sociologist Pierre Bourdieu's theories of cultural distinction. It is intended as an amendment to Bourdieu's notion of 'cultural capital', which is the amount of cultural knowledge/literacy that a person possesses, this also being related to their level of education.[8] Thornton points out that not all forms of cultural knowledge and expertise are shared by an entire culture; some forms of cultural literacy are, in fact, restricted to particular subcultures. Hence Thornton's concept of subcultural capital, which she discusses through an analysis of club culture:

> Subcultural capital confers status on its owner in the eyes of the relevant beholder ... Subcultural capital can be *objectified* or *embodied*. Just as books and paintings display cultural capital in the family home, so subcultural capital is objectified in the form of fashionable haircuts and well-assembled record collections ... Just as cultural capital is personified in 'good' manners and urbane conversation, so subcultural capital is embodied in the form of being 'in the know', using (but not over-using) current slang and looking as if you were born to perform the latest dance style.[9]

Or, translating this idea into a discussion of horror fan subculture rather than Thornton's club culture, relevant subcultural capital can be objectified in a fan's collection of uncut *giallo* films or 'video nasties', or embodied in the same fan's knowledge of horror films and auteurs. Not all fan subcultures have a spectacularly visible 'look' in the way that rave or goth might,[10] although horror fans often tend to display their fandom's "enunciative productivity"[11] by sporting relevant T-shirts at conventions or festivals, where this "choice of clothes ... [is a way] ... of constructing a social identity and therefore of asserting one's membership of a particular fan community".[12] Identifying horror fan culture's versions of its own, distinctive subcultural capital, it is worth noting – given my focus on 'flesh-and-blood' fan communities – that Thornton's examples appear to blur together what might be meant by 'objectified' or 'embodied' subcultural capital. Being 'in-the-know' is said to be 'embodied' subcultural capital, while "fashionable haircuts" are described as an instance of 'objectified' capital. It is quite difficult to see exactly how this distinction is tenable; if I display horror fan knowledge, then is this not an 'object' that indicates my subcultural capital, just as much as it is 'embodied'? And if a haircut is 'objectified' then is it not surely also an embodied component of subcultural capital? Perhaps it is sufficient to note that, other than in the case of material culture and its artefacts – collections of films/books/merchandise and so on – subcultural capital appears to be powerfully linked to embodiment, whether through embodied appearances or through forms of knowledge.

Given this centrality of the body in Thornton's account of subcultural capital, it is curious that the fan body – and gatherings of bodies – have received little theoretical attention in academic work on horror. Even Mark Jancovich, who has profitably applied Thornton's work on subcultural capital to horror and cult fans, has relatively little to say on the matter of fan embodiment and conventions/festivals.[13] And yet it would appear to be difficult to consider subcultural capital without raising the matter of embodiment.

Attendance at horror film festivals or conventions is, I want to suggest, one significant way in which fan knowledge can be embodied and objectified. That is to say, festivals/conventions are a powerful source, and display, of subcultural capital. By virtue of being physically present at such organised events, fans often gain access to film screenings, preview trailers or exclusive 'rough-cut' clips in advance of a finished film's general release (if such a release even occurs). They also have the opportunity to discuss horror texts not only with other fans but also with industry professionals such as writers, effects technicians and directors. Embodied interactions are the key to generating and sustaining high levels of subcultural capital, since the fan can say 'I was *there*', or they can relay to other fans – the relevant beholders for this fan status – their experiences of gaining privileged access to horror filmmakers and/or preview prints.

Why, then, is there such notable fan cultural authenticity constructed around the physical co-presence of the convention/festival? Fans may be able to learn very similar facts about production histories by reading published interviews with directors and actors. They may also be able to watch the films screened at a festival at a later date, either on video/DVD or in the cinema. These alternatives would, on the face of it, allow fans to similarly develop their subcultural capital. And yet convention/festival-going appears to confer greater subcultural capital on its attendees by virtue of being aligned with an ideology of liveness and immediacy, with fans always being hungry to be 'first' to view an eagerly awaited release. As Philip Auslander points out in his study *Liveness: Performance in a Mediatized Culture*:

> [A] ... dimension to the question of why people continue to attend live events in our mediatized culture is that live events have cultural value: being able to say that you were physically present at a particular event constitutes valuable symbolic capital ... One remarkable aspect of performance's position within cultural economy is that our ability to convert attendance at a live event into symbolic capital is completely independent of the experiential quality of the event itself.[14]

Auslander is drawing on Bourdieu's work here, but he uses the term 'symbolic capital' – often taken to relate to matters of 'reputation' achieved through high levels of other forms of capital – interchangeably with the notion of cultural capital. Unfortunately demonstrating no awareness of Thornton's revisionist concept of 'subcultural capital', Auslander instead argues that where fan cultures are concerned, cultural capital (knowledge/literacy) and symbolic capital (prestige) can be equated, *contra* Bourdieu.[15] The idea of 'subcultural capital' does away with the need to prematurely equate these two different terms, since it specifies a type of cultural capital that generates status and prestige, but only within the fan culture concerned. Auslander's examples concerning what he calls symbolic/cultural capital and 'liveness' might therefore, I think, be better reinterpreted as being about liveness and *subcultural* capital. These examples are drawn from rock fan cultures, but make a lot of sense when applied to horror fans attending festivals/conventions:

> In considering the symbolic value of attendance at live performances, rarity, distance in time, and proximity to an imagined originary moment are all determining factors. It is clear, for example, that having seen a Rolling Stones concert in 1964 is worth more symbolic capital within rock culture than having seen the Stones in 1997, for all the reasons I just mentioned. It may even be that having seen the Beatles live is worth more than having seen the Stones, even in 1964, precisely because the Beatles' performing career was relatively short.[16]

Rarity, distance in time, and proximity to an imagined originary moment are all, similarly, determinants of how convention/festival attendance can act as a source of subcultural capital for horror fans; being able to say 'I was there' for the first Shock Around the Clock festival, held at London's Scala cinema in King's Cross, 1987, would hold more subcultural capital than 'being there' for the 2002 London FrightFest at the Prince Charles cinema off Leicester Square. Rarity also plays a part in enhancing subcultural capital due to festivals' limited ticket sales. Likewise, meeting a seldom seen convention special guest would create more subcultural capital than seeing a guest known to attend many collector's fairs and conventions, such as Ingrid Pitt (a regular at UK fan and film fairs). Proximity to an imagined originary moment can also be relevant to horror fan subcultural capital; seeing a special screening of a banned or heavily censored film at a festival years before that same film's eventual certification and re-release would place the fan closer to an 'originary moment' (the history of the film's censorship/banning). Conventions and festivals often also promote themselves, as I will go on to discuss in more detail, through 'premiere' screenings, making the originary moment one of a film's first showing, and hence generating increased subcultural capital for attendees. In this case, the 'liveness' (and thus authenticity) surrounding a film's festival premiere is often created by having the film's director or stars on hand for a festival/convention introduction and post-screening discussion.

Considering the physical co-presence of fan groups and horror genre professionals at festivals, I would suggest that it is the very 'non-imagined' evidence of communal patterns of interpretation, media tastes and affective investments that is important here. Although horror fans may often be reduced to imagining the 'presence and activity' of fellow fans, festivals/conventions provide the opportunity for fans to viscerally experience the accumulation of subcultural capital. Rather than reading (online or offline; in commercial magazines or fanzines) about horror films and their production processes, where subcultural capital can be privately accumulated in a relatively detached manner, subcultural capital becomes very directly embodied and objectified in the case of the festival or convention. Professionals become the objects of fan attention 'live and in person' (Bruce Campbell's billing when he appeared at a back-to-back screening of the *The Evil Dead* films [1982–1992]),[17] just as fans objectify/embody their subcultural capital for fellow fans.

In Thornton's definition of subcultural capital, it is implicitly and logically stipulated that for any object or embodiment to function as this type of capital, it must be apparent to other fans, since status is conferred "on its owner *in the eyes of the relevant beholder*".[18] Therefore, it must be evident to fans that their accumulated capital, carried in objects and embodied, is actually recognised and legitimated *as subcultural capital* by other fans in order for it to function as such. It could, of course, be argued that the subcultural values of horror fandom are mediated by types of niche magazines and fanzines as well as being mediated online.[19] Also, subcultural norms may tend to be internalised by individual fans, meaning that fans could recognise their own subcultural capital, or that they could recognise it through reading around their objects of fandom. These arguments are valuable insofar as they indicate that horror fans' subcultural capital can be affirmed and circulated in specific ways via its mediation, but they also miss the fact that 'liveness' is built into Thornton's original definition and discussion of the term, both given subcultural capital's embodiment, but also its place-bound nature: "Nothing depletes capital more than the sight of someone trying too hard. For example, fledgling clubbers of fifteen or sixteen wishing to get into what they perceive as a sophisticated dance club will often reveal their inexperience by over-dressing".[20] In this account, as throughout Thornton's definition, subcultural capital is a matter of being seen *in situ* (i.e. 'being there' live). But this is not quite the same type of subcultural recognition as that conferred at a distance, via niche mediation.

Given this distinction between 'live' and mediated recognition, subcultural capital needs, perhaps, to be separated into 'potential' and 'actual' forms, or what might be termed 'fixed' and 'circulating' forms of capital. In terms of ideal-types, potential or 'fixed' subcultural capital is that which has been accumulated by a fan – through lone or small-group viewing, where a friendship or family circle may be more important than a fan cultural identity, or through private reading of fanzines/fan commercial magazines – but which has yet to be recognised within the sphere of socially-organised fandom. Again in terms of ideal-types, actual, 'circulating' subcultural capital is that which has been put into play by virtue of its recognition within a socially-organised and periodically co-present fandom. Such a distinction was, arguably, not forwarded by Thornton because of the type of subculture she studied; it makes little sense to write about clubbers who are not, at some point, co-present with other clubbers, where this co-presence depends on a physically embodied knowledge and on time-bound and place-bound performances of subcultural capital (via a dance style carried out at a specific club night). Subcultural capital and its 'live' recognitions are therefore rather more automatically built into club culture in comparison with horror (and other media) fandoms.

In the case of horror, fans might avidly read magazines, consume horror films, and build up what would be thought of as 'subcultural capital' without ever mixing socially with other fans, and without their subcultural capital being recognised as such by 'relevant beholders'. Some fans may even prefer this situation, not wishing to enter the spaces/places of a co-present 'flesh-and-blood genre community', while others may consider that their fan tastes are sufficiently 'recognised' implicitly – though not directly – through the textual mediation of online newsgroups, fan magazines, or by simply sharing a taste for horror with a friend or family member.

However, all this raises a further complication for thinking about subcultural capital; despite Thornton's emphasis on a direct circuit of embodiment/objectification and recognition – seemingly unavoidable in relation to club culture – media fandoms such as horror may more accurately be said to sustain a continuum of forms of capital-recognition, ranging from implied to direct, and thus ranging between potential and actual subcultural capital. This can be represented diagrammatically as follows:

Potential subcultural capital----------------------------------Actual subcultural capital

FIXED CAPITAL   Implied----------Direct recognition   CIRCULATING CAPITAL

/Lone viewer/   /Regular festival or convention-goer/

/Friendship or family viewer/   /Has attended a festival or convention/

/Consumes secondary texts/   /Actively involved in online fandom/

/Writes or has written for offline or online secondary texts /

It should be noted that this continuum implies nothing about the *authenticity* of somebody's experienced fandom; the lone viewer may be as knowledgeable and passionate about horror as the regular festival/ convention goer. But even if this is so, the lone viewer's subcultural capital would remain almost entirely potential/fixed, whereas the festival goer's would be activated through its periodic and 'live' recognition. As we move from left to right on the continuum, we move from forms of horror fan activity where subcultural capital can be accumulated without subcultural recognition (the lone or family/friendship circle viewer), through to subcultural capital that receives implied recognition (the fan is reading about other fans' views), capital that is increasingly recognised via fan interaction (which may be imagined rather than embodied, involving reading fanzines, fan magazines or online material), and from there to subcultural capital that becomes 'actual' capital through its circulation, i.e. through increases in frequency, intensity and/or embodiment of fan interaction. Horror fans' subcultural capital, I'm suggesting here, becomes most fully akin to the 'subcultural capital' discussed by Thornton when her arguments are applied to fans who regularly gather together as a socially-organised 'flesh-and-blood community', since it is this that allows embodied/objectified subcultural capital to be most fully recognised by co-present, relevant subcultural 'beholders'.

By attending a film festival or convention, fans can be assured of 'co-watching' horror films; that is, actually watching horror with a theatre full of like-minded spectators, rather than "forming a fleeting bond with a fellow movie-goer" at a multiplex screening of a horror movie on the basis that this one fellow viewer has reacted as a fan would (laughing at an in-joke) and not simply as part of a more casual audience (cringing at gory effects).[21] The festival/convention experience of being part of a crowd, but nevertheless significantly reacting in sync and in step (as interpretive communities tend to) is a powerful instance of the thoroughly sociable nature of subcultural capital when it is communally recognised, shared and affirmed. Such affirmation can lead horror fans, much like fans of other, science-fiction/fantasy texts, to experience moments of 'communitas' at festivals and conventions. 'Communitas' is Victor Turner's term for the communal fellowship felt by pilgrims – fellowship that cannot be attained in the circumstances of usual, everyday life and its social structures.[22] Horror fan's 'communitas' is, then, a phenomenological by-product of the affirmation and recognition of subcultural capital; fans feel part of a 'flesh-and-blood' community by virtue of the fact that their co-presence and 'co-watching' allows fan subcultural distinctions to be most fully and directly validated/reinforced.

Likewise, being in the presence of films' directors, stars, or actors also allows horror fans at conventions or festivals to feel a sense of communal identification. In this case, fan subcultural capital is partly recognised or affirmed and partly accumulated. Recognition stems from the fact that horror auteurs and directors tend to represent themselves at conventions/festivals as fans as well as professionals – that is, they too share in a discourse and experience of communal 'belonging'. Differences between fans and media professionals are partly elided at conventions and festivals, through an insecurely achieved social proximity that is usually impossible, through codes of courtesy, and through horror professionals' interest in mixing, albeit temporarily and in a highly ritualised manner, with horror fans.

To take one example, Bruce Campbell, star of *The Evil Dead* parts *I*, *II* and *III*, has presented a self-produced and directed documentary *Fanalysis*, included as an extra on the (2002 release) Region 2 DVD of *The Evil Dead*. In this documentary, Campbell uses his own convention attendance as a guest to interview fans about their fandom, and to muse on the social relationships between fans and guests at festivals/conventions.

Here, Campbell talks of having an 'obligation' to fans. His attendance at a convention breakfast, where he engages fans in conversation, is one such obligation, and Campbell's emphasis appears to be on how convention and public appearances can be brought off successfully as social interactions. Similarly, Ted Raimi (brother of Sam) is interviewed for Campbell's documentary, and concludes that there is a specific technique to personal appearances:

> They [the fans] want a certain kind of you, that's what they're paying for . . .
> I can't really hide too much behind a persona, what I have to do is to give
> very specific answers that aren't too personal but not so impersonal so as the
> fans would be disappointed, because they came to see me.[23]

In other words, industry professionals have to negotiate and perform their 'personal' selves without giving away details of their private life that they wish to keep private, but also without too obviously being seen as 'performing'. What fans confront within the 'communitas' that temporarily levels differences of social structure, making celebrity guests (artificially) equal to fans, is thus a type of star/auteur performance. Such a performance stresses the communal bond between star and fan – what Bruce Campbell concludes his documentary by calling the "yin and yang" of celebrity and fan – just as fan-to-fan 'communitas' stresses the fan community's 'flesh-and-blood' recognition of itself.

Performances of the 'family' of horror professionals and fans can also be oriented around a convention or festival's geographical/regional identity. For instance, the DVD of Maurice Devereaux's ultra-low-budget, indie, non-Union, Québécois horror film *$LASHER$* includes a *Making Of . . .* documentary written, edited and directed by Jean-Denis Rouette. This documentary extra includes 'behind the scenes' footage of the film's production process, but it also includes coverage of the festival premiere of *$LASHER$*. This occurred at the horror/fantasy-themed Fantasia Film Festival, in Montreal, in July 2001. By showing director, producer, writer and editor Devereaux being interviewed by local media, this section of the documentary stresses that the film's festival screening was held in front of the auteur's 'home town' audience. Professional-fan communitas is hence supplemented by, and blurred into, discourses of provincial/regional belonging (quite apart from the fact that the film is set in Japan and parodies American reality TV!).

It is striking that both the *The Evil Dead* and *$LASHER$* DVD releases incorporate material from horror conventions or festivals into their secondary texts. Although these DVDs are readily accessible products, such extras nevertheless attempt to interpellate horror's fan-consumers as 'insiders' by capturing, in documentary form, moments from festival premieres and public appearances. As Barbara Klinger has observed, since

> DVDs are mass produced, there would seem to be little potential . . . for pursuing the ultimate collector's commodity – the rare artefact . . . Nonetheless, the language of scarcity permeates . . . discourses . . . [around DVD releases] . . . Media industries attempt to appeal to the collector as a film industry 'insider', privy to a secret world of information about film-making.[24]

This 'secret world', and this language of scarcity, seemingly extend to documenting festival premieres and conventions, demonstrating to horror's DVD consumers that, although perhaps absent from such events, they can still maintain their 'insider' fan knowledge. However, by attempting such a manoeuvre, and invoking notions of 'rarity' and 'exclusivity', these DVD extras remind fans that festivals and premieres are – by dint of involving 'flesh-and-blood genre communities' – *genuinely* rare and exclusive. Such events are, precisely, restricted by their fans' and industry professionals' spatial and temporal co-presence, or by their 'liveness', to recall Auslander's points.

Festivals and conventions therefore make professionals unusually accessible and available to fans. Despite stressing links between fans and professionals, experiences of 'communitas' cannot entirely overwrite or overcome fans' sense of the 'specialness' surrounding horror's subcultural celebrities (that is, celebrities whose status is recognised distinctively or solely by the 'relevant beholders' of the fan culture). It is the extraordinary and ritualised nature of this fan-celebrity social proximity, given that mediation usually means fan-celebrity relationships are socially distant and non-reciprocal which allows fans to accumulate higher levels of subcultural capital, as well as having this form of capital be recognised by fellow fans.[25] Some academic-fans have been no less immune to the sense of an auteur's 'specialness', despite theories of the 'death of the author': film scholar Walter Metz writes of his "emotional experiences" of being "proud to have had a chance to *touch* [shake hands with] the author".[26] Perhaps 'flesh-and-blood genre communities' and ideologies of liveness have as much of a place within academic 'appreciations' as they do within fan cultures.

While festivals/conventions allow fans to interact with other fans and with guests, the nature of exactly *what* gets screened at horror/fantasy film festivals is, of course, also crucial to the generation of fan subcultural capital. The importance of festival screenings within horror fan culture is evident in comments made by film reviewers in UK commercial, horror/

fantasy 'niche' magazines such as *Starburst* and *Shivers*:

> Eight months after it was premiered at FrightFest (on 24 August 2001), director Stuart Urban's restrained, supernatural fantasy [*Revelation*] finally gets a UK release.[27]

> Many of the excellent films on show at this year's Lupo Fright Fest – organised, as in previous years, by Ian Rattray, Paul McEvoy and *Shivers*' own Alan Jones – shared a common theme of perception and vision. This was appropriate, since the Horror fans who packed London's Prince Charles Theatre [http://www.princecharlescinema.com], were there for the sole purpose of viewing the exclusive previews, premieres and oddities from across the world.[28]

The first film review quoted above is written by one of the organisers of London's 'FrightFest', Alan Jones, who perhaps unsurprisingly takes the opportunity to point out an eight month delay between festival screening and general release. The second review – a blow-by-blow account of the 2002 FrightFest – is written by the editor of *Shivers* magazine, David Miller, and points up the 'exclusive' nature of 'premieres'.

In each case, this particular horror-themed film festival (according to Miller "several films fell outside the pure Horror remit")[29] is linked to forms of subcultural capital. Attendees and organisers are more 'in-the-know' than readers of *Starburst* and *Shivers* because, by attending FrightFest, they have already seen what, for most readers and non-attendees, remain as-yet-unseen, forthcoming releases. For example, FrightFest 2000 (originally billed as 'Shock Around the Clock 2000')[30] offered a 'World Premiere' of *Ed Gein*, an 'English Premiere' of *Ring 2*, and a 'London Premiere' of *The Lighthouse*. In the same vein, FrightFest 2001 boasted a 'World Premiere' of *Alone*, an 'English Premiere' of *The Bunker* and a 'London Premiere' of *Trouble Every Day*. Guests scheduled to attend in these two years included Paul Anderson, Chuck Parello (director of *Ed Gein*) and Simon Hunter (director of *The Lighthouse*), while FrightFest 2002's line up featured Danny Boyle with a sneak preview of *28 Days Later*, as well as writer Patrick McGrath discussing *Spider* (filmed by director David Cronenberg, and one of 2002's 'Sneak Preview' screenings).

The importance of 'Premieres' and 'Previews' is apparent from an examination of the programmes for FrightFest 2000 and 2001.[31] Even where a film, or an extract from a film, is screened only a very short time ahead of its general release, it is billed as a 'Sneak Preview', emphasising that it can be seen ahead of its 'mainstream' exhibition. And the notion of a 'Premiere' is also semiotically stretched to cover just about every film screened, including the billing of 'London Premiere', where the superior tags of World/European/British/English Premiere have presumably already fallen through thanks to other festival screenings.

Thus it is not simply the fan knowledge created by attending such screenings that is significant, it is also the timeliness of such knowledge, where even a 'London Premiere' or 'Sneak Preview' can still support a sense of fan cultural distinction. The importance of being what might be termed an 'early viewer' is consistently attested to here; subcultural capital is thus not only embodied/objectified, it is also highly time-sensitive. Online fandoms display a version of this phenomenon, whereby fans posting production details, exclusive photos or spoilers (forthcoming plot/character information), or those who are first to post reviews of new films or television episodes, all demonstrate and accrue high levels of subcultural capital. Elsewhere, I have labelled this "just-in-time fandom".[32] However, such a label does not quite capture the nature of film festival screenings, because in this case the 'first-run' screening is restricted to a highly localised physical place rather than to the potentially vast, disembedded areas of a national television broadcast or a nationwide film release.

The cinemas that regularly play host to horror film festivals and events hence take on a cultishness all of their own, becoming loaded with affective significance and symbolic value within horror fan communities. Kermode and Jancovich both refer to The Scala and The Phoenix cinemas when discussing their own becoming-a-fan stories.[33] And resembling the now-defunct Scala, and East Finchley's Phoenix,[34] the Prince Charles cinema has been described by Thomas Austin as "an independent cinema devoted to repertory and cultish screenings".[35] The fact that FrightFest 2002 was held at the Prince Charles is therefore far from accidental; there is a fit here between a venue with an established subcultural reputation, and the materials of the festival. Just as 'midnight screenings' or 'late-nighters' serve to distinguish cult and horror film screenings from a cinema-going 'mainstream', so too does the screening of films – both regularly and as part of one-off festivals – at specific, independent 'cult'/subcultural venues.[36]

Attending a festival 'premiere' therefore carries such high fan status due to the fact that, by definition, it has rarity and exclusivity; ticket sales are necessarily limited, and fans attending are likely to hail from the local area, or a geographical 'catchment area' of sorts. Hence the UK competition between the London-based Shock Around the Clock/FrightFest and 'Northern' film fests that is mentioned in passing by Kermode.[37] As Jancovich has noted:

> [I]nformation and inaccessibility need to be carefully regulated and balanced. For example, many publications present themselves as guides to an inaccessible 'underground' where knowledge is not only essential

to appreciation and the making of distinctions, but as such, operates as a precious emblem of *insider* status . . . inaccessibility is maintained throughout the scene not only through the selection of materials – they are not for everybody – but also through their virtual unobtainability.[38]

And in the case of horror film festivals and conventions, the 'inaccessibility' of materials occurs as a result of the event's timing (ahead of, or distinguished from, a 'mainstream' film release) as well as its place-bound nature, along with all the physical restrictions of 'liveness' connected to this (and where even media texts can be given a 'live' cachet/distinction by the attendance of a director/star at a premiere). Thus a horror fan's convention/festival attendance becomes one 'authentic' marker of 'insider status'. Given the role of such live events within horror fandom's hierarchies of subcultural capital – something I have explored in detail here – it remains important not to critically ignore, or gloss over, the specificity of this mode of fan 'co-watching' and 'flesh-and-blood' enlivening of media texts.

Notes

1. Rick Altman, *Film/Genre*, London: BFI Publishing, 1999, pp. 160–1.
2. For more on this, see Ian Conrich, 'An aesthetic sense: Cronenberg and neo-horror film culture' in Michael Grant, ed., *The Modern Fantastic: The Films of David Cronenberg*, Trowbridge: Flicks Books, 2000, pp. 35–49, and also 'Killing Time . . . and Time Again: The Popular Appeal of Carpenter's Horrors and the Impact of *The Thing* and *Halloween*' in Ian Conrich and David Woods, eds, *The Cinema of John Carpenter: The Technique of Terror*, London: Wallflower Press, 2004, pp. 91–106. See also Julian Hoxter, 'Taking Possession: Cult Learning in *The Exorcist*', in Xavier Mendik and Graeme Harper, eds, *Unruly Pleasures: The Cult Film and Its Critics*, Guildford: FAB Press, 2000, pp. 173–85.
3. Sarah Thornton, *Club Cultures: Music, Media and Subcultural Capital*, Cambridge: Polity Press, 1995.
4. For more on this issue generally in fan cultures see Matt Hills, *Fan Cultures*, London and New York: Routledge, 2002, pp. 46–64.
5. See, for example, John Tulloch and Henry Jenkins, *Science Fiction Audiences: Watching Doctor Who and Star Trek*, London and New York: Routledge, 1995. See also Jennifer E. Porter, 'To Boldly Go: *Star Trek* Convention Attendance as Pilgrimage', in Jennifer E. Porter and Darcee L. McLaren, eds, *Star Trek and Sacred Ground*, New York: SUNY Press, 1999, pp. 245–70. And see the work of Camille Bacon-Smith, *Science Fiction Culture*, Philadelphia: University of Pennsylvania Press, 2000.
6. See Ian Conrich, Hammer-related book reviews, in *Journal of Popular British Cinema*, no. 2, 1999, p. 165.

7. Mark Kermode, 'I was a teenage horror fan: or, "How I learned to stop worrying and love Linda Blair"', in Martin Barker and Julian Petley, eds, *Ill Effects: The Media/Violence Debate* (2nd edition), London and New York: Routledge, 2001, p. 134.

8. Pierre Bourdieu, *Distinction*, London and New York: Routledge. For Sarah Thornton's development of 'subcultural capital' see *Club Cultures*, 1995.

9. Thornton, pp. 11–12.

10. Paul Hodkinson, *Goth: Identity, Style and Subculture*, Oxford: Berg, 2002.

11. John Fiske, 'The Cultural Economy of Fandom', in Lisa A. Lewis, ed., *The Adoring Audience*, New York and London: Routledge, 1992, pp. 37–8.

12. Ibid., p. 38.

13. Mark Jancovich, '"A Real Shocker": authenticity, genre and the struggle for distinction', *Continuum*, vol. 14, no. 1, 2000, pp. 23–35; and 'Cult Fictions: Cult Movies, Subcultural Capital and the Production of Cultural Distinctions', *Cultural Studies*, vol. 16, no. 2, 2002, pp. 306–22.

14. Philip Auslander, *Liveness: Performance in a Mediatized Culture*, London and New York: Routledge, 1999, pp. 58–9.

15. Ibid., p.58.

16. Ibid., p. 58, n38.

17. See the documentary *Fanalysis* on the 2002 Region 2 DVD release of *The Evil Dead*, 2002 release.

18. Thornton, p. 11, my emphasis.

19. See Jancovich, 'A Real Shocker', pp. 27–9; and 'Cult Fictions', p. 318.

20. Thornton, p. 12.

21. Kermode, p. 129.

22. See Victor Turner, *The Ritual Process: Structure and Anti-Structure* (Piscataway, NJ: Aldine Transaction, 1969); and Porter, 'To Boldly Go', for an interesting discussion of *Star Trek* fan conventions in these terms.

23. See the *Fanalysis* documentary.

24. Barbara Klinger, 'The Contemporary Cinephile: Film Collecting in the Post-Video Era', in Melvyn Stokes and Richard Maltby, eds, *Hollywood Spectatorship: Changing Perceptions of Cinema Audiences*, London: BFI Publishing, 2001, pp. 138–9.

25. See John B. Thompson, *Media and Modernity*, Cambridge: Polity Press, 1995, pp. 219–25.

26. See Walter Metz, 'John Waters goes to Hollywood: a poststructural authorship study', in David A. Gerstner and Janet Staiger, eds, *Authorship and Film*, New York and London: AFI/Routledge, 2003, p. 172, where Metz is writing about introducing a talk by trash-cult director John Waters at Montana State University.

27. Alan Jones, '*Revelation*', *Starburst*, no. 285, 2002, p. 53.

28. David Miller, 'The Lupo Fright Fest' in *Shivers*, no. 100, 2002, p. 46.

29. Ibid.

30. See <http://www.visimag.com/shivers/h77_news.htm>.

31. See <http://www.frightfest.co.uk/programme2001.html>, and <http://www.frightfest.co.uk/programme2000.html>.

32. Hills, p. 178.
33. See Jancovich, 'Cult Fictions', p. 320; Kermode, pp. 128–9.
34. See <http://www.phoenixcinema.co.uk>
35. Thomas Austin, *Hollywood, Hype and Audiences: Selling and Watching Popular Film in the 1990s*, Manchester: Manchester University Press, 2002, p. 179.
36. J.P. Telotte, 'Beyond All Reason: The Nature of the Cult', in J.P. Telotte, ed., *The Cult Film Experience: Beyond All Reason*, Austin: University of Texas Press, 1991, p. 10.
37. Kermode, p. 133.
38. Jancovich, 'Cult Fictions', pp. 318–9.

6

'Trashing' the Academy

Taste, Excess and an Emerging Politics of Cinematic Style

Jeffrey Sconce

> Nobody likes movies like *Teenagers from Outer Space* or *Wrestling Woman vs. the Aztec Mummy* save any loon sane enough to realize that the whole concept of Good Taste is concocted to keep people from having a good time, from reveling in a crassness that passeth all understanding . . . But fuck those people who'd rather be watching *The Best Years of Our Lives* or *David and Lisa*. We got our own good tastes . . .[1]

Written five years before Pierre Bourdieu published his monumental study on the social construction of taste, Lester Bangs' diatribe against a nebulously defined group of cultural custodians epitomises Bourdieu's contention that "tastes are perhaps first and foremost distastes, disgust provoked by horror or visceral intolerance of the tastes of others". "It is no accident", writes Bourdieu, "that when they have to be justified, they are asserted negatively, by the refusal of other tastes".[2] Thus, in the spirit of Lester Bangs, the editors of *Zontar*, a Boston-based fanzine devoted primarily to the promotion of 'badfilm', note that their publication "is *not* for the delicate tastebuds of the pseudo-genteel cultural illiterati who enjoy mind-rotting, soul-endangering pabulum like *Joseph Campbell and the Power of Myth* and the other white-boy 'new-age' puke-shit served up from the bowels of PBS during pledge-week".[3] Meanwhile, a 1990 issue of *Subhuman*, a fanzine featuring articles on cinematic manifestations of "necrophilia, 3-D surrealism, animal copulation, pregnant strippers, horror nerdism, and bovine flatulence", labels itself a journal of "eccentric film and video kulture".[4]

The stridently confrontational tastes espoused by Bangs, *Zontar* and *Subhuman* over this fifteen-year period describe the gradual emergence of a growing and increasingly articulate cinematic subculture, one organised around what are among the most critically disreputable films in cinematic history. Publications devoted to this 'trash' cinema include such magazines, fanzines and makeshift journals as *Psychotronic Video, Zontar, Subhuman, Trashola, Ungawa, Pandemonium*, and the RE/Search volume, *Incredibly Strange Films*.[5] The most visible document of this film community is Michael Weldon's *Psychotronic Encyclopedia of Film*, a subterranean companion to Leonard Maltin's *Movies On TV*, which catalogues hundreds of bizarre titles culled from Weldon's late-night television viewing marathons in New York City. Taken together, the diverse body of films celebrated by these various fanzines and books might best be termed 'paracinema'. As a most elastic textual category, paracinema would include entries from such seemingly disparate subgenres as 'badfilm', splatterpunk, 'mondo' films, sword and sandal epics, Elvis flicks, government hygiene films, Japanese monster movies, beach-party musicals, and just about every other historical manifestation of exploitation cinema from juvenile delinquency documentaries to soft-core pornography. Paracinema is thus less a distinct group of films than a particular reading protocol, a counter-aesthetic turned subcultural sensibility devoted to all manner of cultural detritus. In short, the explicit manifesto of paracinematic culture is to valorise all forms of cinematic 'trash', whether such films have been either explicitly rejected or simply ignored by legitimate film culture. In doing so, paracinema represents the most developed and dedicated of cinephilic subcultures ever to worship at 'the temple of schlock'.[6]

The caustic rhetoric of paracinema suggests a pitched battle between a guerrilla band of cult film viewers and an elite cadre of would-be cinematic tastemakers. Certainly, the paracinematic audience likes to see itself as a disruptive force in the cultural and intellectual marketplace. As a short subject, this audience would be more inclined to watch a bootlegged McDonald's training film than *Man with a Movie Camera*, although, significantly, many in the paracinematic community would no doubt be familiar with this more respectable member of the avante-garde canon. Such calculated negation and refusal of 'elite' culture suggests that the politics of social stratification and taste in paracinema is more complex than a simple high-brow/low-brow split, and that the cultural politics of 'trash culture' are becoming ever more ambiguous as this 'aesthetic' grows in influence. In recent years, the paracinematic community has seen both the institutionalisation and commercialisation of their once renegade, neo-camp aesthetic. Although, paracinematic taste may have its roots in the world of 'low-brow' fan culture (fanzines, film conventions, memorabilia collections, and so on), the paracinematic sensibility has recently begun to infiltrate the avant-garde, the academy, and even the mass culture on which paracinema's ironic reading strategies originally preyed. Art museums that once programmed only Italian Neo-Realism or German

Neo-Expressionism now feature retrospectives of 1960s Biker films and career overviews of exploitation auteurs such as Herschell Gordon Lewis and Doris Wishman. No doubt to the dismay and befuddlement of cultural hygienists like Allan Bloom and James Twitchell, academic courses in film studies increasingly investigate 'sleazy' genres such as horror and pornography. Recently, the trash aesthetic has even made inroads into mainstream popular taste. The ironic reading strategies honed by the badfilm community through countless hours of derisive interaction with late-night science-fiction are now prepackaged for cable in programmes such as *Mystery Science Theatre 3000*. Similarly, Turner Network Television now presents a weekly sampling of the paracinematic pantheon in Friday night, '100% Weird' triple features. Even Blockbuster video, America's corporate bastion of cinematic conservatism, featured a 'le bad' section in many of their stores, where patrons can find the work of John Waters, William Castle and other 'disreputable' filmmakers. Perhaps most incredibly, *Batman's* director Tim Burton recently directed a multi-million dollar biopic of Ed Wood Jr, the director of such paracinematic classics as *Plan 9 From Outer Space* (1959) and *Glen or Glenda* (1953), an artist who himself never spent over a few thousand dollars on any one picture.[7] Clearly, in cinematic circles of all kinds, there has been a significant realignment on the social terrain of taste, a powerful response to what has been termed 'the siren song of crap'.

At first glance, the paracinematic sensibility, in all its current manifestations, would seem to be identical to the 'camp' aesthetic outlined by Susan Sontag some thirty years ago. Without a doubt, both sensibilities are highly ironic, infatuated with the artifice and excess of obsolescent cinema. What makes paracinema unique, however, is its aspiration to the status of a 'counter-cinema'. Whereas 'camp' was primarily a reading strategy that allowed gay men to rework the Hollywood cinema through a new and more expressive subcultural code, paracinematic culture seeks to promote an alternative vision of cinematic 'art', aggressively attacking the established canon of 'quality' cinema and questioning legitimacy of reigning aesthete discourses on movie art. Camp was an aesthetic of ironic colonisation and cohabitation. Paracinema, on the other hand, is an aesthetic of vocal confrontation.

Who, exactly, is the paracinematic audience at war with, and what is at stake in such a battle? Consider the following diatribe from *Zontar*:

Where the philosophical pygmies search the snob-ridden art galleries, flock to the false comfort of PBS-produced pseudo-gentility, WE look elsewhere. We seek the explanations for the decline of Hu-Manity in the most debased and misunderstood manifestations of the IDIOT CULTURE. Monster movies, comic books, cheap porn videos, TV preachers, of course!!! But we search even deeper into the abyss. The Home Shopping Network. Late-Night Cable TV-Product Worship-Testimonial Shows. Tiffany Videos. We leave purity to those other assholes. The search for BADTRUTH is only for the brave few, like you, whose all-consuming HATE is powerful enough to resist the temptations of REFINEMENT, TASTE, and ESCAPISM – the miserable crumbs tossed from the table by the growing mass of REPUBLICAN THIRTYSOMETHING COUNTRY-CLUB CHRISTIAN ZOMBIES who now rule this wretched planet. [8]

The paracinematic audience promotes their tastes and textual proclivities in opposition to a loosely defined group of cultural and economic elites, those purveyors of the status quo who not only rule the world, but who are also responsible for making the contemporary cinema, in the paracinematic mind, so completely boring. Nor does the paracinematic community care much for the activities of film scholars and critics. For example, an editor of *Zontar's Ejecto-Pod*, a sister publication of *Zontar*, encourages readers to hone their knowledge of trash-culture classics ridiculed by the academy (in this case the sword and sandal epic, *The Silver Chalice* [Victor Saville, 1954]), thereby "amazing your friends and embarrassing the jargon-slinging empty-headed official avatars of critical discourse". [9]

At times, factions of the paracinematic audience have little patience even for one another. This rift is perhaps most pointedly embodied by the competing agendas of *Film Threat* and *Psychotronic Video*, two fanzines turned magazines with international circulations that promote rival visions of the 'trash' aesthetic. While *Psychotronic* concentrates on the sizeable segment of this community interested in uncovering and collecting long lost titles from the history of exploitation, *Film Threat* looks to transgressive aesthetics/genres of the past as avant-garde inspiration for contemporary independent filmmaking, championing such 'underground' auteurs as Nick Zedd and Richard Kern. In a particularly nasty swipe, a subscription form for *Film Threat* features a drawing of the 'typical' *Film Threat* reader, portrayed as a dynamic, rockabilly-quiffed hipster surrounded by admiring women. This is juxtaposed with a drawing of the 'typical' *Psychotronic* reader, depicted as passive, overweight and asexual, with a bad complexion.

Despite such efforts at generating counter-distinction within the shared cultural project of attacking 'high-brow' cinema, the discourses characteristically employed by paracinematic culture in its valorisation of 'low-brow' artefacts indicate that this audience, like the film elite (academics, aesthetes, critics), is particularly rich with 'cultural capital' and thus possesses a level of textual/critical sophistication similar to the cineastes they construct as their nemesis. In terms of education and social position, in other words, the various factions of the paracinematic audience and the elite cineastes they commonly attack would appear to share what

Bourdieu terms a "cultural pedigree".[10] Employing the terminology of US sociologist Herbert Gans, these groups might be thought of as radically opposed "taste publics" that are nevertheless involved in a common "taste culture". As Gans writes: "Taste cultures are not cohesive value systems, and taste publics are not organised groups; the former are aggregates of similar values and usually but not always similar content, and the latter are aggregates of people with usually but not always similar values making similar choices from available offerings of culture".[11]

Whether thought of as a subculture, an aesthetic or sensibility, the recent flourishing of paracinema represents not just a challenge to aesthete taste, but the larger fragmentation of a common taste culture, brought about by various disaffected segments of middle-class youth. Although it would be difficult to define the precise dimensions or identify the exact constituency of this particular taste public, I would argue that the paracinematic community, like the academy and the popular press, embodies primarily a male, white, middle-class, and 'educated' perspective on the cinema. Representations of this 'community' are rare, but can be glimpsed, among other places, at the fringes of Richard Linklater's ode to baby-buster anomie, *Slacker* (1991). Linklater documents the desultory activities of bored students, would-be bohemians and miscellaneous cranks, all of whom exist at the economic and cultural periphery of a typical college town.[12] In a more reflexive turn, a fanzine from San Francisco describes the world of 'low-life scum', disheveled men in their twenties manifesting "a fascination with all things sleazy, bizarre, and macabre".[13] Paracinematic interests also often intersect with the more familiar subcultures of science-fiction fandom. Regardless of their individual interests and ultimate allegiances, however, the paracinematic audience cultivates an overall aesthetic of calculated disaffection, marking a deviant taste public disengaged from the cultural hierarchies of their overarching taste culture.

Such acrimonious battles within a single taste culture are not uncommon.[14] As Bourdieu writes: "Explicit aesthetic choices are in fact often constituted in opposition to the choices of the groups closest in social space, with whom the competition is most direct and most immediate, and more precisely, no doubt, in relation to those choices most clearly marked by the intention (perceived as pretension) of marking distinction vis-a-vis lower groups".[15] As the alienated faction of a social group high in cultural capital, the paracinematic audience generates distinction within its own social space by celebrating the cultural objects deemed most noxious (lowbrow) by their taste culture as a whole. Paracinema thus presents a direct challenge to the values of aesthete film culture and general affront to the 'refined' sensibility of the parent taste culture. It is calculated strategy of shock and confrontation against fellow cultural elites, not unlike Duchamp's notorious unveiling of a urinal in an art gallery. As Bourdieu states: "The most intolerable thing for those who regard themselves as the possessors of legitimate culture is the sacrilegious reuniting of tastes which taste dictates shall be separated".[16] By championing films like *2000 Maniacs* (Herschell Gordon Lewis, 1964), *Bad Girls Go to Hell* (Doris Wishman, 1965), and *The Incredibly Strange Creatures Who Stopped Living and Became Mixed-Up Zombies* (Ray Dennis Steckler, 1963), and by associating themselves with home shopping networks, pornography and TV preachers, this community is, in effect, renouncing its 'cultural pedigree' and attempting to distance itself from what it perceives as elite (and elitist) taste.

Despite the paracinematic community's open hostility to the 'jargon-slinging avatars of critical discourse', many scholars see this trend towards the valorisation of 'trash' at work in the academy itself, especially in the realm of media studies. In '"High culture" revisited', for example, Jostein Gripsrud argues that a major segment of contemporary media scholars routinely attacks all forms of high culture while indiscriminately valorising mass culture in its place. As Gripsrud states somewhat sarcastically: "Presenting oneself as a soap-fan in scholarly circles could be considered daring or provocative some ten years ago. Nowadays it is more of a prerequisite for legitimate entry into the academic discourse on soaps in some Anglo-American fora".[17] Gripsrud speculates that this proclivity among many contemporary scholars to condemn high culture and valorise mass culture is a function of their unique trajectory in social space. "Such upwardly mobile subjects are placed in a sort of cultural limbo, not properly integrated in the lower-class culture they left, nor in the upper-class high culture they have formally entered. Since they are newcomers, they are faced with a need to make choices concerning what to do in and with their acquired position".[18] Gripsrud believes that the valorisation of mass culture serves as a form of "symbolic homecoming" that allows such scholars to "strive for or pretend re-integration into the classes they once left, preferably as 'leaders' in some sense, 'voices' for the people".[19]

Gripsrud's depiction of the intellectual in limbo is a particularly apt description of the contemporary graduate student, the figure within the institution of the academy who is perched the most precariously between the domains of cultural, educational and economic capital. Not surprisingly, paracinematic culture is a particularly active site of investment for many contemporary graduate students in film studies. Often, the connections between graduate film study and paracinematic culture are quite explicit, since many students now pursuing an advanced degree in film began as fans of exploitation genres such as horror and science-fiction. Some

9. A matter of taste: Herschell Gordon Lewis's *2000 Maniacs*

students retain their interest in trash culture as a secret, guilty pleasure. Others, however, increasingly seek to focus their work on these previously marginalised and debased forms of cinema. Influenced by the importation of cultural studies to the US during the 1980s, and writing in the wake of film scholars who were increasingly willing to address traditionally 'untouchable' cinematic genres such as horror and pornography, many students in media studies wish to continue pushing the limits of the traditional cinematic canon and the constraints of conventional academic enterprise. At stake is a sense of both institutional and cultural distinction. As John Fiske writes, "many young fans are successful at school and are steadily accumulating official cultural capital, but wish to differentiate themselves, along the axis of age at least, from the social values and cultural tastes (or habitus) of those who currently possess the cultural economic capital they are still working to acquire".[20] As paracinematic texts and concerns increasingly infiltrate film studies, however, many graduate students find themselves caught between the institutional discourses (and agendas) of the film elite as represented by the academy, and the 'fan' activities of the paracinematic community with which they feel a previous affinity. Raised in mass culture, such students are not always willing to give up the excesses of the drive-in for the discipline of Dreyer. The question is what to do with such textual experience and expertise.

Debate within the academy over the politics of the canon is not new. Nor is it unusual for 'fan' cultures to make themselves heard within the academy (most film scholars, one would assume, study the cinema because they were a fan first). What is unusual in paracinematic culture's gradual infiltration of the academy is the manner in which this group so explicitly foregrounds the cultural politics of taste and aesthetics, not just in society at large, but within the academy itself. Graduate students with an interest in 'trash' cinema often find themselves in the ironic position of challenging the legitimacy of the very institution they are attending in order to obtain cultural validation and authority over issues of politics and taste. Such students are struggling to make the transition from a mere fan to an accredited scholar. Though both fan and scholar may be equally dedicated (and even knowledgeable) in their involvement with a particular cultural form, they differ tremendously in terms of their respective status within society as a whole. In a hierarchical social system marked by the differential circulation of cultural economic capital, graduate students seeking to make this crucial transition of accreditation must submit themselves, quite literally, to the *discipline* of film studies in both its institutional and punitive forms. In doing so, the discipline works to shape both knowledge and taste, linking them in a process that is every bit as political in the academy as it is in the culture the academy seeks to study. As Bourdieu notes, "[a]t stake in every struggle over art there is also the imposition of an art of living, that is, the transmutation of an arbitrary way of living into arbitrariness".[21] In this way, the legitimising function of the academy in issues of knowledge, taste and aesthetics works to conceal relations of power and control, both within the institution itself and the society that sanctions the institution's cultural authority.

By challenging this disciplinary authority, the paracinematic audience, both academic and non-academic, epitomises what Bourdieu terms the 'new single autodidact'. As described by Bourdieu, the autodidact is a figure alienated from the legitimate mode of educational and cultural acquisition. Estranged or excluded from legitimate modes of acquisition, autodidacts invest in alternative forms of cultural capital, those not fully recognised by the educational system and the cultural elite. Bourdieu describes two backgrounds typical of this new style autodidact:

'middle-ground' arts such as cinema, jazz, and, even more, strip cartoons, science-fiction or detective stories are predisposed to attract the investments either of those who have entirely succeeded in converting their cultural capital into educational capital or those who, not having acquired legitimate culture in the legitimate manner (i.e., through early familiarisation), maintain an uneasy relationship with it, subjectively or objectively, or both. These arts, not yet fully legitimate, which are disdained or neglected by the big holders of educational capital, offer a refuge or a revenge to those who, by appropriating them, secure the best return on their cultural capital (especially if it is not recognised scholastically) while at the same time taking credit for contesting the established hierarchy of legitimacies and profits.[22]

The autodidact is a person who invests in unsanctioned culture either because he or she can 'afford' to, having already made a successful conversion of legitimate cultural and educational capital into economic capital, or who feel, because of their tentative and at times alienated relationship with 'legitimate culture', that such disreputable investments are more durable and potentially more 'rewarding'.

It should not be surprising, then, that paracinematic fans, as exiles from the legitimising functions of the academy, and many graduate students, as the most disempowered faction within the academy itself, both look to trash culture as a site of 'refuge and revenge'. Such autodidacticism constitutes, for Bourdieu, a form of 'counterculture', one working to free itself from "the constraints of the scholastic market". "They strive to do so by producing another market with its own consecrating agencies", writes Bourdieu, "capable of challenging the pretension of the educational system to impose the principles of evaluation of competencies and manners which reign in the scholastic market".[23] For its audience, paracinema represents a final textual frontier that exists beyond the colonising powers of the academy, and thus serves as a staging ground for strategic raids on legitimate culture and its institutions by those (temporarily) lower in educational, cultural and/or economic capital. Such a struggle demonstrates that battles over the canon, in any discipline, are as much conflicts over the processes and politics by which an entire academic field validates its very existence and charts its own future, fought by groups within the academy as stratified in their institutional power as society at large is stratified in terms of cultural and economic power.

On one hand, it would be easy to explain the turn towards trash cinema as yet another example of the generational politics of the canon in the academy, a struggle that legitimated cinema in the face of literature, Hollywood in the face of art cinema and, most recently, television in the face of Hollywood. But there is more here than a struggle over the canon and the politics of object choice. The study of trash cinema suggests a struggle over the task of cinema scholarship as a whole, especially in terms of defining the relationship between aesthetics and cultural criticism. Whether attacking traditional cultural markets and intellectual institutions as a fan, or attempting to bridge the two worlds as a student, the paracinematic audience presents in its often explicit opposition to the agendas of the academy a dispute over *how* to approach the cinema as much as a conflict over *what* cinema to approach. At issue is not only which films get to be studied, but which questions are to be asked about the cinema in the first place. What I am interested in exploring in the remainder of this essay is the relationship between paracinematic culture and the aesthete culture this group associates with the academy, as well as the place of the contemporary graduate film student in bridging these two often antagonistic sensibilities. How are these groups similar, how do they differ and, perhaps most importantly, how might the trash aesthetic ultimately impact the academy? I am particularly interested in how the two communities approach issues of cinematic 'style' and 'excess'. I will argue that paracinema hinges on an aesthetic of excess, and that this paracinematic interest in excess represents an explicitly political challenge to reigning aesthete discourses in the academy. The cultural politics involved in this struggle, however, can be clarified by first examining similarities between aesthete and paracinematic discourses on cinema.

Counter-cinemas

Throughout the history of cinema studies as a discipline, the cultivation of various counter-cinemas, exclusive cinematic canons that do not easily admit the textual pleasures of more 'commonplace' audiences, has been a crucial strategy in maintaining a sense of cultural distinction for film scholars. Frequently, the promotion of such counter-cinemas has been organised around what has become a dominant theme in academic film culture: namely, the sense of loss over the medium's unrealised artistic and political potential. From this perspective, the cinema once held the promise of a revolutionary popular art form when, as Annette Michelson writes, "'a certain euphoria enveloped…early filmmaking and theory". "[T]here was", she continues, "a very real sense in which the revolutionary aspirations of the modernist movement in literature and arts, on the one hand, and of a Marxist or Utopian tradition, on the other hand, could converge in the hopes and promises, as yet undefined, of the new medium".[24] Instead, these hopes were dashed by the domination of the public taste and mind by Hollywood cinema. And while there has never been a shortage of critical interest in the classical Hollywood cinema, championing counter-cinemas that break with the conventions of Hollywood production and representation remains a central project of film aesthetes and academics. This critical programme proceeds both artistically, by valorising a body of 'art' films over the mainstream, commercial cinema, and politically, by celebrating those filmmakers who seem to disrupt the conventional narrative machinery of Hollywood.[25]

In cultivating a counter-cinema from the dregs of exploitation films, paracinematic fans, like the academy, explicitly situate themselves in opposition to Hollywood cinema and the mainstream US culture it represents. United with the film elite in their dislike of Hollywood banality and yet frequently excluded from the circles of academic film culture, the paracinematic community nonetheless often adopts the conventions of 'legitimate' cinematic discourse in discussing its own cinema. As Fiske notes, fan groups are often "aware that their object of fandom [is] devalued by the criteria of official culture and [go] to great pains to argue against the misevaluation. They frequently [use] official cultural criteria such as 'complexity' or 'subtlety' to argue that their preferred texts [are] as 'good' as the canonised ones and constantly [evoke] legitimate culture . . . as points of comparison".[26] Elite discourse often appears either earnestly or parodically in discussions of paracinematic films. A fanzine review of the obscure 1964 film, *The Dungeons of Harrow*, is typical. The fanzine describes the film as "a twisted surreal marvel, a triumph of spirit and vision over technical incompetence and abysmal production values. The film can be seen as a form of art brut – crude, naïve, pathetic – but lacking the poetry and humour often associated with this style. Perhaps art brutarian would better serve to describe this almost indescribable work".[27]

As in the academic film community, the paracinematic audience recognises Hollywood as an economic and artistic institution that represents not just the body of films, but a particular mode of film production and its accompanying signifying practices. Furthermore, the narrative form produced by this institution is seen as somehow 'manipulative' and 'repressive', and linked to dominant interests as a form of cultural coercion. In their introduction to *Incredibly Strange Films*, V. Vale and Andrea Juno, two of the most visible cultural brokers in the realm of paracinema, describe why low-budget films helmed by idiosyncratic visionaries are so often superior to mainstream, Hollywood cinema.

> The value of low-budget films is: they can be transcendent expressions of a single person's individual vision and quirky originality. When a corporation decides to invest $20 million in a film, a chain of command regulates each step, and no one person is allowed free rein. Meetings with lawyers, accountants, and corporate boards are what films in Hollywood are all about...Often [low-budget] films are eccentric – even extreme – presentations by individuals freely expressing their imaginations, who throughout the filmmaking process improvise creative solutions to problems posed by either circumstance or budget – mostly the latter. Secondly, they often present unpopular – even radical – views addressing social, political, racial, or sexual inequities, hypocrisy in religion or government; or in other ways they assault taboos related to the presentation of sexuality, violence, and other mores.[28]

Such rhetoric could just as easily be at home in an elite discussion of the French New Wave or the American New Cinema. Products of a shared taste culture, paracinematic cinephiles, like the scholars and critics of the academy, continue to search for unrecognised talent and long forgotten masterpieces, producing a pantheon that celebrates a certain stylistic unity and/or validates the diverse artistic visions of unheralded 'auteurs'.

Zontar, for example, devotes almost all of its attention to the work of Larry Buchanan, who is celebrated as "the greatest director of all time" and as a maker of films that must be regarded as "absolute and unquestionable holy writ".[29] Elsewhere, *Zontar* hails Buchanan as "a prophet of transcendental banality...who eclipses Bergman in evoking a sense of alienation, despair and existential angst".[30] As this rather tongue-in-cheek hyperbole suggests, paracinematic culture, like that of the academy, continues to generate its own forms of internal distinction by continually redefining its vanguard, thereby thwarting unsophisticated dilettantes and moving its audience as a whole on to increasingly demanding and exclusive paracinematic films. In its contemporary and most sophisticated form, paracinema is an aggressive, esoteric and often painfully ascetic counter-aesthetic, one that produces, in its most extreme manifestations, an ironic form of reverse elitism. "The fine art of great badfilm is not a laughing matter to everybody", says one fan. "Its adherents are small in number, but fanatical in pickiness. Badness appreciation is the most acquired taste, the most refined".[31]

Invoking Larry Buchanan, the mastermind of films like *Mars Needs Women* (1966) and *Zontar the Thing from Venus* (1966), as a greater director than Ingmar Bergman, however, reaffirms that the paracinematic community defines itself in opposition not only to mainstream Hollywood cinema, but to the (perceived) counter-cinema of aesthetes and the cinematic academy. Again, as with any taste public, this elite cadre of 'aesthetes' cannot be definitively located in a particular author, methodology, or school of academic/journalistic criticism. Paracinematic vitriol also often ignores the fact that low-budget exploitation films have increasingly become legitimised as a field of study within the academy.[32] For purposes of distinction, however, all that is required is a nebulous body of those who do not actively advance a paracinematic aesthetic. As Vale and Juno state broadly in their introduction to *Incredibly Strange Films*:

> This is a functional guide to territory largely neglected by the film-criticism establishment ... Most of the films discussed test the limits of contemporary (middle-class) cultural acceptability, mainly because in varying ways they don't meet certain 'standards' utilised in evaluating direction, acting, dialogue, sets, continuity, technical cinematography, etc. Many of the films are overtly 'lower-class' or 'low-brow' in content and art direction.[33]

Vale and Juno go on to celebrate this cinema for its vitality and then identify what is at stake in this battle over the status of these films within the critical community. In a passage reminiscent of Bangs and Bourdieu, they state, "[a]t issue is the notion of 'good taste', which functions as a filter to block out entire areas of experience judged – and damned – as unworthy of investigation".[34]

Style and Excess

Graduate students entering the academy with an interest in trash cinema often wish to question why these 'areas of experience' have been 'judged and damned' by earlier scholars. But though they may attempt to disguise or renounce their cultural pedigree by aggrandising such scandalous cultural artefacts, their heritage in a 'higher' taste public necessarily informs their textual and critical engagement of even the most abject 'low culture' forms. Gripsrud argues that 'egalitarian' attempts on the part of the culturally privileged to collapse differences between 'high' and 'low' culture, as noble as they might be, often ignore issues of 'access' to these two cultural realms. As Gripsrud writes, "[s]ome people have access to both high and low culture, but the majority has only access to the low one".[35] Gripsrud describes high culture audiences that also consume popular cultural artefacts as having 'double access', and notes that this ability to participate in both cultural realms is not randomly distributed through society. As Gripsrud observes, "[t]he double access to the codes and practices of both high and low culture is a *class privilege*".[36]

The phenomenon of double access raises a number of interesting political issues concerning the trash aesthetic. For example, when Vale and Juno write that these films address "unpopular – even radical – views" and "assault taboos related to the presentation of sexuality [and] violence", this does not mean that paracinema is a 'progressive' body of cinema. In fact, in subgenres ranging from the often rabidly xenophobic travelogues of the 'mondo' documentaries to the library of 1950s sex-loop star Betty Page, many paracinematic texts would run foul of academic film culture's political orthodoxy. But, of course, this is precisely why such films are so vociferously championed by certain segments of the paracinematic audience, which then attempts to 'redeem' the often suspect pleasures of these films through appeals to ironic detachment. Double access, then, foregrounds one of the central riddles of postmodern textuality: is the 'ironic' reading of a 'reactionary' text necessarily a 'progressive' act?[37]

As pivotal as double access is in considering conventional debates over representational politics, the influence of high cultural capital is equally foregrounded in how the academy, the paracinematic audience, and the students who claim membership in both realms attend to the question of cinematic style. Of course, the ability to attend critically to a concept such as style, whether it manifests itself in Eisenstein or a Godzilla movie, is a class privilege, requiring a certain textual sophistication in issues of technique, form and structure. Though paracinematic viewers may explicitly reject the pretensions of high-brow cinema, their often sophisticated rhetoric on the issue of style can transform low-brow cinema into an object every bit as obtuse and inaccessible to the mainstream viewer as some of the most demanding works of the conventional avant-garde. Both within the academy and the paracinematic community, viewers address the complex relationship between cinematic 'form' and 'content', often addressing style for style's sake. This is not to say, however, that the paracinematic community simply approaches trash cinema in the same terms that aesthetes and academics engage art cinema. There is, I would argue, a major political distinction between aesthete and paracinematic discourses on cinematic style, a distinction that is crucial to the paracinematic project of championing a counter-cinema of trash over that of the academy. In other words, though the paracinematic community may share with academic aesthetes an interest in counter-cinema as technical execution, their respective agendas and approaches in attending to questions of style and technique vary tremendously.

For example, film aesthetes, both in the academy and in the popular press, frequently discuss counter-cinematic style as a strategic intervention. In this scenario, the film artist self-consciously employs stylistic innovations to differentiate his or her (usually his) films from the cultural mainstream. James Monaco's discussion of the French New Wave is typical in this regard. "It is this fascination with the forms and structures of the film medium…that sets their films apart from those that preceded them and marks a turning point in film history".[38] Similarly, according to David Bordwell's concept of parametric narration, a filmmaker may systematically manipulate a certain stylistic parameter independent of the demands of the plot. Such films are rare and are typically produced by figures associated with 'art cinema' (Bordwell identifies Ozu, Bresson and Godard as among those having produced parametric films). The emphasis here is on applied manipulation of style as a form of systematic artistic experimentation and technical virtuosity. "In parametric narration, style is organised across the film according to distinct principles, just as a narrative poem exhibits prosodic patterning or an operatic scene fulfils a musical logic".[39]

Paracinematic films such as *The Corpse Grinders* (Ted V. Mikels, 1972) and *She Devil on Wheels* (Herschell Gordon Lewis, 1968) rarely exhibit such

10. Attack of the cat: Fed on minced human flesh, a feline is driven by a craving for more food in *The Corpse Grinders*

pronounced stylistic virtuosity as the result of a 'conscious' artistic agenda. But this is not to say that issues of style and authorship are unimportant to the paracinematic community. However, rather then explore the systematic application of style as the elite techniques of a cinematic artist, paracinematic culture celebrates the systematic 'failure' or 'distortion' of conventional cinematic style by 'auteurs' who are valued more as 'eccentrics' than as artists, who work within the impoverished and clandestine production conditions typical of exploitation cinema. These films deviate from Hollywood classicism not necessarily by artistic intentionality, but by the effects of material poverty and technical ineptitude. As director Frank Henenlotter (of the *Basket Case* series) comments:

> often, through bad direction, misdirection, inept direction, a film starts assuming surrealistic overtones, taking a dreadfully clichéd story into new frontiers – you're sitting there shaking your head, totally excited, totally unable to guess where this is going to head next, or what the next loony line out of somebody's mouth is going to be. Just as long as it isn't stuff you regularly see.[40]

Importantly, paracinematic films are not ridiculed for this deviation but are instead celebrated as unique, courageous and ultimately subversive cinematic experiences. For this audience, paracinema thus constitutes a true counter-cinema in as much as "it isn't stuff you regularly see", both in terms of form and content. Henenlotter continues, "I'll never be satisfied until I see every sleazy film ever made – as long as its different, as long as it's breaking a taboo (whether deliberately or by misdirection). There's a thousand reasons to like these films".[41]

While the academy prizes conscious transgression of conventions by a filmmaker looking to critique the medium aesthetically and/or politically, paracinematic viewers value a stylistic and thematic deviance born, more often than not, from the systematic failure of film aspiring to *obey* dominant codes of cinematic representation. For this audience, the 'bad' is as aesthetically defamiliarising and politically invigorating as the 'brilliant'. A manifesto on acting from *Zontar* further illustrates the aesthetic appeal of such stylistic deviation among this audience:

> Transparent play-acting; mumbling incompetence; passionate scenery-chewing; frigid woodenness; barely disguised drunkenness or contempt for the script; - these are secrets of Zontarian acting at its best. Rondo Hatton's exploited acromegalic condition; Acquanetta's immobile dialogue readings; the drunken John Agar frozen to his chair in *Curse of the Swamp Creature*; - these great performances loom massively as the ultimate classics of ZONTARISM. These are not so much performances as revelations of Human truth. We are not 'entertained', we rather sympathise with our suffering soul-mates on screen. These performances are not escapist fantasy, but a heavy injection of BADTRUTH.[42]

The Zontarian moment of the 'badtruth' is not unlike the Surrealist notion of the 'marvellous' (and indeed, the Surrealists were perhaps the first cinephiles with an interest in bad cinema).[43] As with the marvellous, the badtruth, as a nodal point of paracinematic style, provides a defamiliarised view of the world by merging the transcendentally weird and the catastrophically awful. Thus, rather than witness the Surrealists' vision of the exquisite chance meetings of umbrellas and sewing machines on a dissecting table, the paracinematic viewer thrills instead to such equally fantastic fabrications as women forced to duel in a syringe fight in the basement of a schizophrenic vaudevillian who has only moments earlier eaten his cat's left eyeball (*Maniac!* [Dwain Esper, 1934]), Colonial era witches and warlocks crushed to death by men in Levis corduroys who hurl bouncing Styrofoam boulders (*Blood-Orgy of the She-Devils* [Ted V. Mikels, 1973]), a down and out Bela Lugosi training a mutant bat to attack people wearing a certain type of shaving lotion (*The Devil Bat* [Jean

Yarborough, 1941]), and leaping, pulsating brains that use their prehensile spinal cords to strangle unwary soldiers and citizens on a Canadian rocket base (*Fiend Without a Face* [Arthur Crabtree, 1958]).

Paracinematic taste involves a reading strategy that renders the bad into the sublime, the deviant into the defamiliarised, and in so doing, calls attention to the aesthetic aberrance and stylistic variety evident but routinely dismissed in the many subgenres of trash cinema. By concentrating on a film's formal bizarreness and stylistic eccentricity, the paracinematic audience, much like the viewer attuned to the innovations of Godard or capable of attending to patterns of parametric narration described by Bordwell, foregrounds structures of cinematic discourse and artifice so that the material identity of the film ceases to be a structure made invisible in service of the diegesis, but becomes instead the primary focus of textual attention. It is in this respect that the paracinematic aesthetic is closely linked to the concept of 'excess'.

Kristin Thompson describes excess as a value that exists beyond a cinematic signifier's 'motivated' use, or, as "those aspects of the work which are not contained by its unifying forces".[44] "At the point where motivation ends", Thompson writes, "excess begins".[45] "The minute the viewer begins to notice style for its own sake or watch works which do not provide such thorough motivation, excess comes forward and must affect narrative meaning.... Excess does not equal style, but the two are closely linked because they both involve the material aspects of the film".[46] Thompson writes of excess as an intermittent textual phenomenon, a brief moment of self-conscious materiality that interrupts an otherwise conventional, 'non-excessive' film: "Probably no one ever watches only these non-diegetic aspects of the image through an entire film". But, Thompson writes further, these non-diegetic aspects are nevertheless always present, "a whole 'film' existing in some sense alongside the narrative film we tend to think of ourselves as watching".[47]

I would argue that the paracinematic audience is perhaps the one group of viewers that *does* concentrate exclusively on these "non-diegetic aspects of the image" during the entire film, or at least attempts to do so. Like their counterparts in the academy, trash cinema fans, as active cinephiles practising an aesthetic founded on the recognition and subsequent rejection of Hollywood style, are extremely conscious of the cinema's characteristic narrative forms and stylistic strategies. But, importantly, while cinematic aesthetes attend to style and excess as moments of artistic bravado in relation to the creation of an overall diegesis, paracinematic viewers instead use excess as a gateway to exploring profilmic and extratextual aspects of the filmic object itself. In other words, by concentrating so intently on 'non-diegetic' elements in these films, be they unconvincing special effects, blatant anachronisms, or histrionic acting, the paracinematic reading attempts to activate the "whole 'film' existing...alongside the narrative film we tend to think of ourselves as watching". One could say that while academic attention to excess often foregrounds aesthetic strategies within the text as a closed formal system, paracinematic attention to excess, an excess that often manifests itself in a film's failure to conform to historically delimited codes of verisimilitude, calls attention to the text as a cultural and sociological document and thus dissolves the boundaries of the diegesis into profilmic and extratextual realms. It is here that the paracinematic audience most dramatically parts company with the aesthetes of academia. Whereas aesthete interest in style and excess always returns the viewer to the frame, paracinematic attention to excess seeks to push the viewer beyond the formal boundaries of the text.

This is a shortened version of an article which was originally published in *Screen* vol. 36, no. 4 (winter 1995), pp. 371–93. Permission to reprint was kindly granted by Oxford University Press.

Notes

1. Lester Bangs, *Psychotic Reactions and Carburetor Dung*, New York: Vintage Books, 1988, pp. 122–3.
2. Pierre Bourdieu, *Distinction: A Social Critique of the Judgment of Taste*, Cambridge MA: Harvard University Press, 1984, p. 57.
3. *Zontar's Ejecto-Pod*, vol. 1, no. 1, n.p.
4. *Subhuman*, no. 15, front cover.
5. 'Fanzines' are home-produced, photocopied magazines circulated among fans and devoted to an often narrow area of interest in popular culture.
6. *Temple of Schlock* is another fanzine dedicated to this cinema.
7. In a fittingly perverse tribute to Wood, Burton's film won widespread critical acclaim and yet bombed at the box office, making less than six million dollars on its initial release in the US.
8. *Zontar*, no. 8, n.p.
9. *Zontar's Ejecto-Pod*, vol. 1, no. 1, n.p.
10. For a more detailed discussion of the cultural pedigree, see Bourdieu, p. 63.
11. Herbert Gans, *Popular Culture and High Culture*, New York: Basic Books, 1974, pp. 69–70.
12. In the film's most explicit nod to the paracinematic mentality, one particularly deranged character bases his elaborate conspiracy theories on the 'truth' to be found in late-night, science-fiction movies.
13. *Murder Can Be Fun*, no. 5, n.p.
14. This particular struggle over cinematic taste also takes place in a variety of

cultural contexts. For an account of the cultivation of a disreputable aesthetic in Swedish youth culture, see Göran Bolin, 'Beware! Rubbish! Popular culture and strategies of distinction', *Young: Nordic Journal of Youth Research*, vol. 2, no. 1, 1994, pp. 33–49.

15. Bordieu, p. 60.
16. Ibid., pp. 56–7.
17. Jostein Gripsrud, '"High culture" revisited', *Cultural Studies*, vol. 3, no. 2, 1989, p. 198.
18. Ibid., pp. 196–7.
19. Ibid., p. 197.
20. John Fiske, 'The cultural economy of fandom', in Lisa Lewis, ed., *The Adoring Audience*, New York: Routledge, 1992, pp. 33–4.
21. Bourdieu, pp. 57–8.
22. Ibid., p. 87.
23. Ibid., p. 96.
24. Annette Michelson, 'Film and the radical aspiration', in Gerald Mast and Marshall Cohen, eds, *Film Theory and Criticism*, New York: Oxford University Press, 1974, p. 472.
25. For an influential account of such an agenda, see Peter Wollen's 'Godard and counter-cinema: *Vent d'Est*', in Philip Rosen, ed., *Narrative, Apparatus, Ideology*, New York: Columbia University Press, 1986, pp. 120–9.
26. Fiske, p. 36.
27. *Subhuman*, no. 16, p. 3.
28. V. Vale, Andrea Juno and Jim Morton, eds, *Incredibly Strange Films*, San Francisco: RE/search Publications, 1986, p. 5.
29. *Zontar*, no. 8, n.p.
30. Ibid.
31. Ibid.
32. For examples of work on exploitation cinema produced within an academic context, see Thomas Doherty, *Teenagers and Teenpics: the Juvenilization of American Movies in the 1950s* (Boston: Unwin Hyman, 1988); and Eric Schaefer, *"Bold! Daring! Shocking! True!": A History of Exploitation Films, 1919–1959*, Durham, North Carolina: Duke University Pres, 1999.
33. Vale, Juno and Morton, p. 4.
34. Ibid.
35. Gripsrud, p. 199.
36. Ibid.
37. Such debates, in turn, should not instantly assume that there only exists an impoverished, 'single access' reading of these films within 'low culture', suggesting formations that are without irony. It is difficult to imagine, for example, that an audience of any historical moment or cinematic habitus ever watched Russ Meyer's odes to castration anxiety and breast fetishism with a 'straight' face.
38. James Monaco, *The New Wave*, New York: Oxford University Press, 1976, p. 9.

39. David Bordwell, *Narration in the Fiction Film*, Madison: University of Wisconsin Press, 1985, p. 275.

40. Vale, Juno and Morton, p. 11.

41. Ibid.

42. *Zontar*, no. 8. n.p.

43. For an example of this literature, see Ado Kyrou, 'The popular is marvelous', in Paul Hammond, ed., *The Shadow and Its Shadow*, London: British Film Institute, 1978.

44. Kristin Thompson, 'The concept of cinematic excess', in Philip Rosen, ed., *Narrative, Apparatus, Ideology*, New York: Columbia University Press, 1986, p. 130.

45. Thompson, p. 136.

46. Ibid., p. 132.

47. Ibid., pp. 132–3.

Part Three

Manufacture and Design

7

Culture Wars
Some New Trends in Art Horror

JOAN HAWKINS

When the Korean director Park Chan-Wook walked away with the second-most prestigious prize at the Cannes Film Festival last year, it did more than raise a few eyebrows and critical hackles. It signaled that this wasn't your father's hoity-toity snooze-fest; this was the new, improved Cannes, baby – fast and furious and genre-friendly. Mr. Park's award-winning 'Oldboy', a blood-spattered revenge movie that features death by hammer and other such tasty sport, might have been an exploitation flick, but it was an *arty* exploitation flick.[1]

Culture Wars

In March 2005, BAMcinématek in New York mounted a retrospective honouring Korean director Park Chan-Wook. Park is perhaps best known in the US for *Joint Security Area* (2000), a conventional but surprisingly moving thriller about the politically charged friendships which develop among North and South Korean border guards. Emblematic of a certain kind of US arthouse fare, *Joint Security Area* stresses psychology and human emotion over brutal action, and the violence – when it does come in the film's inevitable climax – is played less for gore than for heartbreak; the fatal result of a tragic geopolitical stand-off.

If Park's subsequent films had followed the same generic pattern as *Joint Security Area*, the BAM retrospective would have opened, as so many do, with little fanfare. There would have been a respectful notice in the *New York Times* and some individual reviews of the films. Perhaps a lament that Korean cinema is not better known in the US – not as well-distributed as Hong Kong action flicks or Japanese yakuza movies. But Park's subsequent films did not follow the same generic pattern. *Sympathy for Mr. Vengeance* (2002) is a violent thriller about organ-theft and kidnapping; *Oldboy* (2003) is a chilling horror-revenge movie that ends

11. The arthouse horrors of the celebrated Asian revenge movie *Oldboy*

with a man cutting off his own tongue. *Oldboy* won a Grand Prix Second Prize at Cannes and solidified Park's reputation as an international auteur, but the graphic elements and general creepiness in this film, as well as in the rest of Park's recent work, have also made him a favourite among cult and horror afficionados. And it is this – his dual status as international arthouse auteur and as cult/horror auteur – which troubled the opening of his BAMcinématek retrospective.

Writing for the *New York Times*, film critic Manohla Dargis used the Park retrospective as an occasion to write a scathing review not only of Park's art-horror films, but also of recent trends in US international arthouse fare.[2] "The ascendancy of Mr. Park in the last few years", Dargis writes in a passage worth quoting at length,

> is partly a testament to his talent. He knows where to put the camera, how to build tension inside the frame and through editing, and he has an eye for how striking fake blood can look pooling over the ground or blooming underwater. *But the filmmaker's success in the international arena, his integration into the upper tier of the festival circuit and his embrace by some cinephiles also reflect a dubious development in recent cinema: the mainstreaming of exploitation* ... Movies that were once relegated to midnight screenings at festivals – and, in an earlier age, grindhouses like those that once enlivened Times Square – are now part of the main event.[3]

In many ways, Dargis's lament is simply a new variation on an old theme. Historically, art horror has troubled critics. It challenges generic assumptions (which are always already under siege both by the rise of generic hybrids, and also, as Thomas Schatz convincingly argues, by the inevitable evolution of genres themselves).[4] But more importantly, it challenges continuing cherished assumptions about culture and taste. What is troubling to Dargis about Park's work is not the violence or exploitation elements *per se*. In fact, Dargis often gives favorable and perceptive reviews of 'pure' horror films (those which are not received at Cannes). She called George A. Romero's *Land of the Dead* (2005) "an excellent freakout of a movie", for example and wrote one of the best pieces on the film that I have read.[5] Rather, what is at stake for Dargis in Park's reception at Cannes, is the erosion of a certain *idea* about art cinema; an idea which elevates art cinema as something culturally superior to and clearly distinct from exploitation. It is *Oldboy*'s "integration into the upper tier of the festival circuit" that bothers her, and the erosion of art/trash distinctions which such an integration implies.

As I have argued elsewhere, the lines between arthouse (high culture) cinema and trash (exploitation, horror, soft porn etc) have never been as clear-cut in the US as taste critics would like to maintain.[6] The midnight screenings and "grindhouses . . . that once enlivened Times Square" – mentioned in Dargis's review – were historically the site where high art and trash cinema commingled in the US. During the period of the Hays Code, all films which did not receive the Breen Office seal of approval were shown outside mainstream theatrical release. In practical terms, this meant that Times Square theaters showing a film by Godard one week frequently showed a biker or J.D. (juvenile delinquent exploitation) flick the following week. Often they showed these films to the same audiences. Further, European art cinema was frequently advertised in ways that called attention to its 'scandalous' and exploitation elements; it was sexier than US cinema and the ads for the films generally featured provocatively posed, lingerie-clad women. A number of American and European films – especially but not solely art-horror movies – routinely migrated between taste categories depending on the titles and distribution they received.[7] And given art cinema's willingness to transgress the boundaries of good taste (cf: the films of Buñuel, to cite just one example), the lines dividing high art cinema from low horror have not always been that easy to see.

The blurring of the boundaries between art cinema and body genres, what Dargis calls "the mainstreaming of exploitation", is not really then "a development in recent cinema". It is part and parcel of the history of art cinema in the US (and even to a degree in the UK).[8] More recently, that blurring has continued in the "guilty pleasures" programs offered at art theatres and in the inventories maintained by the catalogue companies and websites catering to paracinema and art cinema fans.[9] DVD companies have capitalised on the longstanding high-low dialectic with new releases of cult favorites. Criterion, for example, which continues to publicise its dedication "to gathering the greatest films from around the world" has recently added the paracinema classics *Fiend without a Face* (1958). *The Blob* (1958), and *Carnival of Souls* (1962) to its lineup.[10] Facets Multimedia of Chicago – a rental and sales outlet specialising in arthouse, experimental and avant-garde cinema – has long maintained an extensive "guilty pleasures" and trash cinema list, which includes cult classics by Russ Meyer, Roger Corman, John Waters and Ed Wood Jr as well as Elvis Presley flicks, blaxploitation, grade B sci-fi, and trailers and commercials.

In fact, if there is a contemporary trend toward the "mainstreaming of exploitation", it is not happening at the high end of the culture spectrum (arthouses and film festivals), where taste-cultures have always been eclectic. Rather it is happening at the level of DVD sales and stock, and in shopping mall bookstore-DVD chain outlets, such as Borders Books and Music. Films that used to be available in the US only on low-resolution video tape transfers from European laserdiscs are now frequently available as high quality DVDs, complete with all the extras DVDs traditionally offer.[11] Anchor Bay has released an extensive list of titles by European horror favorites Dario Argento, Jess Franco, and Lucio Fulci. BlueUnderground has released Rolf de Heer's cult favorite *Bad Boy Bubby* (1993) as well as a series of drive-in classics. And because the films have been released on commercial DVDs, collectors no longer need to go to specialty companies to find them.

This commercial mainstreaming of exploitation and euroshocker titles has not, however, completely mitigated the need for specialty houses. Sadly, there are still many films – such as the arthouse horrors *Alucarda* (1978) and *Death Walks at Midnight* (1973) – which have not been commercially released for the US home market. Nicheflix, a relatively new DVD rental company, caters to people who own multistandard DVD players precisely because they cannot find everything they want in a US format.[12] Luminous Film and Video Wurks, one of the best and longest running collector companies, has added international region formats to its inventory and its website has links for the "best code free/region free DVD player", the Malata DVP-558 (www.lfvw.com/news.html). Facets Multimedia similarly offers a limited number of imported DVDs to its customers. These include previously unreleased (in the US), unsubtitled films by Henri-Georges Clouzot (*La Prisonnière*, 1968) as well as some cult favourites. And the web is full of collector sites which cater to fans of Asian horror cinema (eday.com, for example).

In addition, there is still a thriving alternative market, where consumers can find many of the art and exploitation films that have not yet been commercially released for home viewing. DVDs burned from the kinds of video products described in my book *Cutting Edge* ossify and fix (literally 'burn in') analog trash aesthetic elements (the 'cool' effects of many collector videos: grainy pictures, washed-out and wandering colors, de-magnetised sound).[13] But the digital process also adds what one of my students has called "new paracinema effects" peculiar to the medium: pixellation, flashing, and other markers of digital reproduction (these are there, of course, whether the DVD was burned from a video transfer or from another source). That is, just as collector videos announce their status as 'rare' objects through markers of home recording, so too rare collector DVDs bear all the signs of being burned on a home system. Discs often come in little white DVD-R sleeves, with the names of the films handwritten in magic marker on the DVD itself.[14] Catalogues are less prevalent now, increasingly replaced with websites and listserv postings. But the catalogue aesthetic has remained dominant, as collector websites maintain the no-frills functional format of the now outmoded print publications. There is frequently (although not always) a digital image from the film and a brief description of the movie. Sites selling commercial DVDs include a list of specs (aspect ratio, languages etc) and of any extras (interviews, author commentary etc) included in the package. Sometimes there are reviews and customer comments; but these are rare. Collector commentary is generally reserved for listserv communiques, blogs, chat rooms and individual websites.

I have written at length about collecting and home viewing because for those of us who cannot afford to go to the prestigious film festivals and who do not live in urban centres, art horror has simply not become mainstream enough. Most of the titles cited in this article received limited theatrical release in the US. I saw all of them for the first time on a home DVD player; many of them I have never been able to see projected (either on celluloid or digitally) in a commercial theatre. Home viewing is not only increasingly the preferred mode of viewing for many American spectators; in many instances it remains the only way the films that Dargis describes in her review can be seen.[15]

Freaky Treasures

As one friend remarked, to work on Asian and European cinema while living in the US is – in the present commercial climate – akin to doing anthropology before ethnography changed the discipline (the time when strange and curious artifacts were exhibited and studied, completely outside of their cultural and social context). Changes in mainstream commercial distribution patterns in the US mean that there is no longer any coherent attempt to bring foreign films to American audiences; certainly not the kind of coherent attempt that companies like New Yorker once made. Instead of buying and distributing groups of films – all of Miike Takashi or all new Japanese cinema, for example, companies pick individual titles that appear to have a marketing hook.[16] Outré sex and violence is one obvious such hook, but there are others. More Afghan and Iranian films were released in the US in the wake of the 9/11 tragedy, for example; and after the fall of the Berlin Wall, there was – temporarily – increased access to Eastern European films. But even when several Japanese or German films are bought and distributed, they are shown as interesting, *individual* artifacts from which the viewer is expected to infer an entire culture and an entire industrial relationship (that is, the individual film's rapport both to world cinema and to its own national cinema). They are shown out of context. Those of us who live outside the festival/cinémathèque beltway frequently do not see the other films – national dramas and genre films, for example – to which these US theatrical releases might be responding. And frequently we know little of the cultural or political tensions within the societies that produce them. As a result, the main selling point about foreign films tends to become their very exoticism. They seem to be in conversation with some other film tradition, with some other culture, which we do not entirely understand. They become, in Chris Anderson's words, "freaky treasures".[17]

The epistemological problems posed by the current US system are a little less severe for those attempting to study the international generic developments in art horror. Although the inclusion of titles (particularly those by unknown directors) in a list can seem haphazard, collector companies and specialty houses do make a coherent attempt to represent national cinemas (within a limited generic scope), generic trends (subgenres) and auteurs. Italian horror and *giallo* are well-represented in catalogues and on websites, for example, and it has been possible to get a sense of the different trends and tensions in their generic development throughout the 1970s–90s. Certainly, it has been easier to get a complete sense of the evolution of Dario Argento's career during this period (since the collector sites also sell tapes of his television productions and interviews), than it is to get a good sense of the evolution of Spanish director Jorge Grau's oeuvre. Claude Chabrol's *Le Cri du hibou* (1987) and other French thrillers of the 1980s were available for purchase from Luminous prior to their mainstream US commercial distribution; so those of us working in art horror could look at the move toward horror themes in Chabrol's career as well as get some sense of the horrific developments in 1980s French *polars* and thriller films (*La Balance* [1982], *One Deadly Summer* [1983]). The fact that the same companies also sold splatter French gorefest movies (Jean Rollin's films, for example) helped to provide some of the cinematic context against which to read the increased violence in thriller/art-horror flicks. Just how transgressive (in the French context) was the violent climax of Chabrol's 1995 *La Cérémonie* and how did it compare with the gory narration ending Nancy Meckler's *Sister My Sister* (1994), a British film based on a similar story? These questions can be approached now, through judicious purchases from the collector catalogue companies.

That is not to say, however, that all the epistemological problems outlined above can be neatly avoided if one sticks with the art-horror genre and turns to alternative DVD sources. Part of the problem US critics have had in reading the recent art horror French formation which James Quandt calls "the new French extremity" (the films of Catherine Breillat, François Ozon, Gaspar Noé etc), for example, rests with distribution problems.[18] While the new French films have been distributed here and are readily available on DVD, the Beur and banlieue films against which (at least in part) they must be read are rarely seen outside the festival circuit.[19] If you do not speak French or Arabic, and you do not have access to a North African or Moroccan store, you will be able to locate only a handful of select banlieue titles in the US. Even within the festival circuit, they can be maddeningly difficult to find; one title one year, one title the next and then one or two years of no titles at all. So it is nearly impossible for American viewers to gain a good sense of the kind of impact they have had on western audiences and young French filmmakers. And, of course, if we do not visit France or Europe all that often, or have regular access to the local media, we can easily forget just how tense the race-class situation has been in Paris.

The current system of distribution should make intelligent critics like Dargis wary of making sweeping qualitative judgements about arthouse cinema and the devolution of taste. At least it should dictate that they frame their comments with the caveat that market forces have helped to delimit and impoverish the range of cinemas which American audiences are readily able to see. Some critics – most notably Jonathan Rosenbaum of the *Chicago Reader* – do routinely remind readers that many of the best Asian and European films do not receive theatrical distribution at all.[20] Or they receive such limited distribution that only critics (those who watch films for a living) or collectors (those who track films as a kind of obsessional avocation) are able to see them.

The New Extremity

The Dargis review of Park's work (with which I began this article) is interesting in the way it links some disparate trends in art horror under one rubric: the new extreme cinema. In part, this naming is itself a function of distribution. As Dargis notes, Park's works are distributed by the British-based Tartan Films, "which puts out works of undisputed artistic worth, genre classics, and pure schlock under the rubric Asia Extreme".[21] Asia Extreme also distributes Breillat's *Anatomie de l'enfer* (*Anatomy of Hell*, 2004), a fact which enables Dargis to link new French "extreme" cinema and Asian horror in interesting ways. So Miike Takeshi's *Audition* (1999) is mentioned here alongside Gaspar Noé's *Irréversible* (*Irreversible*, 2002) and South Korean director Kim ki-Duk's *Spring, Summer, Fall, Winter and Spring* (2003). Along with Park, these directors, Dargis writes, "have earned critical and institutional recognition, partly because of their ability to invent ever more visually arresting ways to turn violence into entertainment".[22]

Certainly, there are similarities that suggest comparison. But while I think Dargis is right that there is a certain extreme quality to the violence in contemporary French and Asian films, I do not think it is helpful to homogenise the traditions – as though all "visually arresting ways to turn violence into entertainment"ultimately mean the same thing, or even have the same visceral effect. Certainly, *Oldboy* invokes a despairing masochism that I am not sure is present in the new French films. In even as masochistic a work as *Dans ma peau* (*In My Skin*, 2002), Marina de Van's film about cutting, mutilation is accompanied by a kind of erotic euphoria rather than the almost unbearable guilt which accompanies it in *Oldboy*. And the reversal of shock effects in *Irréversible* and in François Ozon's *5x2* (2004), both of which foreground rape scenes, yields a totally different affect (and reading strategy) than the shift to violent-horror (in the second half of the film) which *Audition* visits upon its audience.

It is interesting that Park's success with *Oldboy* at Cannes provides the jumping-off point for what ultimately amounts to an invective (by Dargis) against the new extreme cinema – both French and Asian. For, in many ways, *Oldboy* is an extremely old-fashioned film. And it also intersects with other trends in art-horror – trends which I suspect Dargis would find less objectionable than the 'new extremity' and which, sadly, go unmentioned in her critique.

Oldboy begins with a kidnapping. Oh Dae-su (Min-Sik Choi), an unruly drunk, is abducted one rainy night and imprisoned in a room for no apparent reason. Drugged and hypnotised, he spends the next fifteen years in a state of near madness, wondering who is keeping him prisoner

THE ONLY WAY TO WATCH THE
LAST 15 MINUTES OF AUDITION

The UK TV premiere of Audition will expose you to unspeakable scenes of sadistic torture and hilarity. To avoid distress, cut out this mask and wear it over your eyes for the acupuncture, amputation and vomiting scenes.

CUT OUT AND PLACE OVER EYES

12. Promotional tie-in issued by the British broadcaster FilmFour, to aid viewers with watching the horrific final act of *Audition*

and why. Suddenly released (the rationale for his release is as unknown to him as the reason for his capture), he sets out to find his abductor and exact revenge. But his captor has an agenda of his own. He gives Oh Dae-su an assignment. The former captive has five days to find out who instigated his abduction and why, or Mido (Hye-jeong Kang), the young woman who has been helping him and whom he has grown to love, will be killed.

There is a great deal of violence in the film, but surprisingly little gore. As in Quentin Tarantino's *Reservoir Dogs* (1991), the most gruesome scenes actually take place off-screen; the visual suggestion that someone is using a claw hammer to forcibly extract teeth – and revenge – is enough alone to make many viewers look away (it is perhaps no surprise that Tarantino was on the Cannes jury which awarded Park the prize). Much of the violence that does take place on screen has a comic book quality that mitigates the effect. An animated line appears on screen and seems to link Oh Dae-Su to a potential informant at the opening of one menacing moment, for example. And there is a black-humour sequence about suicide that seems almost Monty Pythonesque in its abruptness. In addition, there are continual shifts in register (at one point Mido imagines herself on a subway train with an enormous ant) which work to occasionally blunt (or at least distract us from) the essentially serious humanistic message of the film – that revenge is pointless.

It is this last aspect of *Oldboy* – its lack of a *consistent* humanistic tone – which, I believe, brings it closest to the films that James Quandt has dubbed "the New French Extremity" and which makes it part of the new "extreme" arthouse cinema that so troubles Dargis.[23] Like the affective films of Breillat and Noé, it is difficult to know where on the ideological spectrum to place *Oldboy*, difficult to find anything like the film's "moral center".[24] In that sense, the film itself becomes something of an extension of the jumbled television images that Oh Dae-su sees during his fifteen years of captivity. The serious and the trivial, the deadly and the banal are juxtaposed into one vast sociopolitical cultural jumble.

But the film also taps into another cycle of art-horror movies, the new spate of what, for want of a better term, I will term guilt-trauma films. These include *Bad Boy Bubby*, James Wan's *Saw* (2004), and Brad Anderson's *The Machinist* (2004), films in which male protagonists find themselves imprisoned without fully understanding why. Like the protagonists of *Saw* and *The Machinist*, Dae-su only knows that he is guilty and must discover or (as in the case of Trevor Reznik [Christian Bale] in *The Machinist*) remember what he has done. The incarceration sequence is, in many ways, the strongest and almost the most unbearable of the film. Here we watch Dae-Su struggle to make sense of his situation, escape (by digging a hole in the wall) and keep sane. And, as with all such incarceration films, it becomes abundantly clear here what a tenuous hold on sanity even the most grounded of us really have. Although he has a pencil and is able to keep a sort of prison diary, Dae-su chooses to keep track of time by tattooing lines on his skin (one for each year of imprisonment). In part, this chronicle-on-the-flesh works to ensure that he will not be unmarked by what has happened to him, that – like victims of Nazi concentration camps – he will carry a permanent sign of the arbitrary nature of freedom.

There is a strong tone of existential alienation and angst to each of these films. In that sense they have a great deal in common with the modernist arthouse films of a bygone era. *Saw* unfolds like a horror version of Sartre's *No Exit*, as two men awaken to find themselves chained on opposite sides of a room – with what appears to be a dead body between them. *The Machinist* pays homage to Dostoyevsky's *The Idiot*. And *Bad Boy Bubby* is a sad and terrifying meditation on Sartre's famous dictum that existence precedes essence. Abused and kept locked in a room for thirty-five years, Bubby is the product of his environment. When he finally escapes, he has no point of reference against which to judge the world and can only mimic what others say and do to him. Like *Bubby*, *Oldboy* builds audience sympathy for its main character during the incarceration sequence. Voice-over narration gives us access to his thoughts, and the use of split screen (media images from the television playing on the right, while Dae-su waits on the left) constantly reminds us of his sudden removal from history (and, incidentally, how much time is passing).

In terms of distribution, the guilt-trauma films have fared somewhat better than the European and Asian films discussed earlier in this article.

And since two of them – *The Machinist* and *Saw* – are US films, it is easier to see them within their cultural context.[25] Both films received wide theatrical distribution and the DVDs have been picked up by Blockbuster and other major outlets. *Oldboy* is becoming easier to track since Netflix and Nicheflix have purchased it, but for a long time it was available in the US only as a promise (there were websites, but it was not clear when the DVD would actually become available). And it is still unclear how easy it is for people who do not shop the collector sites to discover the movie (that is, you can find the DVD if you go looking for it, but if you have not heard of the film and do not do a specific search, you are unlikely to find it just by browsing). The Australian made *Bad Boy Bubby* has suffered the most in this regard. Arguably the best film in the cycle, it has received little play in the US, despite winning The Grand Jury Prize at the Venice Film Festival. This is depressing, given the film's artistic and experimental qualities. Using a method similar to the one employed by John Cassavetes, director de Heer shot the film in sequence. In order to build sympathy for the main character, he experimented with aural-perspective, creating a sound scape unlike anything I have heard before in cinema. Finally, he used thirty-two cinematographers to shoot discrete scenes in the film. None of the cinematographers saw previous footage, so the film unfolds as a remarkable series of vignettes or shorts, which are held together (and given continuity) primarily by the sound. From a purely formal point of view, therefore, the film needs to be seen, studied, and discussed. The fact that it also tells a moving and intelligent story simply underscores its importance.

Conclusion

What I have aimed to do in this essay is to open up some of the antithetical impulses in art horror for discussion, and also to revisit and update the taste culture arguments that characterise my book *Cutting Edge*. I have chosen Dargis's review as a point of departure, not out of any desire to paint her as obtuse. Rather, precisely because she is a perceptive critic (particularly in the area of horror cinema), her review of Park seems emblematic of a larger set of cultural blind spots. That there is a continued replay of the age old taste-debate is depressing for scholars who work in this area. But it is also a reminder how almost willfully ignorant of our own cultural history we are. And the ongoing tendency to speak as though everyone in a country such as the US has equal access to festival culture becomes here a necessary reminder of just how class-inflected the debates over taste remain.[26]

Special thanks to Chris Anderson, Nathan Carroll, Ian Conrich, Skip Hawkins, and Greg Waller for their help and encouragement; and to the collectors, specialty houses and *Video Watchdog* who all make it possible for me to do my work.

Notes

1. *New York Times* critic Manohla Dargis on a special screening of Park's work at the BAMcinématek, 'Sometimes Blood Really Isn't Indelible', *New York Times*, 3 March 2005, p. B7.
2. By this term I mean the international films distributed in the US which still play by and large in the festival and arthouse circuit, outside "mainstream" cinemas.
3. Dargis, p. B7. Italics mine.
4. See Thomas Schatz, *Hollywood Genres*, New York: McGraw-Hill, 1981.
5. Manohla Dargis, 'Not Just Roaming, Zombies Rise Up', *New York Times*, 24 June 2005, p. B1
6. Joan Hawkins, *Cutting Edge: Art Horror and the Horrific Avant-garde*, Minneapolis and London: University of Minnesota Press, 2000.
7. Tod Browning's 1932 film *Freaks* is the classic case in point here. Released initially as a mainstream film, then shown on the exploitation and drive-in circuit, and finally resuscitated as an arthouse film. Georges Franju's *Les Yeux sans visage* (*The Horror Chamber of Dr. Faustus, Eyes Without a Face*, 1960) and Michael Powell's *Peeping Tom* (1959) offer further examples. For more on this, see Hawkins.
8. Even the the integration of body genre films into the upper tier of the festival circuit has historical precedent. *Taxi Driver*, which was considered a hyper-violent film whose cultural 'value' was debated at the time of its release, won the Palme d'Or at Cannes in 1976. To be fair to Dargis, though, the Festival traditionally prefers less violent films.
9. Paracinema is, according to Jeffrey Sconce, an elastic category which includes low horror, grade B sci-fi films from the 1950s, hard-to-find European titles, sword and sandal flicks, Asian horror, juvenile delinquent films, exploitation and softcore porn, avant-garde cinema, and historical social guidance films (to name just a few genres). As Sconce has argued, fans with this special cinematic taste, are commonly linked by reading strategies and a certain cultural capital. For more, see '"Trashing the Academy": Taste, Excess and an Emerging Politics of Cinematic Style' in this volume (pp. 103–22) and Hawkins' *Cutting Edge*.
10. Other recent additions advertised on the website include Carl Theodor Dreyer's *La Passion de Jeanne de l'Arc* (*The Passion of Joan of Arc*, 1928), and Anthony Asquith's *The Browning Version* (1951). See <www.criterionco.com>. For more on Criterion's DVDs see James Kendrick, 'Aspect Ratios and Joe Six-Packs: Home Theater Enthusiasts' Battle to Legitimize the DVD Experience', *The Velvet Light Trap*, no. 56, Fall 2005.

11. See Hawkins, pp. 8, 87–116.

12. See <www.nicheflix.com>.

13. See Hawkins, pp. 33–52.

14. Nathan Carroll, *Public Access and Private Archives*, unpublished PhD, Indiana University, Bloomington, 2006. For more on DVDs see the Fall 2005 special DVD edition of *The Velvet Light Trap*, no. 56.

15. According to an Associated Press release, 75% of Americans polled for an American Online survey said they preferred to watch films at home: <http://www.cnn.com/2005/showbiz/Movies/06/17/movies.poll.ap> dated 18 June 2005 (accessed 6 July 2005). For a detailed study of home viewing see Barbara Klinger, *Beyond the Multiplex: Cinema, New Technologies and The Home*, Berkeley: University of California Press, 2006.

16. Currently, even the attempt to sustain the brand-name of an auteur seems to have been abandoned. Companies will buy the rights to an auteur's film and then just keep it in the vault, often for years. Occasionally the film will finally turn up as an extra on a DVD many years later. For more on distribution problems in the US see Jonathan Rosenbaum, *Movie Wars: How Hollywood and the Media Conspire to Limit What Films We Can See*, Chicago: A Capella Press, 2000.

17. I am indebted to Chris Anderson for these observations and the quote.

18. See, for example, Catherine Breillat's *Anatomie de l'enfer* (*Anatomy of Hell*, 2004); François Ozon's *5X2* (2004) and *Regarde la mer* (*See the Sea*, 1997); and Gaspar Noé's *Irréversible* (*Irreversible*, 2002) and *Seul contre tous* (*I Stand Alone*, 1998).

19. James Quandt, 'Flesh and Blood: Sex and Violence in Recent French Cinema' *Artforum*, February 2004, pp. 126–32. Beur is the term applied to second generation children of North African immigrants, who are born in France. Banlieue is the term for suburbs, and refers to the areas surrounding Paris where many people of North African descent live. They are not the only inhabitants, however, and the term 'banlieue film' refers to films set in these troubled areas, which may be made by white filmmakers or members of other (non North African) ethnic groups. Roughly speaking, these films are the equivalent of 'hood films made in the US.

20. See Rosenbaum.

21. Dargis, 'Sometimes Blood Really Isn't Indelible', p. B7.

22. Ibid.

23. Quandt, p. 127

24. The French films which James Quandt links under the rubric "the New French Extremity" are themselves a disparate group and a difficult cultural read. Quandt cannot decide whether they have more in common with the 'épater les bourgeois' spirit of the French Surrealists or with the work of the right-wing anarchist hussards of the 1950s. That is, he cannot determine whether the films of these new cinematic provocateurs align politically with the Left or with the Right, whether they are culturally progressive or reactionary. In a sense, like many of the horror films Robin Wood discusses, they are

both and it is perhaps this imbrication – or perhaps dialectic – of liberal and conservative tendencies which makes the films so deeply troubling.

25. Stephen Holden's review of *Saw* in the *New York Times* discussed the film in terms of the Iraq war, for example. Stephen Holden, 'A Gore Fest, With Overtones of Iraq and TV', *New York Times*, 29 October 2004. Archived at <http://www.nytimes.com/2004/10/29saw.html>.

26. See Pierre Bourdieu, *Distinction: A Social Critique of the Judgement of Taste*, trans. Richard Nice, Cambridge: Harvard University Press, 1984.

8

Making Up Monsters
Set and Costume Design in Horror Films

Tamao Nakahara

This article considers the artists and artisans who generally remain in the background of both films and film history: set and costume designers. Aside from the main award ceremonies and the occasional fanzine or magazine article, attention is rarely paid to the members who – in the case of horror – help vivify nightmares and often define a culture's monsters. One reason for the limited attention paid to designers is the nature of the art and industry itself. As Charles and Mirella J. Affron have noted, to a set designer "the good set" is one that is "essentially and modestly denotative . . . entirely subordinate to the narrative . . . [and that] goes unnoticed".[1] Design's equally scant coverage in film studies is caused in part by the cultural studies trend against earlier practices of close readings and freeze frame analyses – practices that have been criticised for being overdetermined and not indicative of general audience experience of the cinema.

Without relinquishing a cultural studies approach, I aim to examine closely certain design elements and to incorporate those details into a study of the horror film. By doing so, I hope to contribute to the understanding of one part of the vast industry that creates the performance and design of horror. One motivation for this approach is that any undertaking that pays attention to the unsung heroes of film production necessarily warrants a type of close art appreciation of components that make up the whole picture. As C.S. Tashiro contests in this vein, not only must one "be willing to look at pieces of design that would normally go unnoticed", one must also "try to understand the *totality* of the image and recognise the relationship between stories and the outside world as one of constant, mutual exchange and interaction".[2] Secondly, as has been forcefully argued by Thomas Elsaesser on family melodramas, a film can use setting and décor

> so as to reflect the characters' fetishist fixations. Violent feelings are given
> vent on 'overdetermined' objects (James Dean kicking his father's portrait

as he storms out of the house in *Rebel Without a Cause*), and aggressiveness is worked out by proxy.[3]

In the same way that, as Elsaesser historicises, overdetermined readings of melodrama appeared at a time when Freud was widely popularised in the US, the codified groundwork has been laid for horror viewers to attach a range of meanings to objects in the image. The third justification for looking at the details of costumes and sets, therefore, is to acknowledge that fan culture readings are one of many discourses integrated into horror reception. In light of current work on fan culture, overdetermination should be written into cult film practices in which fans rewatch a favourite movie dozens if not hundreds of times, often reading meaning into every detail. They cull through fanzines and biographies noting characteristics of their favourite film, director, or star, and collect DVDs now equipped with clean prints, original trailers, and director commentary.[4] Symbolic (over)interpretation of background objects, by fans (and scholars), while seen for what it is, should be read not as a dismissible practice, but as one of many discourses that contributes to a larger cultural understanding of a film phenomenon.

For the space of this article, I will focus on the case study of works inspired by the real-life serial killer Ed Gein – films in which setting and décor reflect the characters' fetishist fixations, and whose readings now incorporate paratextual elements such as trailers and DVD commentaries. Gein, whose murders, necrophilia, and cannibalism were concentrated between 1954 and 1957, was a veritable 'monster' who still lives vividly in the popular imagination and continues to act as fodder for cinematic exploration. He has an appeal especially because he is an extreme example of a fetishistic collector, one who uses his victims' bodies and body parts to 'decorate' his own body and his home. Among the films that borrow from the Wisconsin killer's gruesome practices, three have been marked by their fame and longevity: Alfred Hitchcock's *Psycho* (1960), Tobe Hooper's *The Texas Chain Saw Massacre* (1974) and Jonathan Demme's *The Silence of the Lambs* (1991).[5] Each example, when translating Gein's characteristics to the screen, employs set and costume design not only to create a theatre in which the monster scopophilically watches his victims perform, but also to fetishise and unite the body of the monster with the body of the house.

Monster's House as Body

In discussing the role of the Manderley house in his film, *Rebecca* (1940), Hitchcock stated that "[i]n a sense the picture is the story of a house. The house was one of the three key characters of the picture".[6] The same could be said of *Psycho*, a film that treats "Set as Narrative", when "decor becomes the narrative's organising image, a figure that stands for the narrative itself".[7] A common visual marker that presents the horrific house as a character or organising image is the use of a long shot of the house as the scene's establishing shot. In the three films noted here as well as in other famous examples such as *The Exorcist* (1973), *The Amityville Horror* (1979), and *Poltergeist* (1982), the house is free-standing and is introduced to the audience with a long shot 'portrait'.[8]

It is noteworthy that, in the case of *Psycho*, the director chose to advertise the movie with a tour of the film sets.[9] Instead of devoting time to promote actors or scenes from the film, "the fabulous Mr. Alfred Hitchcock", the trailer touts, "[escorts] you on a tour of the location of his new motion picture, 'PSYCHO'". At the motel, Hitchcock, our guide, states,

> Here we have a quiet little motel tucked away off the main highway and, as you see, perfectly harmless-looking. When in fact, it has now become known as the scene of the crime. This motel also has as an adjunct an old house, which is, if I may say so, [the camera moves to a low angle shot in which Hitchcock is framed in the foreground next to a long shot of the house] a little more sinister looking, less innocent than the hotel itself. And in this house, the most dire horrible events took place.

Hitchcock's trailer shows that the house's portrait is only the surface that either hints at or hides the murderous activities contained within its body. Such a building is one instance of what Carol J. Clover calls the Terrible Place, a house that is haunting for its "Victorian decrepitude" as well as "the terrible families – murderous, incestuous, cannibalistic" that it holds.[10] Robin Wood similarly labels the house in *The Texas Chain Saw Massacre* a "terrible house", a trope which he views as part of a long line of decaying mansions in the American Gothic literary tradition – mansions marked by, as Andrew Britton notes, disease, incest, corpses, cannibalism, degenerate sexuality, and "a monstrous and perverted family".[11]

Ed Gein's real-life story falls eerily into this American Gothic schemata. The serial killer, who inspired the first fiction rendition of Robert Bloch's book *Psycho* (1959), was raised in an environment dominated by his fervently Christian mother. Indoctrinated in the evils of sex and sinners, Gein purportedly let loose his repressed fantasies once his mother died. While unassuming and neighbourly, he took on habits which included exhuming corpses, necrophilia, cannibalism, killing women, and sewing and wearing the skins and genitalia of his victims. As John McCarty describes, "his crimes were eventually uncovered by a local deputy sheriff who came upon the headless corpse of Gein's own mother hanging on

13. Leatherface pulls a helpless victim into the terrible house in *The Texas Chain Saw Massacre* (1974)

a hook in his squalid farmhouse, which was littered with the bones and flesh of Geins' victims as well as parts of other bodies Gein had recently disinterred".[12]

Psycho, The Texas Chain Saw Massacre, and *The Silence of the Lambs* all rely heavily on their sets to define each monster and to recreate the environment and the shock that the deputy must have felt as he first entered Gein's farmhouse. Clover identifies the first encounter as another generic component of the Terrible Place: "Into such houses unwitting victims wander in film after film, and it is the conventional task of the genre to register in close detail the victims' dawning understanding, as they survey the *visible evidence,* of the human crimes and perversions that have transpired there".[13] The "visible evidence" that the victims and the audience register is provided precisely by the design elements that identify the monster's house and move the narrative forward. In the three examples discussed here, a central design element is the fetishistic residue of the killer's rituals: the victims' flesh and bones. The inner and outer remains of the victims are what the killer uses to furnish his home and fashion his costumes, the remains that unite the body of the monster with the body of the house.

Psycho is the least literal interpreter of the true-life serial killer. It softens Gein's practice, as McCarty explains, of "[making] waistcoats from the skin of his victims and [wearing] them about the house" into a practice of taxidermy.[14] In the film's trailer, Hitchcock makes a point to associate the killer, Norman Bates (Anthony Perkins), with his safe haven and with the birds he sews up: "his favorite spot was the little parlour behind his office in the motel . . . I suppose you'd call this his hideaway. His hobby as you see was taxidermy. A crow here . . . an owl there". During the scene in which Norman invites his future victim, Marion Crane (Janet Leigh), into the parlour for supper, he is visually described by the way that the frame unites him with the various stuffed birds in the room. As the shots and shot-reverse-shots alternate between Norman and Marion during their conversation, the camera remains generally in the same position for all of Marion's shots, while those for Norman change angles to frame him with one bird and then another in the set design. While the conversation is light, the frame shows Norman from the waist up to the right of a dresser with a couple of small birds. As soon as the subject of "mother" is broached, the camera angle changes to show him in a low angle medium shot in front of two paintings (one of a nude) and two menacing spread-winged birds near the ceiling – an image that suggests Norman's conflicted feelings of sexual arousal and self-censure for that arousal. Finally, when Marion suggests putting Norman's mother away in an institution, the enraged Norman is shown in close-up flanked by two birds abutting against his ears. As if to provide a wall ornament for each mood and emotion, Norman's sanctuary, and his behaviour in it, hints at his multiple personalities. The 'costuming' of the walls of the house describes Norman and anticipates the costuming of Norman's body as it appears later in wig and dress. The scene is, furthermore, a prelude to the more explicit proof of Norman's murderous instincts: the sequence in which Marion's sister Lila (Vera Miles), seeking Marion, enters the cement and brick cellar and encounters the mummified and dressed Mrs. Bates for the final unveiling of the Terrible Place.

Psycho's reference to Gein's play with corpses is copied and made more explicit in the slasher, *The Texas Chain Saw Massacre*, as flesh and bone become tangible and visceral fixations of the film's star monster, 'Leatherface' Bubba Sawyer (Gunnar Hansen) and the Sawyer family. The seated skeleton of Norman's mother is mimicked in Hooper's film using the seated and dressed mummy of grandma Sawyer and the not-quite-dead grandpa slumped in a chair beside her. The couple is presented in a similar fashion when the last survivor, Sally Hardesty (Marilyn Burns), like Lila, is briefly comforted by the elderly figures only to find that they are dressed on the outside but dead on the inside. The house's furnishings in *The Texas Chain Saw Massacre* move beyond Norman's orderly taxidermy displays, replacing stuffed birds with live caged chickens, loose feathers and piles of scattered bones.[15] The interior is introduced when the first two victims, Kirk (William Vail) and Pam (Teri McMinn), wander into the Sawyer family home. Kirk first ventures inside intrigued by a red wall decorated with various bones. The details are shown through a type of stylised point-of-view shot in which the wall is shown with long, medium long, then medium shots in quick succession. When Pam wanders in looking for the already butchered Kirk, her point-of-view shots are combined with descriptive shots to provide the most detailed display of the parlour trophy room to the left of the entrance. During the two-minute sequence in the parlour, there are about seventeen shots devoted to the objects in the room and seventeen to Pam's reactions. The combined descriptive, point-of-view, and reaction shots create a scene in which the set – covered with chickens, loose feathers and bones – takes over momentarily as the spectacle. Like Gein's farmhouse with the hanging corpse, the parlour contains chickens and bones suspended from the ceiling with strings, a design choice that effectively fills both the horizontal and vertical spaces of the screen. Finally, when Sally finds herself at the head of the dinner table with the whole Sawyer family, she is surrounded by furniture and ornaments such as a floor lamp made out of a skeleton, a chandelier fashioned out of the skins of human heads, and a dining table dressed with bones and the head of a chicken. Unlike the neatly arranged birds in *Psycho* that reflect Norman's controlled exterior and unstable interior, the messy collection of bones, feathers and spilled blood in *The Texas Chain Saw Massacre* reflects the Sawyers' complete abandon and sloppy killing practices. Similarly, the camerawork in Hitchcock's film is still and held back while the shots in *The Texas Chain Saw Massacre* are frenzied and quickly cut to produce a fast collage of bones, blood and screams.

In *The Silence of the Lambs*, the interior of the monster's house works both to describe him and to create the moment of dawning discussed by Clover. Clarice Starling (Jodie Foster), the FBI recruit who has stumbled upon the killer's house on a hunch, slowly realises where she is and the danger she is in through the visible clues in the set. Demme carefully prepares his identifying objects as Hooper does, but also takes the stylised point-of-view and descriptive shots of *The Texas Chain Saw Massacre* to the next level. The killer, Jame 'Buffalo Bill' Gum (Ted Levine), has already been connected in the narrative to moths and butterflies, images that later give him away. As Clarice slowly makes her way into Jame's lair, she is shown in medium shot walking toward the camera and taking note of objects in the room. The shot cuts to a reverse shot in which the camera shows the back of Clarice and part of what she can see in the set. The next shot returns to show the protagonist's front side, but then wanders to the right to 'look' at an identifying object in the set before Clarice sees it: a painting of a butterfly. By playfully making the viewing eye ambiguous, Demme takes the liberty to move away from restrictive camera conventions and to focus on the set that he has prepared for the scene. In the director's DVD commentary, he frequently discusses the design choices that he and his set decorator, Karen O'Hara, made for *The Silence of the Lambs*. He notes that in this scene:

> the camera takes on a mind of its own here, kind of exploring the place with her, sometimes exploring the place without her. Like when the camera pans off of her for no apparent reason onto a close-up of a painting of a butterfly, a painting executed, by the way, by my wife, Joanne Howard.

> It is only after this ambiguous subjective shot for the audience that the camera presents Clarice's act of looking by showing two point-of-view shots panning and then fixing on a moth intercut with reaction shots registering her moment of dawning.[16]

The use of stylised mise-en-scène draws attention to the objects that decorate the monster's corporeal house: birds for Norman, bones for Leatherface, and moths for Jame. The direction also emphasises, especially in the last example of Demme's wandering camera, the theatrical quality of the corporeal house, a space in which the victim is controlled by the camera-mediated gaze. A discussion of the gaze must necessarily return to Hitchcock's *Psycho*.

Monster's House as Theatre

Preempting fan devotion and believing in the genius and longevity of *Psycho*, Hitchcock in his trailer suggests the artificiality of the set and jokingly invites overdetermined readings of the objects in the décor. At the Bates Motel, he recounts the conversation between Norman and Marion in the parlour:

> An important scene took place in this room. There was a private supper here. And, uh oh, by the way, [pointing to a medium-sized painting on the wall] this picture has *great significance* because ... uh, let's go along to cabin number 1. I'll show you something there.[17]

The director toys not only with an audience that may see itself as film and art savvy, but also with the possibility that the film will become such a hit that fans may see it several times and read too deeply into the meaning of the artwork on the walls. The joke is that, during the feature film, the painting's role is less symbolic than material: its purpose in the parlour is less as a decorative object than as a physical prop that covers up Norman's peephole into Marion's room.

Hitchcock's playing with artifice as well as his reference to Norman's peephole address the scopophilic theatricality of the monster's house in all three films. The house becomes an enclosed space over which the monster has mastery and, most importantly, it is a space in which he can defy physical limitations by freely playing dress-up. This theatricality necessarily highlights the use of set and costume design for affect and artificiality.

In *Psycho*, Norman's mastery is a mastery of vision using the peephole (a practice which has invited volumes of discussion on voyeurism and power-laden subject positions). Marion, in her cabin, is blind to Norman's voyeuristic interests as she undresses in her room and unwittingly provides him with a peepshow. Norman's various rooms in which he plays audience, moreover, are stages on which he also plays performer. Vocally, he recites his 'dialogues' from the house as both himself and his alter ego, his dead mother. Physically, he appears twice in costume as his mother: first in the famous shower scene to murder Marion and second in the end when he attempts to murder Lila. In the former, the costume of Norman dressed as mother in wig and nightgown works to disguise him and maintain his dual identity; in the latter under the basement light, the same costume works to reveal Norman as the killer with a split personality. His performance in costume as mother reveals that he is always performing, that even his controlled personality as Norman in men's clothing is just as much a played role.

The Silence of the Lambs represents a similar killer-victim power dynamic, but Clarice's castration through blindness is made more jarring because she is aware of her danger and her inability to fend for herself. After having found and chased Jame Gum into his basement, she finds herself in complete darkness while Jame enjoys his mastery of vision over her through the assistance of night-vision goggles. The scene is effected by the killer's green-tinted point-of-view shots as he dances around the stumbling Clarice and eroticises his joyful position of power as spectator by pretending to caress her hair.

The costuming in Demme's film is closer to Gein's fetishistic treatment of his victim's corpses. In her investigation, Clarice discovers that Jame is "making himself a woman's suit ... out of real women". In Clarice's climactic encounter with the killer, several staged objects often go unnoticed because of their small size in the screen and the fast pace of the camera in the conflict. In his DVD commentary, Demme has the opportunity to direct viewers' attention to these carefully arranged objects in the background for interpretation. In Jame's basement, Demme first asks, "I always wonder if people notice that there's a half-made suit of human skin sitting there" and in another scene he asks, "do people get that there's a shrivelled old body there?".[18] These questions are followed by the statement that Demme

impresses upon his viewers: *The Silence of the Lambs* is "a movie about skin".
Skin and masquerade are embodied in the character of Jame Gum, as
demonstrated in an important scene in which he dresses up and parades
around in the nude in front of his video camera. The work of the costume
and make-up departments becomes part of the narrative to describe Jame
and to emphasise the fragmented nature of his identity. The scene begins
with an extreme close-up of a hand dabbing a brush into eye shadow
and then cuts to a tattoo of the word 'love'. The following shots focus on
other fragments of Jame's body: a skin wig, extreme close-ups of an eye
being made up, extreme close-ups of painted lips mouthing the words to
a song, a tear drop tattoo, a nipple piercing and a necklace. Once Jame has
put on the various layers of decoration on his already decorated body and
backs up to fill the frame, he temporarily becomes whole. The fragments
of eyes, lips, tattoos and piercings come together as one composite body.
Covered in a robe and surrounded by lush fabrics, a mannequin and a
disco ball, he then completes the picture by recording himself in the
nude as a woman with his penis tucked between his thighs. This is Jame's
temporary masquerade before fulfilling his fantasy of wearing a full body
suit made of women's skin. The killer performs on his own stage complete
with costumes, lights, and music, and becomes his own audience through
the video recording.

Jame Gum is not the only celebrity monster of *The Silence of the Lambs*.
Even more famous is the jailed criminal who helps Clarice in her task, the
cannibal Hannibal Lecter. Hannibal also is portrayed as a monster with
a bent for the theatrical. His surroundings describe him as a talented and
cultured man. His cell has a backdrop of his drawings of the Duomo in
Florence, a desk with books and a swivel chair, *Bon Appetit* magazine, and
a tape recorder playing classical music. Yet his savage nature as a cannibal
justifies one of cinema's most memorable costume images: actor Anthony
Hopkins in orange, strapped to a metal frame and wearing a resin mask
with a wire grid over his dangerous mouth. When granted a special jail
cell in exchange for his services, Hannibal is placed in what Demme calls a
"birdcage stuck in the center of a room", a bright and high-ceilinged stage
ready for his next crime. Hopkins discusses how he requested to wear all
white for the birdcage scenes – a choice that turns the body of Hannibal
into a clean canvas ready to be covered with red. When he does decide to
kill two officers and escape, he hangs one disembowelled officer in front
of a dramatically blinding light, the body with arms spread out like a bird
flying to freedom. Hannibal, who also likes to fashion costumes out of
his victims, cunningly creates a 'mask' out of the facial skin of the officer.
Disguising himself with the mask, Hannibal plays his own form of dress-
up to exit stage left and escape for good.

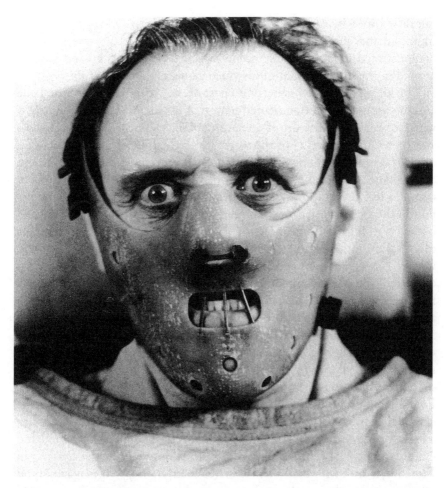

14. The notorious cannibal, Hannibal Lecter, and his memorable restraining mask in *The Silence of the Lambs*

Hannibal's use of a victim's skin for a mask refers to *The Texas Chain Saw Massacre's* Leatherface, cinema's arguably most famous wearer of human facial skins. Leatherface, whose nickname defines him by his practice, is presented as a more grotesque version of Norman as mother: sometimes in a woman's wig and apron, but always with the indispensable dried human skin mask.[19] Leatherface also takes care to alter his appearance three times during the first *The Texas Chain Saw Massacre*. For the butchering of his victims in the beginning of the film, he wears a simple white shirt and tie with his bloody butcher's apron. Halfway through when the Sawyer family is gathered in the house, he takes on the grandmother role by wearing a gray wig, brown shirt and tie, and by speaking in a high pitched voice. In the DVD commentary, the actor Gunnar Hansen who played Leatherface discusses the role with the director:

> Here is Leatherface in his new get-up as the grandma. I think that a lot of people don't know that Leatherface actually has three different masks he wears in the movie and you [to Tobe Hooper] told me that the whole idea is that the mask is because he has nothing inside. I mean that the mask is the personality. So he changes faces depending on what he's trying to do. Now [in this scene] he's being domestic. He's been making dinner and so he's got the old lady mask on, an apron, and a giant wooden spoon. He moves different too.

Excluded footage provided by the DVD, furthermore, shows Leatherface powdering and preparing himself as a woman excited about a formal event. For the dinner, he dresses in his final and most androgynous costume. He wears a black wig and the mask that he has powdered and painted with lipstick, an ensemble to which he gives contrast by wearing a black smoking jacket. The changes in appearance emphasise that Leatherface's identity, like that of Norman and Jame, is always unstable and fragmented, requiring him to perform in his own theatre with different flesh fetish costumes for each occasion and role.

The other Sawyer family members also partake in performances that are highlighted in the penultimate scene in the film. The last surviving victim of the Sawyer family ambush, Sally, wakes up and finds herself at the head of the dinner table toward the end of the movie. She is strapped to a chair and is forced to be a spectator of the members seated for the feast. She is also the star of their evening's entertainment as they jeer, yell and enjoy her screams. Turned into a type of primitive fetish object, she is forced to endure her own ritual killing in which the most senior family member, the mostly dead grandfather, is assisted to clobber her with a slaughterhouse mallet. Finding that the act is more a performance than an effective murder (for the grandfather lacks the strength to hold the mallet), she manages to break free and to burst her way out of the house.

The power of cinema often lies in the visual realisation of certain fetishistic curiosities in the popular imagination. In these horror films, living victims not only are turned into fetishised bodies, but also are altered into material corpses that are not allowed to remain intact. Fragmented into body parts, the pieces of the victims' flesh and bones are used as literal fetish objects – objects worn on the body of the monster or in the body of the house to render him into a temporary whole identity. This identity, however, is always performative, requiring the monster to play dress-up (Norman as mother, Leatherface in the skin mask, Jame in a woman's suit) and to play different roles in the theatre of the monster's domain, the house.

All of these images clearly are not created in a vacuum, but are the result of the hard work of various contributors in the design departments.

The Affrons, in *Sets in Motion*, quote art director, David Rawnsley, who states that "the greatest compliment that a viewer can pass is to say 'Sorry, old man – I didn't notice the settings'".[20] But as films have become more integrated into popular memory and new forums such as fan sites and DVD commentaries increasingly have become part of the filmic experience, film historical and analytical practices must follow suit in their study of the inter-textually connected media. Scholars must also consider Tashiro's contention in *Pretty Pictures*, that all elements of the image – not just the set design – must be taken into account. The image, furthermore, must be studied not only in relation to the narrative, but also as an independent artistic contribution to the film. As a fan, filmmaker, and scholar, Tashiro opens up the possibility of varied interactive readings between the film and the viewer, scholar, and consumer.

The horror genre, whose fanzines and scholarly attention have justified the examination of layered audience readings, is no exception to the arguments presented by the Affrons and Tashiro. Fans continue to contribute their overdetermined readings of elements in the image. As demonstrated in the studies above, directors, set designers, and actors also respond by using inter-textual devices such as trailers and DVDs to reveal the importance of their design choices and to direct their audiences' attention to those choices. They, as Tashiro has emphasised, point to the design elements that go unnoticed and remark on the constructed totality of the image.

Notes

1. Charles Affron and Mirella Jona Affron, *Sets in Motion: Art Direction and Film Narrative*, New Brunswick: Rutgers University Press, 1995, pp. 43–4.
2. C.S. Tashiro, *Pretty Pictures: Production Design and the History Film*, Austin: University of Texas Press, 1998, pp. 12, 9.
3. Thomas Elsaesser, 'Tales of Sound and Fury: Observations on the Family Melodrama', in Marcia Landy, ed., *Imitations of Life*, Detroit: Wayne State University Press, 1991, p. 79. Originally published in *Monogram*, no. 4, 1972, pp. 2–15.
4. Andrew Ross discusses the practices of "overinformed hipsters" in Andrew Ross, *No Respect: Intellectuals and Popular Culture*, London: Routledge, 1989, p. 83.
5. Although Hitchcock's film falls outside the time frame of contemporary horror, its importance to the history of film, horror, and Gein interpretations

such as *The Texas Chain Saw Massacre* and *Silence of the Lambs* warrants close examination.

6. François Truffaut, *Hitchcock*, New York: Simon and Schuster, 1967, p. 94, quoted in Affron and Affron, p. 164, n. 11.

7. Affron and Affron, p. 158.

8. Stuart Rosenberg's *The Amityville Horror* goes so far as to light up the windows of the house to form a façade that imitates the face of a Jack o' lantern.

9. Thomas Schatz mentions how the trailer played off of Hitchcock's monologues in his television show, *Alfred Hitchcock Presents*. The weekly show, which started in 1955, made Hitchcock's face and speaking style familiar to American audiences by the time of *Psycho*'s release five years later. Thomas Schatz, *The Genius of the System: Hollywood Filmmaking in the Studio Era*, New York: Metropolitan Books, 1996, pp. 484–9.

10. Carol J. Clover, *Men, Women, and Chain Saws: Gender in the Modern Horror Film*, Princeton: Princeton University Press, 1992, p. 30.

11. Robin Wood. *Hollywood from Vietnam to Reagan – and Beyond*, New York: Columbia University Press, 2003, p. 14; and Andrew Britton, 'Mandingo', *Movie*, no. 22, 1976, pp. 3–4.

12. John McCarty. *Movie Psychos and Madmen: Film Psychopaths from Jekyll and Hyde to Hannibal Lecter*, New York: Citadel Press, 1993, p. 136.

13. Clover, pp. 30–1. Emphasis mine.

14. McCarty, p. 136.

15. In *The Texas Chain Saw Massacre* DVD commentary Tobe Hooper, director of photography Daniel Pearl, and Gunnar Hansen discuss how they obtained a full human skeleton from India and how they picked out bones from animal carcasses left by a cooperative veterinarian.

16. *The Silence of the Lambs* DVD commentary with Jonathan Demme.

17. Emphasis mine.

18. Demme comments at length on the missed objects in the scene: "we spent a lot of time trying to figure out how to portray Jame Gum. In an effort to make manifest his masculine side that he's trying to escape from by turning himself into a woman, we put on the set a lot of polaroids of Jane Gum posing with topless strippers. Unfortunately they read too small in the frame and I never did inserts which I sort of wish I had done. As the camera moves by him there I wonder sometimes if audiences notice that he's naked in a movie about skin".

19. Ian Conrich observes a similar dependence on masks in the *Friday the 13th* series: "Jason's hockey mask is so much part of his identity – his one essential accessory – that without it he is incomplete and maybe even unable to function convincingly as the executioner". Ian Conrich, 'The *Friday the 13th* films and the Cultural Function of a Modern Grand Guignol', reprinted in this collection, pp. 173–88.

20. 'The Art Director', in Oswell Blakeston, ed., *Working for the Films*, London: Focal, 1947, p. 86, quoted in Affron and Affron, p. 44.

8

They're Here!
Special Effects in Horror Cinema of the 1970s and 1980s

Ernest Mathijs

The Coming of Special Effects and the Return to Form

In 1984, Paul Sammon, a regular contributor to the horror and science-fiction fan magazines *Cinefex* and *Cinefantastique*, wrote that "more than any recent film, *Gremlins* (1984) relied almost as much on its variously conceived mechanical creatures as it did on its live performers".[1] Though certainly not the first time such a comment was made about special effects mechanics and make-up, it serves as a symptomatic marker of the paradigmatic shift in the status of special effects in the early 1980s. As Michele Pierson writes, from about a decade before Sammon's remark fan magazines of science-fiction and horror special effects had been providing

> a forum for directors, special-effects artists, supervisors and technicians (as well as magazine editors and contributors), for assessing the range of special effects that works best, not just for particular kinds of shots, but also for particular kinds of films.[2]

It was in the early 1980s that horror effects in particular were deemed important enough to become a legitimate and respected agent in the critical and academic discourse on the horror film; it was not until these effects proved, almost literally, that they had become "almost as" important as the stories, which they were supposed to support, that they became an active part of debates on the genre.[3]

This chapter argues that the reasons for the rise of special effects in the horror genre need to be understood in relation to their connection with the public debates on and the receptions of the films in which they appear, and the general culture surrounding horror cinema.[4] My main argument is that 'Horror Effects' (or HFX henceforth) becomes a locus of prime importance in cultural discussions of horror in the 1970s and 1980s, two decades in which horror films have occupied a central position. The aim is to show how HFX have been introduced in the public understanding of horror, how HFX have been discussed as aesthetic and textual devices, and how the status of the debate on HFX has changed by foregrounding the position of those responsible for its emergence, the so called 'HFX-auteurs'. The term refers to a small but increasingly significant group of HFX-artists whose reputation has become so important (both aesthetically and as a marketing tool) that it has come to overshadow some of the more traditional elements within the horror genre. While following a (more or less) chronological line throughout, this chapter also focuses on several particular elements, such as the significance of fan magazines in setting the agenda (*Cinefantastique*, *Fangoria*, *L'Ecran fantastique* and *Cinefex* being key examples); the introduction of aesthetic evaluation into HFX reception; personal trajectories of HFX-auteurs like Tom Savini, Rick Baker, Dick Smith, and Chris Walas; and key celebratory moments that have become part of the construction of an HFX canon and HFX film history (in films such as *Scanners* [1981], *The Evil Dead* [1982], *Gremlins* and *The Fly* [1986]).

Fan Magazines and Horror Effects from DIY to Aesthetic Evaluation

It is dangerous to antedate when special effects really became significant in the reception of the horror film, but for the purposes of this discussion a short return to the beginning of the 1970s is necessary. This was the decade in which the first HFX artists received (some kind of) auteurist recognition, in which a new wave of fan magazines aligned itself with the rise in popularity of HFX and devoted critical attention to it, and when special effects became associated with the production values of marketable (cheap or expensive) movies – and indeed with the marketing of films itself.

The real beginning is to be found in the late 1960s, when Dick Smith, who is credited unanimously as the "Godfather" of modern HFX, published *Famous Monsters' Do-It-Yourself Monster Make-up Handbook*, a manual for doing special make up effects, serialised by the American magazine *Famous Monsters of Filmland*.[5] The fact that a DIY guide to special effects making was promoted by a fan publication is the first step towards the convergence between discussions of HFX practice and critical evaluation of HFX that would become so typical for the way in which any public debates of horror, be they in fan magazines or more widely in the general press, addressed special effects. In the early 1970s, this discourse was still a small one. Smith got his first big break working on the make up for Dustin Hoffman in *Little Big Man* (1970), and then worked, with his apprentice Rick Baker, on *The Exorcist* (1973), widely regarded as the first major film to put HFX on the critical agenda.[6] Mark Kermode, looking back on the impact the film left on him, expresses his disappointment about being practically unable to get hold of any information on HFX in *The Exorcist*, other than the "sombre under-stated stills" he found in *Cinefantastique*.[7] More important, however, than the fact that Kermode did not find what he was looking for is that he indicates a connection between the fan press and information on special effects. Though in a different context and through a different argument, this connection is also alluded to by Pierson, when she claims that

> those special effects technologies and techniques that have sought to bring impossible, never-before seen images to the screen have most often been the inspiration for fans' desire to participate in the production of special effects (whether in a professional capacity or in the form of home production).[8]

Pierson's claim echoes the connection (or complicity) between fans and the HFX makers to which Kermode refers. HFX-artist Rick Baker actually makes this connection very explicit when, in a tribute to Smith, he remembers how he made the move from fan (being dropped off at Smith's house in New York to meet his idol) to colleague (when he was asked by Smith to assist him on *The Exorcist*).[9]

The alignment between fan and artist is a key factor in the development of both HFX and the fan horror press in the 1970s, and it is pivotal for its rise from fan subculture to mainstream attention. But there is more than just alignment. With alignment comes a desire to evaluate HFX as an aesthetic element of film, and to create a new canon, one which includes and champions HFX's contribution to the subculture, one which promises to benefit both public (fan) and industry (HFX artist). In the editorial to the first issue of *L'Écran Fantastique*, in 1969, Jean-Claude Michel complains about how other fan magazines ignore the interest fans have in how films are made, promising that *L'Écran Fantastique* will provide topical up to date information from behind the scenes.[10] If this sounds familiar, it could be because almost every other fan magazine that followed in the 1970s makes the same commitment. In the editorial to the first issue, *Cinefantastique* editor Frederick Clarke boldly gives his magazine the subtitle "the magazine with a sense of wonder", and pledges to discuss "those crazy science-fiction films" with "all pretensions intact".[11] Not only does he, like all others, indicate a devotion to the discussion of HFX, he also implies a strong auteurist approach towards the subject, declaring a preparedness to evaluate the efforts of make up and stop-motion artists. Both *L'Écran Fantastique* and *Cinefantastique* try to combine an attitude of alignment with both topic and reader, with a somewhat critical attitude, one which expresses itself most vehemently in the dogged and fierce debates between editors and readers through which both magazines create a canon of the new horror and science-fiction cinema. And *L'Écran Fantastique* and *Cinefantastique* are but two examples of the many fan magazines appearing since the 1970s. *Starlog, Starfix, Fantoom, Halls of Horror, Deep Red, Mad Movies, Samhain, Fangoria* and many other magazines, appearing irregularly, but with increasing circulations, take a similar approach. Moreover, they also initiate a wider debate. While creating their own canon within their own specialisms, they often go into debate with each other (frequently on the instigation of readers, who are often non-discriminatory in their readership), and with the 'official critical press', using cross references to discussions of films, directors, and HFX, to create an overall canon of the subculture of which they see themselves part. Clarke's sneer at the "Big Mainstream Magazines" is a symptomatic example.[12] Because they have so often been derided or ignored by the official press, references to special effects form a vital part of this debate; in fact they become one of the common denominators governing it. Significantly, this mostly happens through interviews and behind-the-scenes accounts, formats implying the DIY attitude and the alignment between fans and artists – in fact turning the debate into the 'us against them' battle for which subcultures are known. Or as *Cinefantastique*'s editor puts it: "stick with us and watch the genre as it grows".[13] So, HFX becomes a key element of contention and admiration in the many publications which start to write about horror and science-fiction film enthusiastically, a tool for aesthetic discrimination, and an expression of an alignment with the (HFX) makers of the films.

By the end of the 1970s this until then largely subcultural debate spills over into mainstream culture, becoming part of the public sphere. There are several aspects to this shift. A first factor, a more or less logical result of the oppositioning of fan press versus official press, is the gradual inclusion of reports on HFX in mainstream public discourses, mostly as part of reports on a 'new wave of horror films'. Typical international examples include Robin Wood's essays on the horror film for *Film Comment*, Lawrence O'Toole's long essay 'The Cult of Horror' in *Maclean's*, and Mark Holthof's essays on horror in *Andere Sinema*.[14] In passing, it is worth noting that O'Toole identifies this new wave as one to which it is "easier to revel than to worry".[15] David Chute's long career article on David Cronenberg in *Film Comment* is perhaps the epitome of this factor, celebrating as it does not just Cronenberg's vision as an auteur, but also stressing the significance of HFX in his work.[16]

A second factor is linked to the industry itself. After the success of *The Exorcist*, HFX quickly gained prominence as a marketable part of a film project, and by the end of the 1970s and the beginning of the 1980s, after the much admired special effects in commercial successes such as *Dawn of the Dead* (1978), *Alien* (1979) and *An American Werewolf in London* (1981) the inclusion of HFX in marketing campaigns became increasingly important, with posters no longer promising psychological but also (and more so) very visceral thrills. This prominence of HFX in the making and selling of films can be illustrated by many examples, but a particularly poignant case is David Cronenberg's *Scanners* (1981), with its infamous 'exploding head' scene. Originally intended for Dick Smith, the HFX for the film were developed by Chris Walas and Stephan Dupuis, who, in the end, called in the help of Smith and Gary Zeller (of *Dawn of the Dead* fame) for some specific scenes, which Cronenberg only added during post production. One of these scenes was the exploding head scene, which caused outright furore upon the film's release. The critical reception of *Scanners* single-mindedly focused on this shot, and on stories of its making, as the film's mark of quality (most of the fan press), or of its lack of ethics (most of the other press), and even its potential cultural dangers (there were stories about how the scene would incite violence and suicide).[17] As Ian Conrich observes:

> *Scanners* opened Cronenberg up to a wider audience and much of this had been due to the considerable promotional support which the film had received. A well-organised advertising campaign in the many foreign markets and, most importantly, in the United States, had exploited dramatic images of the special effects.[18]

The exploding head scene was pivotal to that opening up. Within months, it had become a classic, being cited all across reviews and reports as a HFX tour de force. Actually, in several reviews it occupied a more central place than any special effects shot had ever received. Indicatively, it featured prominently on the cover of the tenth issue of *Fangoria*.[19] Occasionally this even led to the observation that people did not see *Scanners* as a story at all, it was just a 'stunt'; the sensation of the exploding head shot overshadowing all other elements of the film. The fact that HFX's most celebrated artists had collaborated on the film only served to enhance the significance of the special effects scenes. In fact, for the very first time, it foregrounded the effects artists in the mainstream press.[20] As such, it played a vital role in securing HFX a place in any wider debates on horror film culture. In addition, the exploding head from *Scanners* has

15. Cronenberg's classic HFX moment was celebrated on the front page of an early issue of *Fangoria*

become legend and different sources argue over whose creation it actually was (Zeller, Walas, Smith, or Dupuis), its notoriety living on (a recent issue of *SFX* celebrated it as the "most gruesome money shot in horror history").[21]

A third factor is the birth of the fan magazine *Fangoria*. Like *Scanners* became a nodal point for the practice of HFX artistry, *Fangoria* became a similar point of convergence for fan writings on HFX, and the connection between the two might not be that coincidental. Originally published as a spin-off of *Starlog*, it created a distinction between horror and science-fiction (and, after about a year or so, between horror and science-fiction fans, and later even between types of horror fans), and it paved the way for a discussion of HFX not only on aesthetic terms, but as downright auteurist celebration of horror effects. Indeed, as Conrich argues, the place of *Fangoria* is pivotal in any sketch of overall patterns of how (certain) horror film cultures were received. It not only accompanied and reported on the rise to fame of Cronenberg (and his HFX), but also of John Carpenter, and the *Friday the 13th* films, and it became an actual voice for the proliferation of a horror film culture that wished to align itself with a new kind of horror cinema and the new, more crude and 'grand guignol' kind of HFX that threatened to overwhelm the story so typical for *Scanners*, *The Thing* and others. As such it became the flag bearer of a more democratic, more adolescent, type of horror film culture, typified, like the accompanying subculture of heavy metal, by the explicit imagery T-shirt.[22]

The Professionalisation of Horror Effects

Fangoria may have spearheaded the public eruption of HFX, especially its socially dangerous and noisy side, but it was not the only publication discussing HFX. 1980 saw the appearance of yet another magazine discussing HFX: *Cinefex*. Unlike many fan based publications however, *Cinefex* was directed as much towards the industry as to lay readers or fans, and it made no excuses for being specialist, selective and elitist in its exclusive devotion to professional special effects. In 1981, Eric Barnouw published *The Magician and the Cinema*, a book that recounted the importance of special effects in the early days of cinema, and served as a reminder that special effects were far from new in cinema; they had a history.[23] Also in 1984, horror-bestseller Stephen King published his view on horror narratives in *Danse Macabre*, in which he asserted how crucial effects were to (telling and watching) horrific stories.[24] In 1984 the *Famous Monsters Handbook* was finally published in paperback, under the title *Dick Smith's Do-It-Yourself Monster Make-up*, a long-overdue auteurist recognition for the pioneer in the field of modern HFX.[25] There were of course many other signs of the emergence of HFX, but in addressing the sense of history, the professionalisation of the field, the increase of auteurist celebration, and the impact of HFX on horror narratives, these publications typify four key factors of the use of HFX in the 1980s, and its place in the public discourse on horror film.

The most important of these factors is undoubtedly the emphasis on the professionalisation of HFX, neatly encapsulated by the inception of *Cinefex*, founded by former *Cinefantastique* L.A. staff editor Don Shay (with Jordan Fox). As Pierson writes, the magazine had much more in common with the trade paper of the Society of Cinematographers, *American Cinematographer*, than with *Fangoria* or *Cinefantastique*.[26] The stress on first line reporting (a journalistic approach) in the latter are still present in *Cinefex*, in the abundance of inside, first-rate information offered through interviews, close looks behind-the-scenes, and detailed discussions of how HFX are made. In that sense *Cinefex* continues the tradition of the DIY attitude of the 1970s. But throughout the pages of the magazine there is also an increasing indication that the hobby fan is no longer the prime audience. Instead, as Pierson observes, the publication addressed

> all the animators, modelers, puppeteers, makeup artists, and visual effects supervisors and engineers working in the contemporary effects industry [including] all the film, video, and multimedia producers and students who specialise in knowing about the techniques of cinematic illusion.[27]

Pierson may continue that this audience does not necessarily have "a professional stake in this knowledge", but the impression given does invite links with the professional industry.[28] The contributions are lengthy and incredibly detailed, written by specialists (Fox, Paul Sammon, Shay, Tim Lucas) who also write for trade papers (like *American Cinematographer*) and the fan press (like *Cinefantastique*), and the critical tone that was reserved for aesthetic evaluation is now used for making distinctions between types of HFX, and approaches to producing them. The overall tone of *Cinefex* is one of supporting HFX as a professional enterprise. A perfect example is the career article on Rick Baker published in 1984.[29] It is a good indication of the central position that HFX artists were beginning to acquire, not only in the public sphere, but also within the industry. Baker is heralded as one of the most dedicated and consistently innovative HFX artists, and his work on both "low budget offerings" like *It's Alive* (1974) or *Videodrome* (1983), or "loftier assignments" like *Star Wars* (1977), *King Kong* (1976) and *An American Werewolf in London*, is discussed as paradigmatic for the craft.[30] The attention for details in this article is astounding, up to a paragraph long discussion of "a solenoid-controlled valve system that operated via an organ keyboard" for one specific effect in *Videodrome* – one that was eventually not even used in the film.[31] Perhaps the most explicit sign of the professionalist aspirations of *Cinefex* lies in the introduction to the issue, when Fox states that

> When ten-year old Rick Baker began experimenting . . . motion picture make up – the kind that transforms actors into monsters, aliens or even animals – was not at all the stellar occupation it has come to be; and at the time, there was little in the way of instructional materials and enthusiastic novice could draw upon, let alone a clearly marked path toward professional involvement.[32]

Subsequent issues reinforced this approach. In the years that followed the way in which HFX was discussed consistently stressed the specialist aspects of the vocation, resulting in the gradual acceptance of HFX as a *profession*, not just in the critical reception but also on a wider platform. By the late 1980s and early 1990s, this led to a reputation of HFX as a cinematic profession in its own right, and *Cinefex* its near-official trade publication.

The auteurist and professional approaches towards HFX also led to distinctions between types of HFX artists and their arts. Whereas initially only occasional distinctions were made between make-up artists, visual effects supervisors, puppeteers (they were often irrelevant to the polyvalence people like Dick Smith or Rick Baker displayed), the 1980s saw a gradual specialisation in specific tasks within HFX. Gary Zeller was first and foremost a make-up artist, Chris Walas primarily a creature creator. Next to that, variations in status became important – the reputations of HFX artists gradually became measured by their public status. In some way, this division had already been present in the early celebrations of HFX, especially in oppositions between 'veterans' and 'novices' – a relationship perfectly embodied by Smith and Baker. But during the 1980s more sophisticated distinctions arose. The most significant one is that between industry-artists and independent-artists. Both categories encapsulate a degree of professionalisation, but indicate a different attitude towards the profession. The independent artists (such as Mark Shostrom or Greg Nicotero) were the people championed by *Fangoria* and the more obscure fan press, who preferred non-mainstream productions that continued to offer possibilities for DIY and 'hobbyist' attitudes to break new ground, even if this meant working to smaller budgets, and having only the possibility to do a few 'money shots' per film. In return, these artists gained underground and cult reputations.

Undoubtedly the most notorious example of this type of HFX artist is Tom Savini. His big public breakthroughs were *Friday the 13th* (1980) and George A. Romero's *Dawn of the Dead* fittingly a film very much noted for its splatter HFX, but not one which is considered to be at its technical or professional forefront (another way in which it distinguished itself from more slick uses of HFX). Savini's status is as much derived from its HFX work as from his public status as a talismanic figure of independent horror. To begin with, his frequent cameo appearances in films for which he did the HFX work meant that he quickly became a generic signal for fan viewers, a statement of a specific political position in horror culture. As Kermode puts it:

> We understood that when special-effects maestro Tom Savini popped up on-screen as 'third bystander from the left' (as he did with increasing frequency) it was the film-makers' way of winking at the fans in the audience, to which the correct response was a knowing laugh.[33]

In addition, Savini used his public status to give his work a social relevance, commenting on how he felt his HFX work was the result of a personal obsession with the real-life horrors he witnessed during his tour of duty as a GI in Vietnam, something that was, of course, first reported in *Fangoria*.[34] This declaration of cultural inspiration, and of individual creation out of personal experience, perfectly fits the DIY attitude of the original HFX artist. Unwillingly perhaps, it also linked Savini's work to a growing scholarly interest in the horror genre, advanced by Robin Wood, that aimed for establishing connections between horrific representations, and contemporary culture in all its forms.[35] It added to Savini's reputation as an original DIY HFX artist, and gave him, next to a cult reputation, an aura of cultural relevance.

The industry-artists, in contrast, were the people championed by *Cinefex*, who dedicated themselves to working in the mainstream of the film industry, delivering flexible solutions to ready questions, working to (and with) other's agendas, and, usually, with bigger budgets. A good example of this type of HFX artist is Chris Walas, who did the HFX-work for *Gremlins* and *The Fly*, two films which defined HFX practice in the 1980s. As Sammon aptly points out in his discussion of Walas's work on *Gremlins*, his work especially in (but not limited to) the 1980s is often associated with "resounding box-office success" and "mainstream filmmaking".[36] Instead of deriving his inspiration from personal experience, Walas is an exponent of one of the L.A. college film programmes, from where he went straight into the industry. Unlike Savini, Walas is far less of a paradigmatic generic marker, with significant parts of his work (like *Raiders of the Lost Ark* [1981] and *Romancing the Stone* [1984]) located outside the genre. This of course gives him a more marginal position in debates about horror culture. Furthermore, Walas is also often seen as an HFX artist who deals not so much with personal obsessions, but with professional 'challenges'.[37] He also carries with him an aura of 'grandeur', of large-scale production values. As Sammon explains, when Walas became involved in the production of *Gremlins* "it became obvious that the special effects were going to be more expansive and the picture more expensive than Steven [Spielberg] had hoped".[38] However, it should be clear here that this industry connection in no way meant that Walas was regarded as less of an HFX auteur. On the contrary, he was (and is) very much considered to be a prime HFX auteur, with his ability to create large scale cinematic illusions unparalleled (arguably he was the most fêted of HFX artists in the 1980s). By way of illustration, an example of an industry-person who did not really make it to the auteurist A-list is Richard Edlund, HFX supervisor for *Fright Night* (1985) and *Poltergeist* (1982). On both occasions, and notwithstanding celebratory essays on his work in *Cinefex*, and multiple awards for his contributions, the films were regarded in the horror discourse uniquely as Tom Holland and Steven Spielberg and/or Tobe Hooper films respectively.[39]

The Impact of Horror Effects on Narratives

A key factor in the use of HFX in the 1980s is the gradual impact HFX began to have on horror narratives. This factor too is linked to the increasing professionalisation and auteurist celebration. What both types of HFX artists have in common is their ability to use their work in such an effective way that its impact on horror narratives regularly began to outweigh other textual considerations. As has been suggested at the start of this essay, Sammon considered the HFX for *Gremlins* almost as important as the story, and for *The Fly*, the HFX perhaps *are* the story, as most reviews of the film illustrate.[40] Similarly, *The Evil Dead* drew more attention because of its over-the-top HFX than as a result of its storytelling. In fact, most reviews and comments on the film seem to agree that in *The Evil Dead* the HFX disguise the fact that there is not much of a storyline.[41] Together, these three films demonstrate the extent to which Philip Brophy's concept of 'horrality' seems to operate in the mid 1980s.[42] What Brophy does not note, however, are the different ways in which this shift from narrative to HFX display occurs. Basically, I propose there are three forms in which HFX (can) take over classical functions of the narrative: through overkill instead of psychology, through character performance, and by becoming the locus through which the story develops. All three forms are exemplified by *The Evil Dead*, *Gremlins* and *The Fly* respectively.

As suggested above, the HFX in *The Evil Dead* are not really relevant to the story. Even more so, the way in which HFX supervisor Tom Sullivan used HFX was not even intended to fit the narrative. Quite the contrary, the narrative functioned as an excuse to display the technological and formal ability to create over-the-top effects. The use of HFX is, then, an example of overkill: the monsters in the film never seem to give up, which results in an extreme level of mutilation and "claret heavy excesses" according to Jason Arnopp.[43] Very much in the line of what Brophy suggested, *The Evil Dead*'s appeal lies not in how twists and turns in the narrative provide psychological explanations for the horror portrayed; rather it lies in the spectacular experienced by the audience. And the twists and turns are the result of the desire to include yet another thrill, rather than an explanation. In the horror culture of the time this was not seen as a problem, and Sam Raimi and Sullivan found themselves touring the UK to "demonstrate how the special effects in the film were created, showing the live audiences the cinematic art of dismemberment and mutilation", a convincing sign of its relevance to debates on horror.[44] As Kate Egan suggests in her research on the reception of 'video nasties' (of which *The Evil Dead* was considered a prime example), this perceived lack of narrative coherence made the film particularly vulnerable for attacks on its portrayal of splatter: the censors saw no narrative justification for it.[45]

The character related HFX are of a completely different order. They are very much functional to the narrative; they are in fact imperative for the telling of the story. Without the central monsters or creatures of *It's Alive* or *King Kong*, there would not be much of a story. At the same time, however, the monster is only one character in the narrative. This often poses an extra problem for HFX creators, as they are caught between providing a spectacle of monstrosity, and holding back on excess to prevent the monster dominating at the cost of the narrative. In 1980s films like *Gremlins*, this balance becomes a crucial issue, to the point where HFX supported creatures began to weigh heavier than ever before on storylines. The distinction between the good-natured mogwai and the evil-natured gremlin creatures are essential examples of this development. The visible differences between the creatures, and hence the differences in use of HFX materials, became the drive of the narration, replacing the narrative function of live performers and turning them into bystanders. *Gremlins* updated the function as characters in the old tradition of the monster movie (which director Joe Dante of course references), and it proved that HFX could account for both good and bad in a story, and could hence atone for a wide range of narrative functions. This actually lifted HFX's relevance to that of the flexibility usually reserved for live performers.[46] As a result much of the reception of *Gremlins* not only emphasises the function of the creatures as an active agent in the story's development, but it actually also discusses the acting performance of the creatures themselves – one more way in which HFX penetrated any debates about the horror genre.

The way in which HFX becomes the locus through which the story develops is closely related to the previous two forms. Once psychology is replaced by HFX thrills, and once (performances of) HFX characters are as important as live ones, there is no reason why HFX creations, and HFX itself, should not become the major agent through which horror narratives are told. Among the many films that fit this claim, *The Thing* and *The Fly* are perhaps the most prominent. Ian Conrich and Anne Billson have described how much of the critical reaction to *The Thing* concentrated on the preference for, or disgust of, its special effects.[47] I would like to elaborate on the reception of *The Fly*, a crucial example of the evolution of HFX and, by way of its Chris Walas-created effects, a prime marker for the professionalism sketched above. As practically all reviews and reports on the film testify, discussing the HFX for *The Fly* is the only way into making sense of the film.[48] The difficulty film critics have with coming to terms with this evolution is beautifully demonstrated by the fact that most accounts of the film are neatly divided into two parts. In the first part of many *The Fly* reviews much emphasis is put on the psychological background of the story (lonely Seth Brundle tries to impress Veronica but he fails to win her heart, driving him into a doomed experiment), and the gradual display of the HFX-created horrific changes that happen to Brundle are a logical result (and metaphor) of the inner torment he experiences. So far, HFX functions traditionally in these accounts, i.e. they are seen as visually supporting a narrative development. But it is remarkable how the second half of almost every *The Fly* review is dominated by a focus on how HFX moves from supporting to leading the development of the story through different (physical) stages of decay of the protagonist's body, at first hiding the body of actor Jeff Goldblum under layers of make-up, and finally effectively replacing it by a Brundlefly mechanical creature oozing slime and blood. For many critics, this shift is a reason to dislike the film, to dismiss it as "tasteless" and "vulgar", and criticise how the development of the story is halted in favour of a "sick spectacle".[49] Many other critics, however, accept the contribution HFX makes to the story, and treat the transformation of Brundle as the narrative key to the film, hereby granting the HFX the status of prime locus and agent of the story, acknowledging their impact on horror narratives in general, and securing their place in the horror discourse.[50]

16. The Brundlefly spectacle: The HFX of the human-fly hybrid dominated *The Fly* (1986)

Conclusion

The story of HFX does not end with the 1980s.[51] By the beginning of the 1990s, the impact of HFX on any cultural debates of horror, in the fan press or in specialised publications, but also in the wider public domain, was showing itself in a myriad of effects-related jargon use. HFX-artists are classified and discussed as auteurs (both industry-related and cultist ones), artists, veterans, novices, craftsmen, geniuses, mavericks. And the subtle differences between kinds of make-up, puppeteering, pyrotechnics, animatronics, prosthetics and creature creation are all signs of the increasing importance of the HFX industry on (horror) film practice. Apart from the increasing finesses in nomenclature and status, the early 1990s largely confirmed the trends set during the 1980s, with the move to digital effects as a loss or a displacement of handcraftsmanship, and the use of HFX as homage in film style and the introduction of digital effects as noteworthy novel elements.

The use of HFX in stylising homages is closely related to their narrative importance, the difference being that in the case of the early 1990s homages HFX were more often used to invoke a sense of history, rather than push boundaries. Because of the fact their use had been acknowledged for over a decade, it is only logical that the interest in the history of HFX also led to practical applications, in casu celebrating the use of HFX from previous times. Such tributes to history are not at all unusual in the 1990s, a period often labelled as postmodern in its reflexivity and conscious referencing and raiding of past cinema cultures. For HFX, such homages, not just to the craftsmanship of the 1980s, but even further back to 'old school' effects, most notably showed in its contribution to the aesthetic constitution of the short but powerful revival of the Gothic narrative in the first half of the 1990s, with films like *Edward Scissorhands* (1990), *Bram Stoker's Dracula* (1992), *Mary Shelley's Frankenstein* (1994) and *Interview with the Vampire* (1994). A more recent example of this includes the work of Howard Berger's big effects studio KNB FX on the small-budget werewolf films *Ginger Snaps: Unleashed* (2004) and *Ginger Snaps Back: The Beginning* (2004), which Berger saw as opportunities to do "good old school monster movies".[52] It should be no surprise that these films attracted significant attention for HFX artists. The display of HFX's self-awareness with their own history, and its impact on narratives, has given it a status in horror culture similar to that of discussions of mise-en-scène in the film culture propagated by the 1950s *Cahiers du Cinéma*, or of montage in the 1920s formalist debates of film culture: the most significant formal tool in presenting itself as a legitimate cultural debate.

The introduction of digital effects only added to that legitimacy, albeit from a decidedly different angle. For the status of HFX in the horror film culture sketched above, digital effects posed significant challenges for employment (artists being threatened to become mere 'personnel' again), and for technological and production economies. For digital effects, the early 1990s are what Pierson calls the "wonder years", but for HFX they are a mixed blessing.[53] There is no space for elaboration here, but it is telling that even though Pierson is barely discussing horror at all, and even though horror film culture often seemingly antagonises digital effects, her assertion that these years were popular because "they offered viewers the opportunity to participate in a popular cultural event that put the display of the digital artefact – or computer-generated image – at the centre of the cinematic experience" still has validity for HFX, if only in the form of a wider visibility.[54] To me, this mixed blessing is crucial for understanding how the rise of digital effects did not just cause a backlash in the use of (by now) more traditional HFX, at least not initially, and why these years are truly wonder years abounding with interesting experiments, and generally lifting the status of HFX in the horror discourse.

These two elements demonstrate how HFX are increasingly important in contemporary cinema, not just as an aside to 'proper' film aesthetics, but also, and increasingly so, as a powerful part of the synergetic product any horror film is. In addition, and thanks to the efforts of fans, magazines and many social debates on horror cinema, HFX have acquired a central position in any debate on horror films; a sign of its cultural relevance, for better or for worse.

Notes

1. Paul Sammon, 'Never Feed them after Midnight', *Cinefex*, no. 19, November 1984, p. 1.
2. Michele Pierson, 'CGI Effects in Hollywood Science-Fiction Cinema 1989–1995: the Wonder Years', *Screen*, vol. 40, no. 2, 1999, p. 159.
3. Philip Brophy makes this connection in the introduction to his article when he asks what the "notion of special effects in the cinema" is. Philip Brophy, 'Horrality – the Textuality of Contemporary Horror Films', *Screen*, vol. 27, no. 1, January–February, 1986, p. 2. Another early example is John Brosnan, *Movie Magic: the Story of Special Effects in the Cinema*. London: Sphere Books, 1977.
4. I would like to thank Kate Egan, Julian Petley, and Ian Conrich for comments on the topic of this essay.
5. Stan Winston, 'Dear Dick (advertisement)', *Cinefex*, no. 62, June 1995, p. 105; Don Shay, 'Dick Smith: 50 Years in Make Up', *Cinefex*, no. 62, June 1995, p. 112.

6. Shay, p. 120.
7. Mark Kermode, 'I was a Teenage Horror Fan: or, 'How I Learned To Stop Worrying and Love Linda Blair', in Martin Barker and Julian Petley, eds, *Ill Effects; the Media/Violence Debate (Second Edition)*. London: Routledge, 2001, p. 128.
8. Michele Pierson, *Special Effects; Still in Search of Wonder*, New York: Columbia University Press, 2002, pp. 2–3.
9. Rick Baker, 'Rick Baker on Dick Smith', *Cinefex*, no. 62, June 1995, p. 81.
10. Jean-Claude Michel, 'Editorial', *L'Écran Fantastique*, no. 1, February 1969, p. 2.
11. Frederick Clarke, 'Editorial: How's Your sense of wonder?', *Cinefantastique*, vol. 1, no. 1, Fall 1970, p. 3.
12. Ibid.
13. Frederick Clarke, 'Editorial', *Cinefantastique*, vol. 2, no. 4, 1972, p. 3.
14. Robin Wood, 'Return of the Repressed', *Film Comment*, vol. 14, no. 4, July–August 1978, pp. 24–32; Robin Wood, 'Gods and Monsters', *Film Comment*, vol. 14, no. 5, September–October 1978, pp. 19–25; Lawrence O'Toole, 'The Cult of Horror', *Maclean's*, 16 July 1979, pp. 46–7, 49–50; Marc Holthof, 'Alien', *Andere Sinema*, no. 12, October 1979, pp. 22–4; Marc Holthof, 'It's Alive', *Andere Sinema*, no. 21, September 1980, pp. 14–17.
15. O'Toole, p. 47.
16. David Chute, 'He Came From Within', *Film Comment*, vol. 16, no. 2, March–April 1980, pp. 36–9, 42.
17. See Ian Conrich, 'An Aesthetic Sense: Cronenberg and Neo-Horror Film Culture', in Michael Grant, ed., *The Modern Fantastic: The Films of David Cronenberg*, Trowbridge: Flicks Books, 2000, p. 40.
18. Ibid.
19. Ibid., p. 35.
20. Ibid.; Ernest Mathijs, *Referentiekaders van Filmkritiek; een onderzoek naar het gebruik van referneties in de interpetatie en evaluatie van David Cronenberg* (*Frames of Reference of Film Criticism: an Investigation into the Interpretation and Evaluation of David Cronenberg*), unpublished Phd Dissertation, Free University of Brussels, 2000, pp. 327–30, 378–9.
21. Jason Arnopp, 'Ouch! That'll Smart in the Morning', *SFX, Horror Special*, June 2004, p. 49.
22. For an extended discussion of how *Fangoria* aligned itself with HFX, in casu John Carpenter's *The Thing*, see Ian Conrich, 'Killing Time . . . and Time Again: the Popular Appeal of Carpenter's Horrors and the Impact of *The Thing* and *Halloween*', in Ian Conrich and David Woods, eds, *The Cinema of John Carpenter: The Technique of Terror*, London: Wallflower Press, 2004, pp. 91–106.
23. Erik Barnouw, *The Magician and the Cinema*, Oxford: Oxford University Press, 1981.
24. Stephen King, *Stephen King's Danse Macabre*, New York: Everest House, 1981.

25. Dick Smith, *Dick Smith's Do-It-Yourself Monster Make-up*, New York: Harmony Books, 1984.
26. Pierson, *Special Effects*, p. 7.
27. Ibid., p. 49.
28. Ibid.
29. Jordan Fox, 'Rick Baker – Maker of Monsters, Master of the Apes', *Cinefex*, no. 16, April 1984, pp. 4–71.
30. Ibid., p. 3.
31. Ibid., p. 56.
32. Ibid., p. 3.
33. Kermode, p. 129.
34. I owe this reference to Ian Conrich, who pointed out to me how *Fangoria* was instrumental to the creation and maintenance of the reputation of Savini. A more recent source for Savini's comments on how Vietnam inspired his work can be found in the documentary *The American Nightmare* (2000).
35. Robin Wood, 'An Introduction to the American Horror Film', in Andrew Britton, Robin Wood, Richard Lippe and Tony Williams, eds, *The American Nightmare; Essays on the Horror Film*. Toronto: Festival of Festivals, 1979, pp. 7–28.
36. Sammon, p. 2.
37. Ibid., p. 6.
38. Ibid.
39. See Jennifer Benidt, and Janine Pourroy, 'Fright Night', *Cinefex*, no. 25, February 1986, pp. 54–67.
40. See Sammon; Tim Lucas, 'The Fly Papers', *Cinefex*, no. 28, November 1986, pp. 4–29; Ernest Mathijs, 'AIDS References in the Critical Reception of David Cronenberg: It May Not Be Such a Bad Disease after All', *Cinema Journal*, vol. 42, no. 4, 2003, pp. 29–45.
41. See Kate Egan, *Trash or Treasure?: Censorship and the Changing Meanings of the Video Nasties*, Manchester: Manchester University Press, 2007.
42. Philip Brophy, pp. 2–13.
43. Jason Arnopp, 'The Filth and the Fury', *SFX, Horror Special*, June 2004, pp. 100–9.
44. Nick Wenham, 'Putting the H Back into Horror', *Video Trade Weekly*, no. 59, 20 January 1983, p. 7.
45. Egan.
46. See Sammon, p. 2.
47. Anne Billson, *The Thing*, London: British Film Institute, 1997; Conrich, 'Killing Time', pp. 95–6.
48. See Mathijs, *Referentiekaders van Filmkritiek*, pp. 330–1, 433–7, 496–500; Mathijs, 'AIDS References'.
49. Mathijs, *Referentiekaders van Filmkritiek*, p. 435.
50. The fact that *The Fly* is directed by Cronenberg, whose 1980s reputation is a synonym for horror auteurship, obviously helps in securing this status. See Mathijs, *Referentiekaders van Filmkritiek*, pp. 436; Mathijs, 'AIDS References'.

51. For an extended discussion of HFX in the 1990s, see Ernest Mathijs, *Bloody Ugly: A Cultural History of Special Effects in the Modern Horror Film*. Working paper, Centre For Research into Extreme and Alternative Media. University of Wales, Aberystwyth.

52. I thank Emily Perkins and Howard Berger for sharing their views on the HFX of the *Ginger Snaps* trilogy with me.

53. See Pierson, 'CGI Effects'.

54. Ibid., p. 157.

9

The *Friday the 13th* Films and the Cultural Function of a Modern Grand Guignol

IAN CONRICH

The Theatre of the Grand Guignol, the Parisian performance space associated with horrific drama, ran from 1897 to 1962. The graphic manner in which the plays were enacted involved the foregrounding of moments of torture, mutilation, surgery and execution. The popular performances attracted a regular audience who became known as 'Guignolers'; a group of bloodthirsty devotees who exhibited an insatiability for brutality and gore.

A modern comparable can be found in the series of *Friday the 13th* films, which to date number twelve instalments. I would argue that the greatest significance of this series was its influence on the slasher film, a form which dominated the horror genre between 1980 and 1984, and which often featured a faceless killer stalking and chopping down a seemingly endless series of victims. The popular view is that the slasher films of the horror New Wave began with *Halloween* (1978). The importance of this film is undeniable, yet the commerciality of *Friday the 13th* (1980) showed that the success of *Halloween* was repeatable and it was only from this position that there was an explosion in the number of slasher films produced. But by 1984, this subgenre had collapsed and the fourth *Friday the 13th* film, in what was already then the longest running slasher series, was announced to be the last – 'The Final Chapter'. The success of the post-slasher *A Nightmare on Elm Street*, in 1984, appears to have inspired the release of *Friday the 13th Part V – A New Beginning*, and by 1993 and the production *Jason Goes to Hell: The Final Friday*, there had been nine films in the series in total, as well as a television series, and a cultural trade in Jason related merchandise. The tenth film in the series, *Jason X* (2001), mixes horror with science-fiction as a frozen Jason is thawed in 2455 A.D. and stalks a spaceship full of teenagers; the eleventh film pits two horror icons in *Freddy vs. Jason* (2003); whilst 2009 sees a revisiting and remaking of the original legend in *Friday the 13th*.[1]

Despite the repetitive nature of these films, they have acquired a cult following demonstrated perhaps, today, by the number of devoted websites. The reduction of the story for each of the films in this series results in a recounting of the methodical slaughter of each helpless individual; what has been termed the 'body count'. The doomed teenagers have names, but they appear of less importance than the omnipotent executioner, Jason Voorhees. What does matter in these films is the character who is Jason's next victim and the manner in which they are despatched. On several websites a record of the deceased is maintained, though it would appear not out of respect for the dead but as a celebration of the executioner's brutality and inventiveness.[2] Each victim is numbered, named (almost always by first name only) and listed in order of death with a brief description of the manner in which they were killed – for example, for *Friday the 13th Part 2* (1981), "1: Alice – stabbed in the temple with an ice pick"; "6: Mark – macheted in the face".[3] There exists a relationship between Jason, the executioner, and the various teenagers, his victims. There is also, though, the relationship between the films, the site of execution, and the audience, the filmgoer, who pays for and thereby supports the continuance of the brutality. It is the reception of the *Friday the 13th* films within popular culture, and their function as a modern grand guignol, that will be addressed within this discussion.

The Theatre of the Grand Guignol

In Mel Gordon's study of Grand Guignol, he argues that there were approximately 1,200 dramas and sketches produced for the famous Parisian Theatre and its competitors. He focuses on the 100 most popular and most performed productions – which often lasted no more than one act – and divides plots into Horror Plays, Comedies and Farces, and Dramatic Plays. The Horror Plays are then subdivided into nine categories: Helplessness, Infanticide, Insanity, Mutilation, Mysterious Death, Suffering of the Innocent, Suicide, Surgery and Vengeance. Furthermore, Gordon notes six subsidiary themes: Exoticism, Hypnosis, Imprisonment, Parisian Lowlife, Play-Transforming-Into-Terror and Prostitution.[4] In the 'mutilation' plays *The Garden of Torture* (1922, written by Pierre Chaine) and *A Crime in the Madhouse* (1925, André de Lorde and Alfred Binet) facial disfigurement appears a forte with a knitting needle and heated sharp implements used to pierce eyes, and a woman's face charred as it is thrust against a hot stove plate; in *The Little House in Auteuil* (1907, Robert Scheffer and Georges

Liguereux) a bound man's teeth and nails are extracted and his eyes burnt. A celebrated performer was Maxa, and as Gordon writes:

> During her relatively brief career, she was murdered more than 10,000 times and in some 60 ways. A few examples: devoured by a ravenous puma, cut into 93 pieces and glued back together, smashed by a roller-compressor, burnt alive, cut open by a travelling salesman who wanted her intestines; she was also raped over 3000 times . . . [it was] calculated that on the stage, Maxa cried "Help!" 983 times, "Murderer!" 1,263 times, and "Rape!" 1,804 and $\frac{1}{2}$ times.[5]

The horrific nature of such performances was cushioned by moments of black humour, or comedy sketches which, as Gordon observes, would alternate in a regular evening's programme – "three comedies (and farces) and three horror plays (or psychological dramas). The patented whiplash effect . . . known as 'hot and cold showers'".[6]

The Theatre of the Grand Guignol – a former chapel for a Jansenist convent – retained the wood carvings and designs in the ceiling and doors created during the earlier occupancy, which added to the Gothic atmosphere of the venue. Though it was the style of the gruesome effects which managed most dramatically to heighten the tension of the performance. The wounds and severed limbs, and the retractable weapons that appeared to penetrate a performer's body, were realistic and were the tricks of the act. As Gordon writes, a company manager

> frequently purchased different animal eyeballs from taxidermists – not only for visual realism, when characters eye's [sic] were gouged out, but for the organ's ability to bounce when they hit the stage floor.[7]

The believability of such gory effects ensured the shocked reactions of the audience – a strong performance was gauged by the numbers of fainting patrons – whilst also often sustaining their morbid curiosity.

Modern Horrific Tricks

Body horror marks the style of the neo-horror film, which had emerged in the late seventies. As I have written "the horror New Wave demonstrated a desire for producing spectacular set pieces, which were designed to parade the fantastic anatomical creations of special effects technicians".[8] Aiding the realisation of these persuasive body aberrations were the advances being made in effects technology, the implementation of new foam latex application and the ever-innovative design of prosthetics. The *Friday the 13th* series began in neo-horror's late formative period and initially displayed the effects 'wizardry' of Tom Savini (*Friday the 13th*), and Carl Fullerton (*Friday the 13th Part 2*). Both were interviewed in the early issues of the premier horror fanzine, *Fangoria* – Savini in issue 6, and Fullerton in issue 13 – where they discussed their craft for these films.[9]

What is striking from the interview with Savini (which includes a discussion of his work for *Dawn of the Dead* [1978]) and Fullerton (which includes his work for *The Wolfen* [1981]) is the care and attention given to attaining realistic detail for achieving the required effect. Savini states that when he "first started working with foam latex, it was so hard to get it to look right, getting the right porous skin texture, or to get that thin edge, so you don't get a line between latex and skin area".[10] Fullerton explained that for his effects he "didn't saturate the wounds with blood . . . in many films of this type, the make-up artist will just cover everything with blood so that there's no chance to *see* his craftsmanship".[11] The craft is a learning process – particularly with technology that was then still in its infancy – and presents constant challenges – "learning effects is sometimes just a matter of making every mistake there is to make before you get the technique down", Savini confesses.[12] As with the graphic effects employed at the Theatre of the Grand Guignol, knowledge, technique and resourcefulness manage to combine for the creation of an horrific moment that is designed to be seen and believed. Sean S. Cunningham, the director, producer and writer of *Friday the 13th* said that Savini's work was so good "that you find yourself wanting to leave in more of an effects scene than you should to get a strong shock effect. It can go over the border of shock; gore itself isn't scary, it's disgusting".[13]

The desire to better the effects of each previous instalment has lead to the immoderation of the *Friday the 13th* series. Not only a desire to better the number of killings but the manner of each murder. Style and invention was very much a consideration of Fullerton's when working on the effects:

> I always knew that there would be a comparison between *Part II* and the first *Friday the 13th*, so I wanted to have something in the film that *had not* been seen before. That's why I wanted to have the double pinioning. We saw an after sex murder in the first one, but that was through a guy's neck. This killing was through two *full* bodies.[14]

Fullerton then details, at great length, the creative process of this effect. *Fangoria*'s estimated readership included a significant number of 'wannabe' filmmakers and effects fans and such text supported by graphic illustrations was part of the fanzine's identity. At one point an adolescent glee is almost apparent as Fullerton satisfyingly recounts his achievement:

We got the blood to spurt by using two different types of blood pumps. One was a standard plastic or metal syringe. The other was an actual garden pump that is used to spray plants. We cut off its end and we got what is called "a trombone action". It sprayed blood *everywhere*. Another thing that made the back effect so terrific was that in addition to the blood pouring out, we had flesh pushing out of the wound made from gelatin. The entire sequence was extremely graphic.[15]

Credit for this particular method of murder, however, belonged to the *giallo* terror-thrillers of Mario Bava. The double pinioning referred to by Fullerton, where copulating teenagers, one on top of the other, are skewered together, had been filmed previously in *Ecologia del Delitto* (1971).[16] Furthermore, the mask that Jason rejects moments before on the stairs, appears as a reversal of the beginning scene of *Halloween*.

Body Counts

Within a heredity of the slasher film, the influences for *Friday the 13th* are John Carpenter's *Halloween* – itself influenced by *Psycho* (1960) – and *Ecologia del Delitto* – an extension of Bava's style that was most startling in *Sei Donne per l'Assassino* (1964).[17] There are similarities between aspects of Carpenter's horror and Bava's terror-thrillers: the use of a prowling or stalking camera, voyeuristic camera positions, fluid camera movement. But there are also notable differences and the early *Friday the 13th* films can appear more influenced by Italian than American cinema. If *Halloween* offers story development, then Bava's terror-thrillers are basic plots offering a systematic series of murders. *Halloween*'s violence was distinct and brutal but, in comparison to Bava, largely blood-less and less stylised and centre-screen. The killer's weapon of choice, in *Halloween*, remained relatively focused – a large knife – whilst Bava's killing implements could be more unique and scene specific.

The *Friday the 13th* films offer a thread-bare story – Tim Pulleine writing on *Friday the 13th* describes the "narrative sense" as "less than riveting"; and writes that *Friday the 13th Part 2* is "no less feeble in plot".[18] On this are built the moments of grand guignol – interventions that allow for the graphic executions and the showcasing of the special effects. The importance of these moments is clear in the publicity for the films. Posters for slasher films such as *The Burning* (1979), *Halloween II* (1981) and *Alone in the Dark* (1982) – the former featuring a man desperately attempting to run from a menacing and shadowy figure, the second displaying a superimposed image of a demonic skull and a pumpkin, the latter the image of an eye, terrified, peering through a slight opening in a door –

17. Foregrounding brutality, murder, and the mask of the executioner, Jason Voorhees, in the British posters for the films in the *Friday the 13th* series

carried in their narrative image a message of panic and fear. In contrast, the British and American posters for *Friday the 13th Part 2*, *Friday the 13th Part 3 (3D)* (1982), *Friday the 13th – The Final Chapter* (1984), *Friday the 13th Part V – A New Beginning* (1985), *Friday the 13th Part VII – The New Blood* (1988), and *Friday the 13th Part VIII – Jason takes Manhattan* (1989) foreground brutality and murder through a weapon – a blood-dripping axe, a penetrating knife, or a machete, poised and ready.

Jason's hockey mask, the executioner's disguise which he first wears in part 3, appears on all the subsequent posters and is part of the signified threat. Yet, in the posters for parts 2 and 3 the weapons are wielded by a simple sketched and blackened figure. I would propose with these posters, that the iconic figure of Jason only begins with the fourth instalment in the series – the first film to carry a design featuring Jason's mask, and an image that is such a strong signifier that it can appear solo. Each of the subsequent five posters displays the mask prominently. Prior to the iconic presence of Jason, the posters simply emphasised slaughter – a fact reinforced on the poster for part 2, which declares "The body count continues . . .". Never has the British or American poster image for a *Friday the 13th* film promised anything less than the attraction of an executioner, and a series of executions.

Executioner/Executions

"13 is an unlucky number . . . but out here so are 1 through 12", declares the trailer for *Friday the 13th Part 3*. In a manner similar to the trailers for parts 1 and 2, a series of numbers (1–12 for parts 1 and 3, 14–23 for part 2) flash up on screen accompanying an image of a victim-to-be.[19] The trailer for part 3 also announces "Jason – you can't fight him. You can't stop him". Jason can be stopped and he is assailed with a variety of weapons throughout the series. Killing Jason is the problem and it was not until part 4 – 'The Final Chapter' – that he was finally terminated, macheted and his body repeatedly hacked by an uncontrollable Tommy Jarvis. A vengeful medic, Roy Burns, adopts the Jason disguise – easily acquired and exchanged – for part 5. But with part 6, and the addition of a supernatural element – Jason dramatically revived from his tomb with a bolt of lightning – the series entered the realm of post-slashers such as the *Nightmare on Elm Street* (1984–2010), *Hellraiser* (1987–2005), *Child's Play* (1988–2004), *Puppetmaster* (1989–2004) and *Candyman* (1992–1999) films, where the killer continues to live after death through possession, transference, alternative dimensions, the imaginary, the hyperreal, and freakish and bizarre twists of science and nature. With such plot 'logic' Jason can now be utterly destroyed – at the start of part 9 he is blown into pieces – but appear increasingly indestructible and powerful. In part 9, Jason's heart is eaten by the coroner who becomes possessed; others are possessed by Jason through penetrating extensions that facilitate transference from one body to another. In part 8, Jason is revived by a high electrical charge from a submerged cable, and in part 7, he emerges from his watery grave thanks to the psycho-kinetic powers of a young woman.

With the *Friday the 13th* series so dependent on its spectacle of a series of executions, the maintenance of an ever-present omnipotent executioner is essential. Like *Halloween*'s Michael Myers, and *The Texas Chain Saw Massacre*'s Leatherface, the executioner's mask establishes a cold, mechanical and faceless killer devoid of personality.[20] The mask also aids the detachment that the executioner – the professional killer – requires in order to function unhindered. Jason's hockey mask is so much part of his identity – his one essential accessory – that without it he is incomplete and maybe even unable to function convincingly as the executioner. Such is its importance that at the start of *Jason Lives: Friday the 13th Part VI* (1986) it is not just the bolt of lightning that revives Jason, but seemingly the discarded hockey mask tossed into his opened grave. Bernard Welt writes that here the mask has become "a magic talisman",[21] but he also argues that "the mask *is* Jason's real face";[22] if so it is then the face without expression, the face devoid of muscle, the face of rigor mortis. Throughout *Friday the 13th Part 2*, Jason's face is hidden beneath a flour sack, and even though this is not the later trademark hockey mask the disguise still suggests a potent threat. In Elias Canetti's work on crowds and power he writes that

> the mask is distinguished . . . by its rigidity. In place of the varying and continuous movement of the face [the mask] presents the exact opposite: a perfect fixity and sameness . . . To fixity of form is added fixity of distance What gives the mask its interdictory quality is the fact that it never changes. Everything behind the mask is mysterious . . . Above all it *separates* . . . It threatens with the secret dammed up behind it . . . the unknown that it conceals.[23]

I would argue that in the slasher film, more frightening than the mask is the concealed face, which is often revealed in the climactic conflict (and sometimes in the prelude) – the 'face shot' that audiences expect. *The Friday the 13th* series is no exception with the mask never able to impart the ultimate horror of what lies beneath. In one scene, near the end of *Friday the 13th Part VIII*, Jason emerges from a subway in Times Square, Manhattan, and kicks over a cassette player owned by a gang of youths. "You're dead meat, slime bag", declares the gang leader, to which Jason turns around to face the youths, lifts up his mask and reveals off-screen his hideous face – shocked, the gang flee. The *Friday the 13th* series is tied to revealing, at different stages of deterioration, the increasingly distorted and putrefied features of Jason. Eyes peering through holes in his mask deceptively suggest recognisable normal features, but each of Jason's facial unveilings – in situations in which he has become most vulnerable – is shocking for the way in which he is shown to be a human aberration. By the point in the series where he has become supernatural, his body has been damaged by so many final fights that he has lost much of what there ever was of Jason Voorhees, and is instead a monstrous hulk. He is more an 'It' than a 'He'.

In Welt's essay on Jason he proposes that "through its association with sport, the mask also transforms the monster into an angry god playing a game with human life".[24] But Jason is not "playing a game", as his compulsion to kill is too strong and cannot allow for any delays or deviations. His victims are mainly selected whilst isolated or vulnerable giving him the greatest chance of executing a quick, uncomplicated and successful death. Crucially, he exhibits no desire to torture his victims or extend their pain. His weapon of choice is practical, often requisitioned, and sometimes quite inventive. Where practical, his weapon – a meat cleaver, machete, spear, hunting knife, or axe – is employed for its effectiveness in penetrating, slicing and splitting flesh and bone. Readily available, some of these weapons are carried in *Jason Lives: Friday the 13th Part VI* in his tool belt which only emphasises his commitment, professionalism, and organisation. The weapons that Jason requisitions are found at the killing scene and put to use – this includes any of the above, but allows for one-off weapons that are tools and equipment taken out of a domestic or work context: a knitting needle, fireplace poker, ice pick, deep-fat fryer, garden shears, pitchfork, scythe, barb wire, and a saw. The moments of invention occur most when Jason uses his bare hands – the head that he squeezes until an eye pops out in *Friday the 13th Part 3*; the sheriff's body bent backwards in half in *Friday the 13th Part VI,* or the boxer's head that Jason severs with one single mighty punch in *Friday the 13th Part VIII.*

Jason's 'Guignolers'

As Jason approaches his victims – at the start of many of the executions – there is an audible, non-diegetic phantom chant on the soundtrack. It is partly a "ch-ch", "ah-ah" sound and partly "kill-kill" and "kill-kill ah-ah".[25] Never is the chant connected to an on-screen individual or group, and the instruction to "kill" is certainly not established to be within Jason's mind. If this chant is to be traced then I think it is to the film audience. Followers of the *Friday the 13th* series are drawn to the spectacle of Jason's brutality. Here, there are aspects within the series that could be recognised as offering the pleasure and attraction; there are the voyeuristic camera positions, point of view shots, and the sharing of the killer's gaze, which Vera Dika discusses in detail, and then there are the moments of nudity and titillation and the passages of perceptual transference in which the audience is physically jolted by the screen terror (what Kim Newman calls the "boo!" message).[26] Sean S. Cunningham, the director of *Friday the 13th*, described his film as a "rollercoaster" ride and an experience similar to a visit to a "funhouse".[27] What if the audience for the series was to be compared to spectators at an execution and considered as modern 'Guignolers'?

In Gordon's study of the Grand Guignol, he writes that most of the performances "traded on sensationalistic plots and the exploitation of their audience's visceral curiosity . . . in a way, they acted as fantasy substitutes for the guillotine and its public executions".[28] The relationship that the *Friday the 13th* films has with its audience is also dependent on exploiting a visceral curiosity; a desire to view the body modified and pushed beyond the limits of normality and acceptability. And the humour that can be discerned in *Friday the 13th Part 3*, and which is first made explicit with *Friday the 13th Part V*, exhibits a similar effect to the Grand Guignol performances with their "hot and cold showers", in that horror is designed in combination with comedy.

The films with their systematic series of executions are also modern substitutes for the effect of the guillotine. Jason establishes moments of execution, in which characters are signalled to be 'next' and given a 'platform' for their dramatic yet rapid demise. The audience's thrill of seeing the next victim for execution is transferred to the film and non-diegetically echoed by the soundtrack's instructions to "kill". But there is another relationship between the executioner, Jason, and the voice that commands the execution. The film viewer can be viewed as the spectator but perhaps it can also be regarded as the sovereign authority. The film viewer's position is privileged and its commands to "kill" are unfailingly met by the obedient and compliant executioner. Maybe here Jason is similar to actual executioners in European history who, as Jonathan Sawday writes, stood at the moment of execution as "the sovereign's representative".[29]

Whether the audience is the spectator or the sovereign power, or even both, Jason remains the executioner, and like many of the actual figures which precede him in European history, he is assumed to be endowed with special powers. As Sawday writes, the hangman or executioner who had a "potency over the bodies of individual members of the community", was

> the focus of certain fears. His trade with the dead, his existence as the corporeal representative of the final stages of the law at its most extreme and rigorous, and the fact that he was *de facto* the last incarnation of sovereign power over the body, all conspired to construct a finely poised network of taboos and jurisdictions around his person.[30]

According to Sawday "the executioner's touch produced 'infamy'" and individuals "were tainted by coming into contact with the executioner's person, or even objects associated with him".[31] In contrast, the popular executioner in the *Friday the 13th* films is regarded quite differently within his community. Jason's special powers have endeared him to his film fans to the point where he has become idolised and his mask – this executioner's most distinctive feature – fetishised. Here, the Jason look is easily copied, such is the uniformity of the hockey mask and its availability from sports shops. In *Friday the 13th Part VIII*, there is a neat moment when Jason, upon finally arriving at Manhattan, immediately sees a billboard promotion for ice hockey. Foregrounded on the advert is a large centralised image of a hockey mask – "Meet the Competition – Eastern Hockey League", the poster announces. Jason, unable to comprehend the image, tilts his head slightly downwards to his left and briefly exhibits a rare moment of contemplation.

Jason generally lacks the coolness of such contemporary monsters as Freddy Krueger and *Hellraiser*'s Pinhead, though within the *Friday the 13th* series there are distinct moments when Jason is given the power of parody and irony. At the start of *Friday the 13th Part VI* he is firmly established as the film's star with style, as the opening signature image from the James Bond films is copied and Jason walks on-screen centred within the pupil of an eye. A position from which he then turns, faces the camera and slashes at the screen with his machete turning it red.

The iconic status of Jason led to *Friday the 13th* related merchandise which began in the mid 1980s with poster images of the hockey-masked killer. But *Friday the 13th* merchandise never reached the heights of the *Nightmare on Elm Street* series, which became a phenomenon of popular culture in the late 1980s and early 1990s.[32] Around this time, with the success of Freddy products, similar merchandise was released and this included the 'Jason and Victim Spitballs'. Made in 1989 by LJN toys, as a copy of the 'Freddy and Victim Spitballs', the two ping-pong size squeezy spheres in the shape of faces were meant to be briefly immersed in water, filled with liquid, and then pressed allowing those within distance to be squirted and soaked. "They're a gruesome twosome that can spit water up to 18 feet!", declared the advertising. Worryingly, as with the Freddy merchandise, the toy was aimed at children who were below the classified viewing age of the films – "Ages 4 and Up", the packaging advises.

Later Jason products moved away from the relationship between killer and victim and, instead, were concerned with solely the iconic executioner. New Jason products of the late 1990s are largely the retro merchandise of companies such as McFarlane, who have made an impact with a series of popular models and figurines that now includes David Cronenberg's Brundlefly creation (from *The Fly* [1986]), the shark and fishing boat from *Jaws* (1975) and, even, Dr Caligari from *The Cabinet of Dr Caligari* (1919). The recent celebration of the *Friday the 13th* films includes dolls, snowstorms and a diecast toy car from Matchbox – Jason astride a four-wheel drive vehicle, machete in hand. These are mainly toys for adults who presumably grew up with the *Friday the 13th* films, during the peak of the

18. Popularising Jason: *Friday the 13th* toys and merchandise

horror New Wave. And as collectable models, they are replacements for the Jason toys that never were.

With a narrow range of Jason products available in 1985, a fan wrote into *Fangoria* with "the greatest idea":

> everyone knows how successful Kenner's "*Star Wars* Action Figures" have been. Well, how about "*Friday the 13th* Action Figures". Give it some thought, wouldn't it be great? I think it would be. There would be Jason, Mrs. Voorhees and all the victims of the films! They can come with the weapons that they were killed with. The weapons will have a way of being attached to the figures . . . Take Mark from Pt II, he could come in a little wheelchair with a machete that will fit over his face.[33]

Jason and the *Friday the 13th* films were extremely popular amongst the horror-hungry readership of *Fangoria*, and such a range of action figures would have proved attractive. The publishers of the publication were acutely aware of the interest in the films and they devoted more "pull-out" posters – an A3 or A2 size, folded colour reproduction of a notable film image of the body monstrous – to the productions, than any other film or series. The posters began with issue 26, and within two issues (number 28) a graphic enlargement of the macheted wheelchair victim, Mark, from

Friday the 13th Part 2, was celebrated. Posters for *Friday the 13th* (issue 32), *Friday the 13th Part V* (issue 44), and again *Friday the 13th* (issue 53) followed.

In issue 39 of *Fangoria* the results of a "Maniac Match-up" contest were published – a monster bash that invited readers to submit comic-strip depictions of an imagined fight between Jason and *Halloween*'s Michael Myers, with the victor meeting Leatherface in the final.[34] The winning comic-strip, a brilliantly drawn fantasy by readers John Arnold and Linwood Sasser, establishes a battle in which Jason plunges his axe into Michael's shoulder, pours boiling fat over him, cuts his body open with a tree saw and removes his internal organs. Jason appears distinctly in control, but he is then distracted by a passing *Star Trek* fan, which gives Michael Myers enough time to rise up and decapitate Jason. Michael Myers then moves onto the showdown with Leatherface who is split in two when he is unable to start his chainsaw.[35] *Fangoria* was a magazine which had exhibited a partial interest in wrestling, and this connected with one reader, William Boblett, who suggested this movie monster death-match between Jason and Michael, in *Fangoria* 34: "a real battle of the heavyweights. Wouldn't you think so? I do. They both seem so indestructible".[36] This "no-holds-barred battle of the terror titans!" was initiated by *Fangoria* two issues later, with entries being judged on "both artistic skill and dramatic imagination".[37]

The battle of the terror titans was as much the result of fans imagining the omnipotence of their screen heroes – a contest that was to broaden after 1984 with the successful introduction of Freddy Krueger in *A Nightmare on Elm Street*, and which later saw Freddy battle with Jason on screen in *Freddy vs. Jason* – as it was the conflicting opinions of followers regarding the value of the various contemporary monsters as figures of popular interest.[38] The *Friday the 13th* films generated a large debate and divided the *Fangoria* readership with opinion reaching a peak around the release of *Friday the 13th – The Final Chapter*. James Stephens wrote to express his anger that in issue 38 there had been "a full page of letters" devoted to the film and "none of the letters were negative . . . what blows me away is, you never did any of this for the Shape [Michael Meyers] . . . the *Halloween* movies were much better (and a lot more believable. . .)".[39] Another reader, with the pseudonym 'Grossed Out', complained about the fans of the series: "It's the thought of people idolizing Jason that gets me. Isn't there something wrong with people like that?".[40] A reader in a later issue articulated further concerns:

> Why do these people insist on worshipping Jason? . . . I don't know what they could possibly see in him. I have only see the first three *Friday the*

13th movies, and that was two too many! The first one was all right, but the others lacked energy and emotion, and they just don't warrant all the adulation and praise poured on them by misguided Fangorians.[41]

Such feelings continue in the readers' messages in the classified ads which appear towards the back of *Fangoria*. These brief non-commercial advertisements commenced with issue 12 of the fanzine and were free to first-time subscribers and readers who renewed their subscription. With the presumed death of Jason in 1984 messages included "Jason dead? About time!" and "Jason – Good Riddance", but on the same page there were also messages such as "Romero, Savini, *The Evil Dead, Dawn of the Dead* and *The Brood* kick ass! Blackfoot rules! We miss you Jason!".[42] If the results of a mini poll conducted by *Fangoria* are to be believed then Jason was certainly missed: 92.18 per cent voted for "Jason lives to kill again!", whilst just 0.24 per cent voted for "Jason is dead; it's all over", and 0.03 per cent for "Jason learns to be nice like Godzilla".[43]

"Jason lives forever in our hearts. King and Bottin Rule", reads one fan's message.[44] The adoration of Jason is evidenced by those fans who call themselves "Kristal Layke", who write with the initials "J.V." messages such as "Your tax-deductible contribution will help send these children to camp. Please be generous", or declare "Jason lives!!! I know because I sewed his head back together".[45] The fans desire an affiliation to Jason, but they are also attracted to his performances of screen violence and the extreme acts of gore and horror. There are the occasional bizarre fan announcements: "*Friday the 13th* and Kermit the Frog #1", and "Jason, Michael and the Pointer Sisters are #1".[46] But many fan messages emphasise the splatter: "I LOVE GORE AND BLOOD AND *FRIDAY THE 13TH. CHUD* IS MASSIVELY WEIRD", "Fangoria is #1, so is *Friday the 13th*. Long Live Horror, Blood and Guts. This is Dr. Blood Signing Off.", "Gore: *Friday the 13th* and any other horror movies – I want info. Send to Gore, 1354 . . .", and "*Dawn of the Dead, Friday the 13th* and Tom Savini rule [blood & guts forever]".[47] It is here, where the films function culturally as a modern grand guignol, that arguably the greatest attraction of the series exists.

Notes

1. *Friday the 13th* (2009), breaks so many of the conventions of the series that it is best viewed as detached from the preceding films. Amongst the character and plot revisions, Jason is now an expert archer, takes victims captive, and plans death predicaments in the style of the *Saw* (2004–2009) movies.
2. An excellent website, and a good example, is <www.fridaythe13thfilms. com>.

3. See <www.fridaythe13thfilms.com/saga/bodycount2.html>.

4. Mel Gordon, *The Grand Guignol: Theatre of Fear and Terror*, New York: Da Capo Press, 1997, revised edition, p. 51. For further discussion see also Richard Hand and Michael Wilson, *Grand-Guignol: The French Theatre of Horror*, Exeter: University of Exeter Press, 2002.

5. Ibid., p. 26.

6. Ibid., p. 51.

7. Ibid., p. 47.

8. Ian Conrich, 'An Aesthetic Sense: Cronenberg and Neo-horror Film Culture', in Michael Grant, ed., *The Modern Fantastic: The Films of David Cronenberg*, Trowbridge: Flicks Books, 2000, p. 36.

9. Bob Martin, 'Tom Savini: A Man of Many Parts', *Fangoria*, no. 6, June 1980, pp. 11, 50–2; James H. Burns, 'Carl Fullerton', *Fangoria*, no. 13, June 1981, pp. 53–6. Tom Savini returned to the series for *Friday the 13th – The Final Chapter*. See R.H. Martin, 'Savini and *Friday the 13th – The Final Chapter*', *Fangoria* no. 36, July 1984, pp. 56–9.

10. Martin, 'Tom Savini: A Man of Many Parts', p. 52.

11. Burns, p. 53. Emphasis in the original.

12. Martin, 'Tom Savini: A Man of Many Parts', p. 52.

13. Bob Martin, 'Friday the 13th: A Day for Terror', *Fangoria*, no. 6, June 1980, p. 16.

14. Burns, 'Carl Fullerton', p. 56. Emphasis in the original.

15. Ibid. Emphasis in the original.

16. The machete sliced into the face in *Friday the 13th Part II*, also appeared originally in *Ecologia del Delitto* as a woman with an axe inflicted facial wound.

17. See Ian Conrich, 'How To Make A "Slasher" Film', *Invasion*, no. 11, July 1995, p. 48.

18. Tim Pulleine, *Monthly Film Bulletin*, no. 558, July 1980, p. 132; Tim Pulleine, *Monthly Film Bulletin*, no. 570, July 1981, p. 138.

19. These numbers are inaccurate as there are 9 victims of Pamela Voorhees (Jason's mother) in part 1, 10 victims of Jason in part 2, and 12 victims in part 3.

20. Post-slasher killers often do not wear a mask, and as I have written on the *Nightmare on Elm Street* series "by contrast, Freddy is the confident performer, the host, the showman and the comic. He is ostentatious, 'courteous', even courtly and is constantly cracking jokes". Ian Conrich, 'Seducing the Subject: Freddy Krueger, Popular Culture and the *Nightmare on Elm Street* Films', in Alain Silver and James Ursini, eds, *The Horror Film Reader*, New York: Limelight Editions, 2000, p. 226.

21. Bernard Welt, *Mythomania: Fantasies, Fables, and Sheer Lies in Contemporary American Popular Art*, Los Angeles: Art issues. Press, 1996, p. 82. Emphasis in the original. The book collects together a series of short essays by Welt, which includes 'Jason Voorhess, R.I.P.', pp. 78–83.

22. Welt, p. 83.

23. Elias Canetti, quoted in Tim Marshall, *Murdering to Dissect: Grave-robbing,*

Frankenstein *and the anatomy literature*, Manchester: Manchester University Press, pp. 303–4.

24. Welt, p. 81.

25. A reader of *Fangoria*, Joseph Shea, wrote to the publication asking about this sound: "my friends say that it's the words 'kill her'". *Fangoria* responded with the advice that if the movies were played backwards "it sounds like someone saying 'Fango Rules!'". 'The Postal Zone', *Fangoria*, no. 38, October 1984, p. 7.

26. Vera Dika, *Games of Terror: Halloween, Friday the 13th, and the Films of the Stalker Cycle*, London: Associated University Presses, 1990, pp. 67–84; Kim Newman, *Nightmare Movies*, London: Proteus Books, 1984, p. 96.

27. David B. Nichols and Bob Martin, 'An Anatomy of Terror', *Fangoria*, no. 10, January 1981, p. 22.

28. Gordon, p. 7.

29. Jonathan Sawday, *The Body Emblazoned: Dissection and the Human Body in Renaissance Culture*, London: Routledge, 1995, p. 80.

30. Ibid., p. 81.

31. Ibid., pp. 81–2.

32. I have discussed the *Nightmare on Elm Street/* Freddy Krueger merchandise at length elsewhere. See Conrich, 'Seducing the Subject'.

33. Letter from Don Wilson, 'The Postal Zone', *Fangoria*, no. 42, February 1985, p. 7.

34. 'Battle of the Maniacs!', *Fangoria*, no. 39, November 1984, p. 26.

35. 'The 1st *Fangoria* Splatterbowl!', *Fangoria*, no. 39, November 1984, pp. 27–30, 38.

36. 'The Postal Zone', *Fangoria*, no. 34, June 1984, p. 8.

37. 'The Postal Zone', *Fangoria*, no. 36, August 1984, p. 7.

38. The two characters had previously appeared briefly in the New Line Cinema produced *Jason Goes to Hell*, where the concluding image is of a Freddy glove rising up through the ground and grabbing Jason's abandoned mask.

39. 'The Postal Zone', *Fangoria*, no. 40, December 1984, p. 7.

40. Ibid.

41. 'The Postal Zone', *Fangoria*, no. 52, March 1986, p. 8.

42. 'Classified Ads', *Fangoria*, no. 41, January 1985, p. 67.

43. 'The Postal Zone', *Fangoria*, no. 42, February 1985, p. 8.

44. 'Classified Ads', *Fangoria*, no. 39, November 1984, p. 67.

45. 'The Postal Zone', *Fangoria*, no. 53, May 1986, p. 8; 'Classified Ads', *Fangoria*, no. 45, June 1985, p. 66; 'Classified Ads', *Fangoria*, no. 39, November 1984, p. 67.

46. 'Classified Ads', *Fangoria*, no. 45, June 1985, p. 66; 'Classified Ads', *Fangoria*, no. 49, November 1985, p. 67.

47. 'Classified Ads', *Fangoria*, no. 43, March 1985, p. 67; 'Classified Ads', *Fangoria*, no. 38, October 1984, p. 67; 'Classified Ads', *Fangoria*, no. 53, May 1986, p. 67; 'Classified Ads', *Fangoria*, no. 45, June 1985, p. 67.

Part Four

Boundaries of Horror

10

'Parts is Parts'
Pornography, Splatter Films and the Politics of Corporeal Disintegration

Jay McRoy

Introduction: Wet Work

The aesthetics and the ideological implications of both hard-core pornographic cinema and the goriest offerings of the splatter film genre have long been the focus of contemporary film scholarship.[1] Feminist critics like Andrea Dworkin, Laura Kipnis, Anne McClintock and Linda Williams have advanced important, albeit theoretically divergent studies of the 'pornographic' mise-en-scène and its impact on a wide variety of potential spectators. Likewise, film scholars such as Barbara Creed, Carol J. Clover, Judith Halberstam and Harry M. Benshoff have addressed the influence of graphically violent images and representations of physical alterity upon radically diverse audiences. However, while much of the critical debate over hard-core pornography in film has centered on the socio-cultural implications of the genre's propensity for depicting the human form as fragmented and decontextualised, relatively few analyses of splatter, or body horror films have ventured beyond the most elementary gender- and class-based considerations of who does the butchering, who gets butchered, and how the butchering is received by audience members.

In *The Reality Effect: Film Culture and the Graphic Imperative*, Joel Black posits that pornography, in its "fragmentation" of the "desired object" into "body parts",[2] initiates a process of visual and ontological disassembly that not only renders inconsequential the identity of the film's characters (and the actors who portray them), but also promotes conceptualisations of the body as molecular and contingent, revealing "the schizoid nature of everyday reality".[3] Consequently, in articulating the difference between pornography and its far less explicit cousin, eroticism, Black states: "Eroticism conceals what pornography reveals".[4] Curiously, one can easily apply a similar formulation to works of cinematic horror, especially those most gruesome of texts structured around the bloody dismantling of the human physiognomy: conventional horror films conceal what splatter films reveal. In the pages that follow, I argue that in their depiction of the body in fragments, both hard-core pornography and splatter films, while eliciting a myriad of complex and uncomfortable 'pleasures' in their viewers, nevertheless reveal the artificiality of socio-cultural paradigms informed by modernist myths of organic wholeness. In the literal and figurative deconstruction of the discrete human form, these oft-vilified film genres can be understood as progressive in that their aesthetics of corporeal disassembly allows for the creation of an infinitely inclusive model of film spectatorship, while also providing important avenues for imaging social resistance.

Skin Flicks and Sex Machines: Bodies, Pornographies, Intensities

In a 1999 interview with Novella Carpenter, Steven Shaviro notes that much of the similarity between pornography and horror films results from not only the cinematic traditions' explicit preoccupation with bodies, but also the impact of these corporeally-charged imagery upon the audiences that view them:

> [Pornography and horror films] are both visceral. They both are about things happening to human bodies, [and about] having bodies on an intense sensoral level. Part of the point of those films – often precisely because they are exploitative – is to get the audience to react in the same visceral manner as [the bodies] depicted on screen. [5]

Although Shaviro elaborates only briefly upon this connection between pornography and horror films,[6] he ultimately suggests that there may be something to "value"[7] rather than merely criticise within these texts, an observation that gestures towards an understanding of these oft-disparaged genres as potentially progressive rather than merely exploitative.[8] This is not to suggest that the vast majority of the films arising from these deceptively rich cinematic traditions set out to contest, rather than reinforce, dominant systems of disciplinary power. Indeed, such an argument, while virtually indefensible, also vastly exceeds this chapter's critical scope. What the pages to follow do contend, however, is that 'body genres' like hard-core pornography and the splatter film produce what Gilles Deleuze, in his writings on cinema and other aesthetic creations (including literature), calls *affect*, a disruptive intensity that "skew[s] or scramble[s] the faculties", impacting the viewer's ability to imagine "a meaningful world that is there for us all".[9] Such reconsiderations of previously held notions of ideological (and biological) cohesion can be unsettling and even frightening, but they can also prove fertile, allowing audiences to understand both the films they view, as well as the very act of viewing films itself, as contributing to a process of continual transformation – a perpetual becoming that reveals the extent to which everyday experience is informed by illusory structures and binary logics.

Hard-core pornographic cinema is one of fragmentation and immanence, the very aesthetic of which derives from a play between the (social) imaginary and the 'real', between the perpetuation of illusion and a drive towards documentary authenticity that, as Linda S. Kauffman notes, evokes comparison to "films of open heart surgery".[10] In most hard-core pornographic films, the excessive sexual coupling and re-coupling of bodies punctuates thinly developed and highly derivative plot lines that function primarily to contextualise the films' carnal activities. Indeed, it is the genre's very *excessiveness* that generates much of its affect. By way of illustration, consider the form and function of the following visual tropes commonly mobilised within hard-core pornographic cinema:

> *The extreme close-up* of graphic intersection(s) between genitalia, or between genitalia and other bodily zones (the fingers/hand, the mouth, the anus) coded as erogenous.
>
> *The 'orgy' sequence*, during which actors/characters engage in graphic sexual unions with multiple, interchangeable partners.
>
> *The application of specific editing techniques* applied within, and between, sex scenes – including jump cuts, cross-cutting, cutting to continuity, and, sometimes, the blatant recycling of previously viewed footage for the lone purpose of extending a sequence's action.

Such an analysis will reveal hard-core pornography's aesthetics of fragmentation, a visual logic resulting from both the prominence of the "fragmented body" as a visual motif within "the hard-core regime of representation",[11] as well as the way such radical visions frustrate conventional viewing practices and, consequently, "short-circuit . . . the sensory-motor schema that governs our perceptions".[12]

Perhaps few techniques more completely capture the visual fragmentation of the human body in hard-core pornography than the use of extreme close-ups to present the genre's abundance of physical couplings, corporeal collisions, and intimate intersections. Lensed so that the camera and, by extension, the viewer assumes an almost clinical proximity to the bodies in congress, the compositions' telescopic detail frequently makes it difficult to designate precisely where one body ends and the next begins. Consequently, these extreme close ups expose the union of bodies within the frame as little more than soft machines engaged in "an ambisexual charade".[13] As such, body parts, in the words of Berkeley Kaite:

> form a textual closure in their manifestation as *one* physical reality. There is a loosening of boundaries around the body's immanence ... A body doubles as its other. The two [or more] corporeal entities are feigned as one, a unity in a circuit of desire.[14]

The use of the term 'circuit' is particularly instructive here, as extreme close-ups of intercourses in hard-core pornography often assume an almost bio-mechanical aesthetic. Consider, for instance, the standard mise-en-scène adopted during the filming of double-penetration scenes in films geared predominantly towards 'straight' and 'bisexual' markets. Penises pump like pistons into a woman's vagina and anus, orifices that, at extreme close range, seemingly lose all anatomical specificity. Similarly, as Kaite convincingly posits, scenes of anal sex (especially when lensed in extreme close up) contain the potential to eradicate, at least temporarily, notions of difference predicated upon the "boundaries of masculinity and femininity",[15] especially since the anus, as a sight of "penetration, aggression, expulsion",[16] occupies a space outside of traditional gender difference. Hence, in its potential to disintegrate the corporeal and gendered body, hard-core pornographic cinema is among the "most revealing" and "apocalyptic ... of all fleshy discourses".[17] Additionally, by dividing the body into fetishised fragments, it exposes the body's various 'parts', or 'zones', as simultaneously biological and mechanical. Rather than an imaginary, impermeable construct, the body, revealed as indiscrete and open to a multiplicity of combinations and recombinations with other physiognomies, is exposed as a liminal construct that, as Gertrude Koch reminds us, "refers [embodiment] back to the world of machines, of interlocking systems and cogs, in which everyone, ultimately, is caught up".[18] As a substantial component of the pornographic mise-en-scène, the extreme close-up exposes a multiplicity of potential sexual conjunctions and possibilities for carnal 'exchange'.[19] Such shots reveal pornography as a mode of representation that functions through visual "disorientation" designed both to produce a "psychic dislocation"[20] and to "multiply the possibilities of [sexual] exchange".[21]

Perhaps no pornographic sequences better illustrate this filmic tendency towards the depiction of the human body as simultaneously molecular and mechanised than orgy sequences. Alternating between extreme close ups and medium shots of the actors performing, the pornographic mise-en-scène exposes the rhizomic complexity of the various anatomical (re)assemblages. Consequently, the images the viewer encounters depict a multiplicity of disassembled and amalgamated desiring machines. The viewer witnesses a graphic display of variable physiognomies at once coherent and fragmented, individuated and merged. Thus, bodies in hard-core pornographic films, as always already partial, form what Gilles Deleuze and Felix Guattari call "free multiplicities", "syntheses" that "constitute local and nonspecific connections, inclusive disjunctions, [and] nomadic conjunctions".[22] This corporeal indiscernibility allows the spectator to imagine a plurality of identities that at once contain and exceed 'either . . . or' notions of gender and sexuality. Orgy sequences, then, can be understood as a filmic discourse that, in Deleuze's words, reaches "the body before discourses, before words, before things are named";[23] these sequences visualise the amalgamated pornographic body as a plane of 'immanence', a constant becoming rather than a fixed or naturalised entity.

Furthermore, when considering how these corporeal representations impact conventional viewing practices, the pornographic film's potential as an ontologically disruptive force becomes increasingly apparent. Cinematic compositions that obfuscate corporeal specificity destabilise paradigms dependent upon comprehensions of the corporeal and narrative body as an organic whole. This destabilisation is further exacerbated when these scenes emerge as part of a larger, yet equally disruptive, sequence of events sutured together through editing techniques as varied as jump cutting, cross-cutting, cutting to continuity, and the strategic application of mechanical distortions (for instance slow motion, the repetition of previously-viewed footage). Transitions between scenes transpiring in separate locations and time frames, for instance, often feature reverse zooms that pull back slowly from the ambiguous junction of bodily zones, revealing the actors only briefly before cutting to a close up of new bodies in variable congress or, in some cases, jump-cutting to a radically different angle of the same bodies metaphorically *renewed* through physical and visual reconfiguration. In other instances, shifts between ostensibly concurrent sex scenes are linked both aurally and visually by changes in soundtrack accompanied by a cut from a medium shot of one pair/group of actors to an extreme, de-personalised, and fragmenting close up of a new physiological conjunction.

Cinema is an art form wholly comprised of schisms, and visual and temporal ruptures that filmmakers and audiences variously mesh together to create meaning. Hard-core pornographic films, in their excessive displays of corporeal fragmentation, are particularly intensive texts in that they produce an abundance of disruptive affect. They are, as 'libertine feminists' like Susan Sontag[24] and Angela Carter[25] posit, 'transgressive' in their subversive 'excess';[26] at the very least, even when the films are infused with the most overtly sexist or homophobic premises, the pornographic mise-en-scène, coupled with the genre's most frequently employed editing techniques, provides audiences with avenues for imagining identities that exceed conventional notions of embodiment predicated upon the most "obvious biological and discursive difference".[27] Creative rather than merely representative, hard-core pornographic cinema exceeds the physiological and ontological boundaries imposed by its more socially acceptable cousin, the soft-core film. Rather than neatly recuperating the ideological framework from which it frequently arises, hard-core pornography 'fucks with' conventional notions of the corporeal and social body.

Meat Flicks and the Splattering Subjectivities

Along with pornography, horror cinema is arguably the mode of filmic discourse that most frequently takes the body as its primary focus. It is a cinema literally obsessed with corporeality; revelling in the body's "intensive and insistent materiality",[28] horror films often create fear by exploiting the all-too-human trepidation over the potential loss of physiological integrity, a dread that – as Linda Williams and others have argued – manifests itself through the spectator's body as it squirms and writhes in its seat, assuming terrified postures akin to those projected upon the screen.[29] Consequently, as many scholars of contemporary horror cinema have noted,[30] it is possible to view the horror genre as providing a valuable arena for the promotion of conservative agendas, allowing for the apparent recuperation of the status quo through the eradication of radical/'monstrous' alterity. This conceptualisation of contemporary horror cinema as largely reactionary is understandable, as most works of filmic terror still conclude with the (if only temporary) defeat of the fantastical or virulent threat to the equally imaginary social order. In contrast, some recent horror films, like Clive Barker's *Nightbreed* (1990) and John Fawcett's *Ginger Snaps* (2000),[31] can be read as promoting more overtly progressive visions, at once depicting the 'monster' as heroic (rather than merely sympathetic), and exposing the dominant culture as maintained by an assortment of corrupt – if not decidedly oppressive – institutions. Such texts, however, remain very much in the minority.

The discussion that follows, then, endeavours to answer the following question: Is it possible to understand the nightmarish figures and violent actions within even the most 'socially conservative' works of contemporary horror cinema as ultimately irreducible to a politics of ideological re-inscription? In other words, do graphic displays of cinematic terror inevitably confound, if not outright escape, humanist notions of a consolidated corporeal and social body?

Horror cinema is informed by a disruptive aesthetic that reveals the body – of the 'monster'/killer, of the 'victim' – as fragmentary, rendered cohesive only through a process of imagining wholeness. Consequently, horrific images *horrify* because they disrupt audience assumptions of what is and is not 'fixed' or 'normal'. As Judith Halberstam explains in *Skin Shows: Gothic Horror and the Technology of Monstrosity*, horror "disrupts dominant culture's representations of family, heterosexuality, ethnicity, and class politics", ultimately producing "models of reading . . . that allow for multiple interpretations and a plurality of locations of cultural resistance".[32] Furthermore, if contemporary horror cinema, as Philip Brophy tells us, "tends to play not so much on the broad fear of Death, but more precisely on the fear of one's own body, of how one controls and relates to it",[33] it is to those horror films in which the threat of corporeal disintegration is most explicitly foregrounded that this chapter now turns. In a genre obsessed with bodies and the integrity of their 'boundaries', no better assemblage of texts exists upon which to focus a critical lens than those works of 'body horror'[34] most obviously dedicated to the depiction of the human form dis- (and sometimes re-) assembled – the splatter film.

As texts designed around excessively gory displays of the human form ripped open or disintegrated, splatter films frequently rely upon special effects rather than tightly constructed – or even remotely logical – narratives to produce an impact upon an audience. Long after the final reel (or the DVD) has ceased spinning, it is often not the minutia of the film's plot points that remain in the viewer's memory, but the most extreme sequences of corporeal disintegration – the intestines spilling from a gaping abdominal wound, the crimson arterial spray jetting from a slit throat. As Michael Arnzen observes, not only is gore "the only part of the film that is reliably consistent", but any semblance of formal "stability" results from "a consistency of genre expectations, not of text".[35] Like works of hard-core pornographic cinema, plot is pretense, an excuse for an intensive focus on the body's very materiality that, through an aesthetic informed by fragmentation and violence (both physical and semiotic), produces affect. As a result, it should come as no surprise that the camera work and editing techniques adopted by the directors of some of the genre's most notorious offerings bears a striking resemblance to those found in pornographic cinema. In particular, extreme close-ups of bodily trauma, medium shots of mutilated or reconfigured corpses, and the application of disorienting editing effects add to a cinema of fragmentation in which the body of the viewer (re)enacts that horror on the screen, and in which closure is resisted with the gruesome emergence of every new fissure.

By way of illustration, consider the aforementioned splatter film aesthetic as mobilised within two representative, and particularly gruesome, offerings from the genre: J.G. Patterson Jr's *The Body Shop* (aka *Dr. Gore*, 1973), and Juan Piquer Simón's *Pieces* (1981). Filmed roughly a decade apart, each text unfolds with an almost self-reflexive awareness of its status as an exploitation film, depicting the graphic dismemberment of (primarily female) bodies as a blood-soaked, and, at times, darkly humorous refrain. Obviously financed with the slimmest of budgets, as evidenced by their modest sets and small casts of little renown (and even lesser talent), these films offer viewers a series of progressively gory set pieces framed by storylines that are unapologetically simplistic and contrived. *The Body Shop* and *Pieces* recycle the Frankenstein motif by depicting psychotics seeking to disassemble a series of bodies in order to stitch together an idealised female form. Although the former presents its material with tongue planted firmly in cheek and the latter borrows heavily from both the Italian *giallo* and American 'slasher' film traditions, both tales make up in spectacle what they lack in storyline.

Deleuze's ruminations upon the function of cinema prove instructive here, for the horror we experience from these films resides largely "in our own sensory affect, in our jarred and confused optic and aural nerves and our . . . projections of other sensations engendered by cinematography and sound".[36] Extreme high, low, and oblique angles constitute much of the films' mise-en-scène as spine-jarring shrieks and screams accompany torrents of bright red stage blood. Like many works of hard-core pornographic cinema that use extreme close ups to fragment the human form and, in the process, render it ambiguous, *The Body Shop* and *Pieces* capitalise upon similarly intimate displays of open wounds and freshly severed appendages to create affect within the viewer. Thus, while the overwhelming percentage of the recipients of physical violence in these films are women, a detail that one can hardly fail to recognise in any analyses of these notorious works, the use of extreme close ups to capture the sanguine immediacy of the dismembered body parts and viscera spewing gashes remove the bodily zones, if only momentarily, from their prior corporeal and gendered context. Impaling the viewer "on the present moment, emptying out the past and forestalling the future",[37] these scenes/schisms provide instances of pure intensity that reveal not only the "spectator's own materiality as a receptive and responsive organism",[38] but also demonstrate the power of horror to expose the artificiality of the constructs that govern our perceptions and, in the words of Georges Bataille, "break everything that stifles".[39]

A visual (and ideological) discourse of fragmentation underlies *The Body Shop*. Explicit in its presentation of the human body violently dismantled, Patterson's aesthetic is so closely aligned with the films of director Herschell Gordon Lewis that his film plays like a self-conscious homage to, and playful parody of, the works of his infamous predecessor. As mentioned, *The Body Shop*'s plot, which evolves around an insane doctor/mad scientist (complete with a halting, Igor-esque assistant) and his ill-fated quest to build the 'perfect woman', is little more than an excuse for scenes of spectacular violence and moments of sophomoric humour. Indeed, at no time does the film make even the slightest gesture towards presenting itself as anything other than what it is – a low budget gore fest aimed clearly both at fans of the genre who, like many viewers of hard-core pornographic cinema, watch almost exclusively for the spectacle embedded within the narrative, as well as at an audience of viewers seeking to be titillated and repulsed by vivid portrayals of physiognomies disembowelled and dismembered. Thus, whether achieved through extreme close ups, or by way of extended medium shots that reveal a formerly cohesive body reduced to a collection of scattered parts, the representation of gore in *The Body Shop* overwhelms the audience, contributing to an atmosphere of disruptive intensity that results not only in the fragmentation of the viewer (who is at once compelled to look and 'hide his or her eyes'), but also in the viewer's notion of a stable, cohesive identity.

Like the pornographic body discussed by Berkeley Kaite in *Pornography and Difference*, the splattered body in Patterson's *The Body Shop* is, both literally and figuratively, the sum of its parts. In other words, the splattered body and its "corporeal fragments are so strongly discursive that they place the body into the 'meta-anatomical' and threaten to transgress the discursive limits of the biological corpus . . . if not annihilate the body altogether".[40] Furthermore, as an intensive and heterogeneous de-formation, the splattered body resembles the pornographic body's multiplicity and potential for promiscuous conjunctions and reconfigurability; it is a perpetually malleable physicality, a corpus in the process of continual de/re-construction. Thus, although emerging within a discourse frequently coded with conservative or reactionary notions of corporeal and social embodiment, the splattered body, through its very fragmentation, rejects the idea of fixed borders and totalising systems.

The Body in Pieces

Juan Piquer Simón's *Pieces* is a particularly fitting text with which to conclude this exploration of the body and its 'boundaries' in hard-core pornography and splatter films, as the filmmaker's graphic representations of carnage and gore not only create affect within the audience, but also contribute to the narrative's over-riding thematics of the human body as an assemblage of 'segments' or 'parts' that can be variously dismantled and re-integrated. A hybrid amalgamation of body horror traditions, *Pieces* sutures tropes from the pioneering splatter films of Lewis, the formulaic slasher/'teenie-kill-pics' of the late 1970s and early 1980s, and the black-glove whodunit chills of the Italian *giallo* to tell the tale of a chainsaw-wielding maniac dismembering college girls in an attempt to fashion a three-dimensional human jig-saw puzzle. Like in *The Body Shop*, the premise of *Pieces* is transparently misogynistic in its narrative of male violence enacted upon the female body, as well as unabashedly clichéd in its hackneyed quasi-Freudian representation of the killer as an emotionally castrated and matricidal maniac whose banal insanity – signified by his crazed stare and rumbling chainsaw/phallus – is only slightly more compelling than the boring mask of sanity he dons throughout the majority of the film. Nevertheless, in its meshing of three related yet distinct traditions within the horror genre, the film variably gestures towards, and at the same time eludes, simple generic classification. As a result, this stylistic modulation conditions the film in such a way that it escapes reductive dismissals as 'just another horror film'. Like *The Body Shop*, *Pieces'* most abject representations of corporeal disintegration expose the potential splatter films possess for rupturing notions of organic wholeness, including those that relate directly to the imagining of identity, even as socio-cultural paradigms achieve brutal reiteration in both the film's lack of most hackneyed sequences, and the text's (over)reliance upon master-narratives like psychoanalysis and the sexist objectification of women.

Compared to *The Body Shop*, *Pieces* is the more explicit in its resemblance to the aesthetics of hard-core pornographic cinema. Throughout *Pieces*, scenarios seemingly lifted from the plots of adult films precede inevitably gruesome climaxes: a woman clad only in a pair of black panties swims alone in a dimly lit indoor pool before beckoning her eventual killer to join her; a lone female aerobics student jazzercises seconds before boarding an elevator with a trenchcoat-clad stranger; in a blatantly gratuitous sequence, a female tennis player erotically lathers herself in the shower of a dark and seemingly empty locker room. Even the film's central prop, a jigsaw puzzle, is a piece of pornography. Adorned with the likeness of a nude woman, her genitalia obscured by a bloody smear, it is this puzzle that the killer assembles as he butchers his victims to obtain the 'pieces' needed to create a grisly patchwork corpse held together with surgical thread. Perhaps no prop better illuminates the fragmentation of the human form within pornography and splatter films, a filmic syntax that reduces bodies to a compilation of 'parts' variably removed, via editing and carefully composed mise-en-scène, from their previously cohesive arrangement.

Like Patterson before him, Simón's direction contributes to these moments of physiological and ontological disintegration. In one of the film's more grotesque moments, his camera lingers – in a high angle long shot – above the dismembered body of the lone female swimmer, the ambiguous yet carefully stacked segments of blood-soaked tissue rendered even more indistinct by their encasement within transparent plastic bags. Later, while filming the killer's assault on the tennis player, Simón cuts to an extreme close up of the woman's bare midsection as the chainsaw's blade chews through her flesh and into her entrails, spraying a nearby wall with blood. Simón then abruptly cuts to a series of shots filmed outdoors, the only link to the violent bisection coming in the form of the marching-band music on the film's soundtrack. Such editing serves to dislocate the viewer from the previous image of corporeal disruption, an event that, lensed in extreme close up, momentarily dissociates the violent act from the victim's sexual specificity, allowing both male and female viewers to assume a strong, physical response to the graphic depiction on the screen. Thus, although a later shot of the woman's upper body resting in a pool of blood and viscera relocates the corporeal violation within the context of an attack upon a specifically female physiognomy, Simón disallows such a connection immediately following the instance of corporeal penetration, contributing to a sense of rupture designed to create affect within the audience. As spinning metal teeth rip through abdominal wall, or an arm bagged in plastic is raised to expose a nub of white bone surrounded by damp red meat, we are once again presented with images that can be understood as resistant to 'closure' through their very indifferentiating immanence.

Conclusion: Becoming Radically Other

Despite the frequent re-inscription of oppressive ideologies or rigid cultural codes within their narratives, hard-core pornography and splatter films, through their creation of affect within viewers, reveal the body's corporeal and ontological boundaries as imaginary. Flesh – the 'border' most explicitly crossed/violated in both hard-core pornography and splatter films – is fantasy; skin, the very organ that seemingly defines the parameters of the human by separating us from that which is 'not us', is in fact an expansive permeable membrane that, stretched over arrangements of muscle, cartilage, and bone, functions at once as a point of contact, a site of resistance, and a method of transference. Our bodies are not unified;

they are not closed systems. They are, rather, bodies in flux – immanent, becoming. Likewise, pornographic and splattered bodies contest and disrupt conceptualisations of identity as fixed and literal. In their representation of biological conjunctions and incoherence, these infamous body genres expose the potentials of a 'radical otherness' that exceeds mere difference.[41] They reveal, in short, an understanding of the physical and philosophical as intensive and ever-differentiating, allowing viewers to experience a sense of psychic dislocation and the thrill of transgressing boundaries that were always already illusory.

Notes

1. In this essay, the term 'hard-core pornography' refers to explicit cinematic depictions of sexual acts choreographed to appeal to, and across, a variety of subjective viewing positions, including straight, gay, lesbian and transgendered.
2. Joel Black, *The Reality Effect: Film Culture and the Graphic Imperative*, London and New York: Routledge, 2002, p. 107.
3. Ibid., p. 88.
4. Ibid., p. 107.
5. Novella Carpenter, 'Avant-Prof: An Interview with Steve Shaviro', *The Write Stuff [Interviews]*. <http://www.altx.com/interviews/steven.shaviro.html>, 26 May 2003, para. 7.
6. Shaviro is by no means the only scholar to note this connection. See also, among others, the writings of critics like Linda Williams, Carol J. Clover (*Men, Women, and Chain Saws: Gender in the Modern Horror Film*, New Jersey: Princeton University Press, 1992), Isabel Christina Pinedo (*Recreational Terror: Women and the Pleasures of Horror Film Viewing*, Albany: State University of New York Press, 1997) and Linda S. Kauffman (*Bad Girls and Sick Boys: Fantasies in Contemporary Art and Culture*, California: University of California Press, 1998).
7. Carpenter, 'Avant-Prof: An Interview with Steve Shaviro', para. 7.
8. Curiously, although hard-core pornography and films depicting graphic violence have both met with vocal detractors frequently mobilised in the name of 'family values', the horror genre and the erotically charged independent film (often labelled as either 'erotic' or as filmic exercises dedicated to that nebulous genre known as 'erotica') have met with perhaps the most vehement social resistance. In her essay 'Slippery When Wet: The Shifting Boundaries of the Pornographic (A Class Analysis)', Rebecca Huntley proposes that such movements to censor content may have as much to do with mainstream exposure to such texts as they do with content; in other words, it may not be the films' content that is dangerous so much as their accessibility through video stores, cable television, and other mass outlets. As Huntley notes: "The distinctions between pornography and erotica vary across time periods

and cultures. Debates about censorship are inevitably about this boundary between art and smut, reality and fantasy, legitimate and illegitimate cultures" (*Continuum* vol. 12, no. 1, 1998, p. 69).

9. Claire Colebrook, *Gilles Deleuze*, London and New York: Routledge, 2001, p. 39.
10. Kauffman, p. 105.
11. Berkeley Kaite, *Pornography and Difference*, Bloomington and Indianapolis: Indiana University Press, 1995, p. 46.
12. Colebrook, p. 39.
13. Kaite, p. 47.
14. Ibid., p.47.
15. Ibid., p. vii.
16. Ibid., p. 61.
17. Ibid., p. 62.
18. Gertrude Koch, 'The Body's Shadow Realm', in Pamela Church Gibson and Roma Gibson, eds, *Dirty Looks: Women, Pornography, Power*, London: British Film Institute, 1993, p. 37.
19. Susan Sontag, 'The Pornographic Imagination', in *Styles of Radical Will*, New York: Picador, 2002, p. 66.
20. Ibid., p. 47.
21. Ibid., p. 66.
22. Gilles Deleuze and Felix Guattari, *Anti-Oedipus: Capitalism and Schizophrenia*, Trans. Robert Hurley, Mark Seem and Helen R. Lane, Minneapolis: University of Minnesota Press, 1983, p. 295.
23. Gilles Deleuze, *Cinema 2: The Time Image*, trans. Hugh Tomlinson and Robert Galeta, Minneapolis: University of Minnesota Press, 1987, p. 173.
24. See Sontag, pp. 35–73.
25. See Angela Carter, *The Sadean Women*, London: Virago Press, 1979.
26. See Sophia Phoca and Rebecca Wright, *Introducing Postfeminism*, London: Icon Books, 1999.
27. Berkeley Kaite, 'The Pornographic Body Double: Transgression is the Law', in Arthur and Marilouise Kroker, eds, *Body Invaders: Panic Sex in America*, New York: St Martin's Press, p. 165.
28. Anna Powell, 'Kicking Away the Map: *The Blair Witch Project*, Deleuze and the Aesthetics of Horror', *Spectator: The University of Southern California Journal of Film and Television Criticism*, vol. 22, no. 2, 2002, p. 66.
29. Linda Williams, 'Film Bodies: Gender, Genre, and Excess', in Leo Braudy and Marshal Cohen, eds, *Film Theory and Criticism: Introductory Readings* (fifth edition), New York and Oxford: Oxford University Press, 1999, p. 704.
30. For a particularly compelling analysis of contemporary cinema's "cooptation of the horror film's radicalism", see Christopher Sharrett, 'The Horror Film in Neoconservative Culture', *Journal of Popular Film and Television*, vol. 21, no. 3, 1993, pp. 100–10.
31. See, respectively, Jay McRoy, 'There Are No Limits: Splatterpunk, Clive Barker, and the Body *in extremis*', *Paradoxa*, no. 17, 2002, pp. 130–50; and Kat

Reany, 'Ginger Snaps: Puberty Ain't No Bed of Roses', *Monsterzine*, October–December 2002, <http://www.monsterzine.com/200210/ gingersnaps.php>.

32. Judith Halberstam, *Skin Shows: Gothic Horror and the Technology of Monstrosity*, Durham: Duke University Press, 1995, p. 23.

33. Phillip Brophy, 'Horrality – The Textuality of Contemporary Horror Films', in Ken Gelder, ed., *The Horror Reader*, London and New York: Routledge, 2000, p. 280.

34. Body horror is, as Kelly Hurley notes in her essay, 'Reading Like and Alien' a "hybrid genre that recombines the narrative and cinematic conventions of the science fiction, horror, and suspense film in order to stage a spectacle of the human body defamiliarised, rendered other". It is a genre, she explains, that "seems to inspire revulsion – and in its own way pleasure – through representations of quasi-human figures whose effect/affect is produced by their abjection, their ambiguation, their impossible embodiment of multiple, incompatable forms", Judith Halberstam and Ira Livingston, eds, *Posthuman Bodies*, Indianapolis: University of Indiana Press, 1995, p. 203. Paul Wells echoes this definition when he remarks that body horror allows for the recognition of "new physiological configurations and redefinitions of anatomical norms", *The Horror Genre: From Beelzebub to Blair Witch*, London: Wallflower Press, 2000, p. 114.

35. Michael Arnzen. "'Who's Laughing Now?": The Postmodern Splatter Film', *Journal of Popular Film and Television*, vol. 21, no. 4, 1994, p. 179.

36. Powell, p. 66.

37. Geoffrey Galt Harpham, *On the Grotesque: Strategies of Contradiction in Art and Literature*, New Jersey: Princeton University Press, 1982.

38. Powell, p. 59.

39. Georges Bataille, *Visions of Excess: Selected Writings, 1927–1939*, Minneapolis: University of Minnesota Press, 1985.

40. Kaite, *Pornography and Difference*, p. 37.

41. See Jean Baudrillard, *The Transparency of Evil: Essays on Extreme Phenomenon*, London: Verso Books, 1993.

12

Nazi Horrors
History, Myth, Sexploitation

Julian Petley

In contemporary culture, the Nazis have become such all-purpose, short-hand signifiers for everything that is vile and depraved that they regularly feature as icons of the monstrous in horror movies. Certainly, Alvin Rosenfeld's remarks about Adolf Hitler apply equally to representations of Nazis in general:

> Hitler is today all around us – in our loathing, our fears, our fantasies of power and victimisation, our nightmares of vile experience and violent endings . . . Because he has taken up residency in some of our deepest apprehensions and stands today as the incarnation of our wildest and most fearful imaginings, he has become a convenient touchstone for writers of suspense and horror fiction, who know that merely to evoke his name is readily to garner sensations of a horrific sort.[1]

As Steve Neale has argued, the horror genre is centrally concerned with images of the monstrous, with that which "disrupts and challenges the definitions of the 'human' and the 'natural'", and does so in a context involving frequently graphic bodily violence.[2] It is thus unsurprising that Nazis have regularly featured not only in war films and political dramas but in horror movies too. But in what ways are the Nazis represented as monstrous in such films? And do these representations reveal anything significant about Nazism, or are they rather more revealing of contemporary concerns, not least how the horrors of the Third Reich are frequently regarded today? As Saul Friedlander asks: "Is such attention fixed on the past only a gratuitous reverie, the attraction of spectacle, exorcism, or the result of a need to understand; or is it, again and still, an expression of profound fears and, on the part of some, mute yearnings as well?".[3]

The Occult Reich

On one level, many horror movies featuring Nazis can be related to that literature which seeks to explain the Third Reich in occult terms. Such were the terrible crimes committed by Hitler's regime that some have argued that it must be considered as an example of metaphysical evil. Thus the historian Norman Davies writes of there being a "demonological fascination with Germany"[4] and Nicholas Goodrick-Clark argues that, to many, the Third Reich "frequently appears as an uncanny interlude in modern history", the intrusion of an order "generally considered both monstrous and forbidden upon the familiar world of liberal institutions".[5] Both writers are sceptical of such an approach, but from the perspective which they criticise it is but a short step, particularly given certain Nazis' known fascination with arcane and esoteric beliefs (occultism, theosophy, World Ice Theory, the lost Aryan civilisations of Atlantis, Lemuria and Thule to name but a few) to asserting that they were in contact with and agents of supernatural evil forces. As the equally sceptical Alan Baker puts it:

> Just as early *völkisch* occultists took various elements of prehistoric mythology to construct a totally spurious history for the Germanic 'master race' so many occult-orientated writers have taken the image of the Nazi black magician and his diabolical allies and with it have attempted to create an equally spurious history of the Third Reich.[6]

Such attempts encompass both fiction and non-fiction, but it is cinematic incarnations of the former which are of concern here.

There is, in fact, nothing particularly new in fictional works which exploit Nazism's dabblings in the occult – for example, Dennis Wheatley's 1941 novel *Strange Conflict*. In such works, the Nazis are presented in supernatural or metaphysical terms, in the sense that the events surrounding them "defy the principles both of common sense and of science".[7] One of the first examples of a film in this category is *They Saved Hitler's Brain* (1963), which tells how Hitler's head has been kept alive on the fictional Caribbean island of Mandoras in anticipation of the day when the Nazis will rule the world. Parts of this film were actually shot by Stanley Cortez (*The Magnificent Ambersons* [1942], *Night of the Hunter* [1955]) and their shadowy mise-en-scène stands out strikingly from the other material, but, from the point of view of this chapter, the film's chief interest is as a very early exploitation of the 'Fourth Reich' theme – the idea that the Nazis would one day emerge again from a distant part of the world (usually South America) and take over the planet. This fear also animates *The Frozen Dead* (1966) in which Dana Andrews plays Dr Norberg, a

Nazi scientist working in England trying to reanimate, by means of a live human brain, the bodies of top Nazis placed in cryogenic suspension at the end of the war. The film has clear affinities with the Frankenstein story, but the peculiarly melancholic and disturbing scenes with the severed head anticipate Dennis Potter's British television miniseries, *Cold Lazarus* (1996), and the animated arms which finally despatch Norberg recall the scene in *Repulsion* (1965) in which Catherine Deneuve is menaced in a corridor by arms protruding from the walls. Meanwhile, in *Flesh Feast* (1970) Veronica Lake is Dr Elaine Frederick, who is attempting to breed maggots which will slow the ageing process. Unbeknownst to her, those funding the experiments wish to rejuvenate Hitler who, though decrepit, is still alive and is living in South America. Once Hitler is brought to her laboratory, Dr Frederick uses the maggots to kill him – in revenge, it is revealed, for her mother dying in the course of being experimented upon in the Ravensbrück concentration camp. This was the last film starring Veronica Lake, who also served as its executive producer, and it is an ill-fitting swansong. The film's title is an obvious cash-in on the infamous exploitation horror *Blood Feast* (1963) and the horrific element consists mainly of the body parts, stolen from hospital morgues, on which the maggots are fed. The Ravensbrück element provides a link with the experiment camp films discussed below, as do at least two other 'Fourth Reich' films: *The Boys from Brazil* (1978) and *Angel of Death* (aka *Commando Mengele*, 1986) in both of which Dr Josef Mengele is shown continuing his horrific experiments, except now in South America. However, these play more in the generic register of the crime and adventure movie rather than that of the horror genre.

If such films play upon the fantasy of the Nazis returning to dominate the world, others posit their return at a more limited, local level. The most effective in this respect is *Shock Waves* (aka *Almost Human*, 1977), in which a crew of zombies wreaks havoc on an island off the US coast. These are the last remnants of the *Totenkorps*, invincible soldiers developed by the Nazis from criminal elements. At the end of the war, in order to avoid discovery, they were despatched from Germany by submarine. Near the US the boat was scuttled by its captain (Peter Cushing), who took to living on an island near the wreck, and whose charges have now been revived and unleashed by a storm. Low on gore by comparison with George A. Romero's zombie horrors, but high on mood and atmosphere, the film's repeated shots of the zombies looming out of the water and advancing with seemingly unstoppable momentum are actually extremely effective in communicating the brutally invincible quality so often conjured in war films and documentaries by images of the Nazi *Blitzkrieg*. Also effective in a metaphorical sense is *Death Ship* (1980), in which a former SS torture vessel, now driven by a need for human blood, roams the seas in search of victims. The ship is impressively threatening and doom-laden, and the film works well as an evocation of the permanent, ineradicable stain that is Nazism. In one scene, the ship's passengers discover a projector showing newsreel footage of the Third Reich. Even though they destroy both the screen and the projector, the images keep playing on the walls, seemingly animated by a malign and unstoppable life of their own. Here, as at other moments in the vessel's wanderings, one is reminded of David Britton's novel *Motherfuckers* (1996) in which he evokes "vast tidal hurricanes, sweeping all before them, emanating in unceasing waves from the point of suffering, staining, polluting the core of the Earth: Auschwitz, Dachau, Belsen, roasting hells forever travelling through the earth".[8]

Shock Waves spawned a brief Nazi zombie cycle. In *Night of the Zombies* (1981), German and American troops are still fighting in the mountains of Bavaria, kept 'alive' by a gas invented during the war by the US Army, which preserves life by putting the wounded into a state of suspended animation. However, as well as the gas, the zombie soldiers need to consume human flesh to prevent decomposition. The opening and closing scenes feature Hitler's speeches playing over images of German armour driven by zombies – a nicely ironic take on the Thousand Year Reich and the Master Race. In *Le lac des morts vivants* (*Zombie Lake*, 1981), German soldiers killed and thrown into a lake by the French Resistance come back as zombies and take revenge on the local population (and especially the naked girls who repeatedly swim in the eponymous lake). Finally, in *Las tumbas de los muertos vivientes* (*Oasis of the Zombies*, 1983) zombiefied German soldiers are guarding a shipment of gold which, in life, they were transporting across an African desert until killed by allied troops. The film features a great deal of war footage lifted from *Kaput lager gli ultimi giorni delle SS* (*Achtung! The Desert Tigers*, 1977), in which the survivors of an allied commando raid on a German oil compound in Africa during WWII find themselves imprisoned in a torture camp (thus placing the film within the 'Nazi sadism' cycle discussed below).

In these films, the Nazis function as little more than ciphers through which fantasies about the 'Fourth Reich' and evil, superhuman powers are played out. Some might argue that to expect anything other from horror films is foolish, but whilst, obviously, it would be unwise to look to such films for political or ideological analysis, other, more imaginative forms of illumination might be hoped for. After all, as Tom Eliot puts it in *Motherfuckers*: "To me, psychopathology and romance manifested on a political level equals fascism. It's the disease of the Twentieth Century. Its sick appeal is best understood within a horrific, dark fairy tale".[9]

19. The zombiefied German soldiers of the horror-war film *Las tumbas de los muertos vivientes*

Such hopes are definitely raised by Michael Mann's *The Keep* (1983), based on F. Paul Wilson's novel, in which German troops, led by the non-Nazi Captain Woermann, are sent to occupy a vast keep overlooking the strategically important Dinu Pass in the Carpathian Alps. Unwittingly they unleash an ancient and evil force named Molasar (in one of the film's most vertiginous *tours de force*), who can be stopped only by the equally elemental Glaeken Trismegistus. During the film's pre-production, Mann himself stated that:

> What I want to personify here is basically the conflict between psychopathological disease (i.e. the psychopathology of Nazi Germany) and its antithesis. The overt politics interest me less than the states of mind: the specific kinds of aberration that explain why a lower-middle-class bourgeois in Munich would be attracted to the Waffen SS in 1933. What attractions would it hold? What inner fears and insecurities is he not dealing with, but avoiding by the romantic leap into something promising deliverance? That romantic notion of having objective reality dealt with for us – that's the horror this thing's about. Romanticism in painting, in literature, is terrific; but stick it into politics, and you get fascism every time. There are a lot of other factors involved here, that manifest themselves in the movie, dealing with the meta-politics, the psychology and culture of fascism in the 30s and 40s.[10]

And indeed, at one point in the film, Captain Woermann does tell the fanatical SS Major Kaempfer that: "All that we are is coming out here in this keep . . . You have scooped the many diseased psyches out of the German gutter . . . You have infected millions with your twisted fantasies. What are you meeting in the granite corridors of this keep? Yourself". However, so elliptical is Mann's treatment of Wilson's novel (which is rendered even more gnomic by studio-imposed cuts) that these themes are barely developed at all, and are largely subsumed by what increasingly becomes a battle, albeit a visually striking one, between two mysterious and unexplained supernatural forces.

A dark fairy tale character, namely an elf, also dominates the action of *Elves* (1990), in which a young American woman, Kirsten, the offspring of an incestuous union between her mother and her former Nazi grandfather, is being lined up by her grandfather's erstwhile comrades to be impregnated on Christmas Eve by an elf in order to propagate the master race. As a Dr O'Connor explains:

> The elves were a genetic engineering experiment . . . Each elf was to house the haploid gene structure in its sperm cells to produce the master race . . . Driven to select the genetically perfect human mate, the proverbial virgin

of course ... the elf mates with the virgin on Christmas Eve to produce the
master race, and it will eventually rule the world.

How the stunted, hideous elf could actually produce the master race is
indeed puzzling, but the attitude of the film (and indeed of most of those
discussed in this chapter) towards the Nazis is perhaps best summed up
by a Dr Fitzpatrick who states that: "They [the Nazis] believed in a lot of
things. You know, if you could ignore their brutality you'd have to say that
they were just a bunch of crackpots".

Much more cinematically satisfying, however, is *Puppetmaster III:
Toulon's Revenge* (1991), from Charles Band's ever-reliable Full Moon
Pictures. Set in 1941 in Berlin this is a prequel to the other *Puppetmaster*
films, and tells of the Nazis' Death Corps project, which involves inventing
a drug to reanimate the dead, thus enabling German soldiers to march into
battle shielded by zombies. When the Nazis find out that puppetmaster
Andre Toulon has discovered how to animate his puppets, they try to
capture him and steal his secret. Here the by now hackneyed theme of
diabolical Nazi experiments serves as a springboard for a film which most
imaginatively plays, in a fairy tale-like manner, on the simultaneously
charming and sinister qualities of puppets. Furthermore, it features a wry
anti-Nazi puppet show, in which Hitler is despatched by a cowboy.

In its amusing way, this also points up the generically hybrid quality
of many of the films discussed above. For example, the films involving
medical experiments can be regarded as having links with the science-
fiction genre and *Las tumbas de los muertos vivientes* plays for part of its
length as a war movie. Meanwhile, *Le lac des morts vivants* strays regularly
into soft-core sex film territory. This brings the discussion on to the most
controversial, and equally hybrid, of horror films featuring Nazis, those
making up the 'Nazi sadism' cycle.

The Erotic Reich

During the 'video nasty' era in the UK in the early to mid 1980s, one of
the exhibits cropping up with monotonous regularity was *Lager SSadis
kastrat kommandantur* (*SS Experiment Camp*, 1976), whose lurid cover
featuring a naked woman hanging upside down in the context of Nazi
and prison camp iconography probably did more to stimulate prosecution
than the film's actual content, which was, in fact, relatively tame. 'Relatively'
because *SS Experiment Camp* does not have the field to itself in the 'Nazi
sadism' stakes, and is, in fact, part of a cycle, whose main components are
Love Camp 7 (1968), *Ilsa She Wolf of the SS* (1974), *Le deportate della sezione*

20. The exploitative *Lager SSadis kastrat kommandantur*, one of the most
controversial of the 'video nasty' covers

speciale SS (*Deported Women*, 1976), *KZ9 lager di sterminio* (*Women's Camp 119*, 1976), *Le lunghe notti della Gestapo* (*Red Nights of the Gestapo*, 1977), *La bestia in calore* (*The Beast in Heat*, 1977), the aforementioned *Kaput lager gli ultimi giorni delle SS*, *SS lager 5 l'inferno delle donne* (*SS Camp 5 – Women's Hell*, 1977), *Casa private per le SS* (*SS Girls*, 1977), *La svastica nel ventre* (*Nazi Love Camp 27*, 1977) and *L'ultima orgia del Terzo Reich* (*The Gestapo's Last Orgy*, 1977).[11]

As is obvious from their very titles, these films belong as much to the sexploitation as to the horror genre, and they also contain elements of the war film and even the documentary (in the case of the inserts in *SS lager 5 l'inferno delle donne* and *La svastica nel ventre*). However, it is the conjunction of Nazi and sexual elements which is their defining feature, and which accounted for their being banned as 'nasties' in Britain, thus accentuating their credentials as horrific movies. These really are *films maudits*, and even a level-headed and well-informed guide to Italian exploitation cinema calls them "some of the most distasteful examples of exploitation ever committed to film ... the lowest form of trash culture".[12] But it is worth pausing at this point to enquire if these films are so radically 'other' as they might first appear.

First, these are actually variants on the 'women in prison' subgenre of sexploitation, whose roots lie in the perfectly respectable social consciousness drama *Caged* (1950); the rather more lurid *Women's Prison* (1955) followed, and paved the way for sexploitation titles such as *99 mujeres* (*99 Women*, 1969), *Women in Cages* (1971) and *The Big Doll House* (1971). Second, the particularly notorious *Ilsa* is largely a development of the 'roughie' Olga series, sparked off by *White Slaves of Chinatown* (1964) in which Audrey Campbell played a sadistic lesbian vice queen.

Third, the representation of sadism in a specifically Nazi context long predates *Love Camp 7*. Take, for example, the two films made in 1943 about Reinhard Heydrich, the 'Reichsprotektor' of Czechoslovakia. In *Hitler's Madman* (1943), the first American film by Douglas Sirk, Heydrich's sadistic treatment of women is particularly evident in the scene in which he terrorises a group of female students at Prague University by selecting some of their number for the brothels on the Eastern front, during the course of which one young woman leaps to her death from a window. In Fritz Lang's version of the same story, *Hangmen Also Die* (1942), which also features a syphilitic, homosexual Nazi officer, the characterisation of Heydrich is even more demonic than in Sirk's film, as Jean-Louis Comolli and François Géré point out:

> The character is designed by the fiction to contrive within a single scene, to convene and concentrate in his person, through his body, his face, his

attitude, the signs of a radical negativity, everything necessary to make him instantly and externally hateful to the spectator. This body, this voice, these eyes bear death, castration, abnormality, sexual ambiguity. No hint of amiability; quite the contrary, in fact something equivocal, venomous, petty even in his extremes of cruelty . . . A body that is sexless and ageless, man-woman-child; but for that reason, in addition to the fact of his authority, an erotic body.[13]

Other examples of wartime films which represent the Nazis in a specifically sadistic fashion include *Till We Meet Again* (1940), in which a Nazi officer threatens to send a nun to the military brothels; *Hostages* (1943), where a Nazi remarks that "the tears of a young girl make the salt of the earth"; *The Cross of Lorraine* (1943), which has a prisoner chained to the wall and whipped by Nazi guards, one of whom says afterwards that "we amputated his enthusiasm"; and *Enemy Of Women* (1944), a portrait of Goebbels which accentuates his oppressive treatment of women to whom he is attracted.

In *Sealed Verdict* (1948), one of the first Hollywood films to indicate what happened in the camps, the scene in which a father describes his daughter's degradation has a distinctly sadistic sexual ring to it: "At the camp, they put a whip in her hand. Push her into big room with many women, all naked. Her mother too . . . They force her to lash all the people, her mother. They all dance. Germans laugh. They dance till they can't stand up; then Germans turn on the gas". Outside Hollywood at this time, the sexual dimension of Nazism was touched on by Roberto Rossellini in both *Roma, città aperta* (*Rome Open City*, 1945) and *Germania anno zero* (*Germany Year Zero*, 1947). In the former, the Nazi commander is a sadistic torturer and his female assistant a lesbian, whilst the unrepentant Nazi schoolteacher in the latter is a paedophile. And, on a very different note, in *She Demons* (1958), a former Nazi doctor, now living on a desert island, is trying to restore his wife's face by transferring the genes of young women to her body. The 'donors' are kept semi-naked in cages, horribly disfigured, and flogged to death if they try to escape.

Fourth, publishers had begun to exploit the pornographic possibilities of Nazi iconography within a few years of the end of the war. Thus as early as 1949 the French publisher Juillard was putting out in its Capricorn series novels such as *Gretchen en uniforme* and *Gretchen sans uniforme*, which were little more than pretexts for scenes of sex and violence against a Nazi backdrop. Their success spawned around sixty imitators during the 1950s, including one entitled *La chienne de Buchenwald*. The recipe was taken up again in 1973 by the war story publisher Les Editions de Gerfaut, with lurid titles such as *Fraulein SS* and with equally lurid covers to match, and by France-Europe-Presse, with books like *Filles de SS* and *Section des femmes*. The US began to exploit this strain in the 1960s in pulp magazines such as *New Man* (one of whose typically sensational covers shows two Nazis torturing a scantily clad woman, with the caption "ride the Nazis' swing of agony, lovely maiden"), *Men Today* ("I blasted Hitler's super sin and spy brothel"), and *Man's Book* ("The death ballet of the Nazis' tortured virgins"). And then, in Italy in 1970, the publishing house Elvipress gave birth to a series of adult *fumetti* featuring the Ilsa-like Hessa, "the virgin of the Third Reich", with similar scenarios cropping up in succeeding series such as *Guerra e sesso, Terror, Oltretomba colore, Storie blu* and so on.

By the late 1960s and early 1970s, the eroticisation of Nazi iconography had spread further afield, not least into the fashion industry and various sexual subcultures. As Susan Sontag observed in 1974 in her seminal essay 'Fascinating Fascism': "Much of the imagery of far-out sex has been placed under the sign of Nazism. Boots, leather, chains, Iron Crosses on gleaming torsos, swastikas, along with meat hooks and heavy motorcycles, have become the secret and most lucrative paraphernalia of eroticism".[14] In her view, this was because

> Between sado-masochism and fascism there is a natural link. "Fascism is theatre", as Genet said. As is sado-masochistic sexuality: to be involved in sado-masochism is to take part in a sexual theatre, a staging of sexuality. Regulars of sado-masochistic sex are expert costumers and choreographers as well as performers, in a drama that is all the more exciting because it is forbidden to ordinary people.[15]

This was certainly true of sections of the gay community, but Siouxsie Sioux and other punks' use of Nazi iconography, and the penetration of the mainstream fashion market by SM gear via the popularisation of punk styles, show that this was also part of a much wider phenomenon. In particular, it relates to the postmodern practice, in the realm of representation, of disregarding contextual specificity and draining signifiers of their historical content, foregrounding spectacle over substance and circulating signs without the burden of their history. By this means, as Sontag presciently noted in pre-po-mo times: "Nazi material enters the vast repertory of popular iconography usable for the ironic commentaries of Pop Art".[16]

The above considerations also demonstrate that the 'Nazi sadism' cycle is not, as is often claimed, simply a rip off of 'art' films such as Luchino Visconti's *La caduta degli dei* (*The Damned*, 1969), Liliana Cavani's *Il portiere di notti* (*The Night Porter*, 1974), Tinto Brass's *Salon Kitty* (1976) and Pier Paolo Pasolini's *Salò o le 120 giornate di Sodoma* (*Salo*, 1976). But in what sense can the components of the cycle be regarded as, in part at least, horror films? There are two answers to this question, involving the level of violence in these films, and the manner in which the Nazis are represented.

Just as it is the amount and the extremity of the violence in historical witch-hunt films such as *Witchfinder General* (1968) and *Hexen bis aufs Blut gequält* (*Mark of the Devil*, 1970) that propels them into the horror genre, so it is the case here. Much of the violence, torture and degradation is directed against women, but many of these films also feature castration. In *Ilsa*, the eponymous commandant of Medical Camp 9 castrates men who fail to give her sexual pleasure, thus making her an absolutely literal incarnation of the *femme castatrice*. In *Lager SSadis kastrat kommandantur*, by contrast, it is the camp commandant who has been castrated (as a result of forcing a Russian woman to have oral sex with him), a lack which he eventually overcomes by making one of his sergeants undergo a testicle transplant. Meanwhile, in *Le deportate della sezione speciale SS*, one of the female prisoners fixes a razorblade onto a cork which she pushes up her vagina before having sex with the camp commandant, with predictable results.

The violence to the human body in these films is presented quite differently from that which is seen in documentary films about Nazi concentration camps. Here there are no terrifyingly skeletal bodies, no ghastly evidence of mass murder on an industrial scale. Admittedly in *Lager SSadis kastrat kommandantur*, *SS lager 5 l'inferno delle donne* and *L'ultima orgia del Terzo Reich* we do see, briefly, bodies being cremated (live in the last example), *KZ9 lager di sterminio* contains a gas chamber scene (in which the victims are shown as having defecated in their death agonies), and both *SS lager 5 l'inferno delle donne* and *KZ9 lager di sterminio* contain footage of real concentration camp scenes. But this is hardly the content of 'entertainment' films, even ones such as these, and the violence here is inflicted on healthy bodies and on a limited, even intimate, scale, mostly taking the form of an extremely familiar horror movie ingredient – torture.

In some cases, the tortures are part of medical experiments, or of research programmes designed to aid the armed forces. In others, they are a form of punishment, or simply carried out at the whim of the Nazis. The most extended and explicit examples of such scenes occur in *Ilsa* (decompression, boiling alive, infection with syphilis, gas gangrene and typhus, flogging, electrodes attached to nipples, insertion of an electrically charged dildo into the vagina); *SS lager 5 l'inferno delle donne* (finger nails pulled out, fingers set on fire, a head crushed in a vice, branding, a stomach ripped open with a sharpened knuckle-duster, the extraction of a tongue); and *L'ultima orgia del Terzo Reich* in which, after a dinner party at which a Professor advocates turning the Jews into meat for human consumption, and proves the point by serving up "a pot-roast of unborn Jew", a girl is laid out in a huge dish, doused with cognac and set alight (shades of the banquet in Peter Greenaway's *The Cook, the Thief, His Wife and Her Lover* [1990]). Such scenes irresistibly bring to mind the violently misogynist fantasies of *Freikorps* officers analysed by Klaus Theweleit – for example, the novel *Die letzten Reiter* (1935) by Edwin Dwinger, in which the body of a dead Latvian woman soldier is described as "a bloody mass, a lump of flesh that appears to have been completely lacerated with whips and is now lying within a circle of trampled, reddish slush".[17]

These films contain only one monster in the literal sense of the term, and that is in *La bestia in calore*. Here the Ilsa-like Dr Krast is carrying out experiments as part of the Nazis' plans to create a master race. As part of her efforts to create a sexually untiring being (in the interests of eugenics rather than pleasure) who "would make the god Eros green with envy" she has created a sex-crazed half-man-half-beast which rapes women to death. (As in the case of *Elves*, how this relates to creating the master race remains a mystery). However, the Nazis themselves in these films are clearly represented as monsters in a metaphorical sense, and their monstrousness is represented primarily in sexual terms – as sadism. Indeed, *L'ultima orgia del Terzo Reich* even contains some distinctly sub-Sadeian philosophising. But the sexual elements of the cycle also include homosexuality (the camp commandant in *Le deportate della sezione speciale SS*, and some of the soldiers in *Kaput lager gli ultimi giorni delle SS*), impotence (the commandant in *Lager SSadis kastrat kommandantur* and chief Nazi in *Casa private per le SS*), sado-masochism (the commandant in *Nazi Love Camp 27* and *L'ultima orgia del Terzo Reich*), and urolagnia (the general in *Ilsa*).

But do these films' representations of the Nazis as sadists actually say anything significant about Nazism itself? The short answer is 'no'. As George Mosse states: "The Nazi attitude towards sexuality, with its emphasis upon the home, the family, restraint, and discipline, is at first glance almost a caricature of bourgeois respectability", and consequently one of the greatest sins in Nazi demonology was sexual 'decadence'.[18] It is true, of course that Himmler and Martin Bormann both practised bigamy, and that Goebbels had a taste for starlets, but these are less instances of flouting bourgeois morality than particularly hypocritical examples of bourgeois double standards, especially in the case of the notoriously rigid and conventional Himmler. No wonder, then, that Michel Foucault was led to ask:

How is it that Nazism, represented by shabby, pathetic, puritanical characters, laughably Victorian old maids, or at best smutty individuals – how has it now managed to become, in France, in Germany, in the United States, in all pornographic literature throughout the world, the ultimate symbol of eroticism?[19]

The answer to this question does say something about the Third Reich, but a great deal more about why it is now often perceived in the terms of the 'Nazi sadism' cycle.

The Reich of Shadows and Myths

During the Weimar period, the opposition press in Germany frequently highlighted the sex lives, real or imagined, of particular Nazis in an attempt to denounce their puritanical party as hypocritical – in much the same way that certain British newspapers attempted to undermine Mrs Thatcher's crusade for 'Victorian values'. And during WWII in Britain the Political Warfare Executive (an offshoot of the Special Operations Executive) specialised in 'black propaganda', aimed at demoralising German soldiers and civilians by alleging, among other things, that leading Nazis were engaging in sexual conduct at odds with Nazi ideology. (The work of this unit was brilliantly dramatised by David Hare in his television film *Licking Hitler* [BBC, 1974]). Such work was also undertaken in the US by the Office of Strategic Services (part of the Morale Operations Department). Particularly important here was the report produced by the psychologist Walter Langer – *A Psychological Analysis of Adolph Hitler, His Life and Legend* – whose detailing of Hitler's supposedly deviant sexual practices, particularly those involving his niece Geli Raubel, though now largely discredited, has done a great deal to fuel the imaginings explored in the latter part of this chapter. It also needs to be borne in mind that this sexualised representation of the Nazis drew on an already-existing repertoire of anti-German images which had circulated amongst the allies during the First World War. As Laura Frost has pointed out in an exceptionally interesting account of fantasies of fascism in literary modernism, during that war the Germans were depicted in allied propaganda as having violently and atavistically abandoned all the civilised practices of democracy. Foremost amongst these were sexual restraint, and hence "Germany's sexual practices are imagined to be as aggressive and undemocratic as her politics: Germany is a nation of rapists and sadomasochists".[20] In particular, the German invasion of Belgium was consistently represented as metaphorical rape, and endless atrocity stories depicted its female inhabitants as victims of the real thing. As Frost concludes: "The images of Germans with whips, of Germans as atavistic, sado-masochistic masters, and of Germans dragging half-naked women out of their homes became the tropes of eroticised fascism".[21]

However, these imaginings do have some, albeit tenuous, basis in historical fact. For example, it is true that the head of the SA, Ernst Röhm, was a practising homosexual who denounced certain Nazis' "absurd excrescences of prudishness", argued that the "German revolution" was not won by "philistines, bigots and sermonisers" and forbade his men from becoming "the stooges of perverse moral aesthetes".[22] There was indeed homosexual activity amongst the SA but, six weeks after uttering these words, Röhm was murdered, along with many other SA members, by Himmler's SS in the 'Night of the Long Knives', which was dramatised in *La caduta degli dei*. However, this was not on account of homosexuality but because Hitler feared Röhm and the SA as a rival source of power, and needed to silence talk of a 'second revolution' if he were to keep the German establishment, not least the Reichswehr and the upper echelons of German capitalism, on side. This, of course, was not the official reason given for the so-called Röhm *putsch*; as the Reich Press Office duly put it: "His notorious and unfortunate proclivity gradually became such an intolerable burden that the Leader of the Movement and Supreme Commander of the SA was himself forced into the gravest conflicts of conscience".[23] But paradoxically, if understandably, it is the iconography of the sinister but elegant SS, not that of the *lumpen* SA, which has gone on to become such a potent source of erotic fantasy.

On 23 February 1933, the new German government issued an ordinance which proscribed all organisations which had defended homosexuals, and the same measure also banned pornography. Such a measure, of course, had its roots in the Nazis' eugenic policies – above all in their desire to increase the German birth-rate. Of course, at the same time, the Nazis' veneration of traditional notions of maleness and their creation of *Männerbünde* (male communities) such as the SA, SS and Hitler Youth, clearly ran the risk of encouraging homosexuality. (Not the least of the absurdities in the 'Nazi sadism' films is the spectacle of female SS officers). Indeed the Hitler Youth did have a relatively high rate of expulsion for homosexuality. The difficulty was further exacerbated by the persistence of more 'radical', anti-bourgeois elements within National Socialism. One typical way out of this ideological conundrum is illustrated by an article in a 1936 edition of the SS paper *Das Schwarze Korps*, which, on the one hand, condemned the dictates of the "pettifogging morality of yore" and argued that bourgeois, religiously-inspired calls for denial of the "healthy instincts stirring inside a young man" could all too easily lead to "lapses into aberrations which cannot be termed wholesome, still less normal".[24] On the other hand, it suggested that the old dictates should simply be replaced by self-discipline motivated by a sense of duty to the *völkisch* community. In 1937 Himmler decreed that any member of the SS convicted of homosexuality would be executed, and during the war the definition of homosexual acts was widened to include caressing (even if fully dressed), with men who kissed each other also facing death.

Another key ingredient of the erotic Reich is the *Lebensborn* project. As Hans Peter Bleuel puts it:

> Fantastic rumours surrounded the *Lebensborn* or 'Fount of Life' association (motto: 'Every mother of good blood is our sacred trust'), not only during the Third Reich but even more so after its downfall. SS brothel or stud-farm, or a cross between the two – such were the sensational constructions put upon it.[25]

But inevitably, as Bleuel is at pains to explain, the truth was considerably less lurid. The *Lebensborn* association was founded in 1936 under the auspices of the SS Race and Resettlement Bureau, with the aim of helping SS officers to produce healthy families of at least four children. But its role was also to "care for mothers of good blood and tend mothers in need of help and children of good blood".[26] As the last phrase suggests, unmarried mothers could participate in the scheme as long as they and their offspring were 'racially pure'; such was the demand for population growth that it outweighed conventional moral considerations. The ratio of wives to unmarried mothers in the *Lebensborn* homes was 60:40. In other words, these were perfectly 'respectable' maternity homes, except for the fact that unmarried mothers were not stigmatised: "The National Socialist state no longer sees in the single mother the 'degenerate'... It places the single mother who has given a child life higher than the 'lady' who has avoided having children in her marriage on egotistical grounds".[27] And Hitler stated that: "A girl's object is, and should be, to get married. Rather than die as an old maid, it's better for her to have a child without more ado! Nature doesn't care the least bit whether, as a preliminary, the people concerned have paid a visit to the registrar. Nature wants a woman to be fertile".[28] He also enthused about "honourable houses of love" in which the finest specimens of Aryan man- and woman-hood would mate to produce new members of the Reich.

The rumours were fuelled, however, by the secrecy surrounding the homes (which was largely to protect the reputations of the unmarried mothers), and by unguarded remarks about the project by leading Nazis. For example, Himmler revealed that: "I have made it known privately that any young woman who is alone and longs for a child can turn to the *Lebensborn* with perfect confidence ... As you can imagine, we recommend only racially faultless men as 'conception assistants'".[29] Similarly Walther

Darré, one of the architects of the 'Blood and Soil' mythos, and Minister of Agriculture and Head of the SS Race and Resettlement Bureau, added fuel to the fire by putting forward the idea of 'farm reservations' in which 'superior' racial types would be encouraged serially to reproduce. In June 1942 the Reich Director of Health, Leonardo Conti, published a paper entitled 'Raising the Birth Rate by Marital Introduction, Marriage Guidance and Fostering'; among other things, this proposed an artificial insemination scheme in order to make the best use of 'racially pure' male semen – with the *Lebensborn* helping out single women who had made use of the scheme.

The *Lebensborn* project is mentioned in *Le deportate della sezione speciale SS* and plays quite a prominent role in *La svastica nel ventre*, which features ludicrous scenes of regimented breeding amongst Nazi iconography to the strains of Wagner. But again, all of this was prefigured in wartime Hollywood, namely in *Hitler's Children* (1943) and *Women In Bondage* (1943). In the former, the *Lebensborn* centres are obliquely described as 'rest homes' where the select "may meet and decide to share the experience that makes them worthy of the Führer", but the film does contain an absolutely key moment in the annals of Nazi sadism in the scene in which the heroine Anna is tied to a flagpole and flogged by the SS. Meanwhile in the latter, the members of the German Girls' League are told that: "Love doesn't matter in selecting your mate. Yours is the greatest destiny, to create the master race". And in the scene in which the girls, dressed only in sheets, prepare for an "examination for motherhood", are prefigured all the obligatory 'medical inspection' scenes in the 'Nazi sadism' cycle – except there, of course, the girls are completely naked.

Most of the camps featured in the 'Nazi sadism' cycle function, at least in part, as brothels for the SS and the regular army. It is true that because Himmler was concerned about the levels of sexually transmitted disease amongst SS members (which could decrease their potency), and was keen to keep homosexuality at bay, in 1939 he did indeed order medically-supervised brothels to be established for all SS units – but not, as in these films, staffed by 'undesirables', and most certainly not Jews, which would have run directly counter to the 1935 Nuremberg Laws on citizenship and race. From 1941, there were brothels staffed by prostitutes recruited from the occupied territories, but these were for the increasing number of foreign workers employed in the Reich and existed in order to avoid 'miscegenation' and to protect 'pure' German blood. Lynn Rapaport quotes a number of German sources to back up her claim that by the end of 1944 at least eleven concentration camps actually had brothels – the idea being to give an incentive to hard-working, non-Jewish prisoners, and especially the *Kapos*, to work even harder.[30] According to Laurence

Rees, the prostitutes in Auschwitz were mostly selected from the nearby Birkenau camp, and, although forced to have sex, were otherwise treated relatively well. However he also details instances of the rape of prisoners by SS guards at Auschwitz.[31]

As for the existence of Ilsa-types in the camps, the best known example is Ilse Koch, the 'bitch of Buchenwald', who was the wife of the camp commandant. It was she who made lampshades and gloves from human skin, and these practices feature in *L'ultima orgia del Terzo Reich* (which also includes knickers made from human hair). Psychiatrists who examined her prior to her trial for crimes against German nationals declared her to be a "perverted, nymphomaniacal, hysterical, power-mad demon".[32] In Auschwitz, Irma Griese, one of the few female guards, engaged in sado-masochistic practices with the prisoners, and Alison Owings details sadistic behaviour on the part of some of the 2,000 female assistants who, along with SS guards, ran Ravensbrück, a largely female camp.[33]

In terms of the medical horrors represented in the cycle, the disgraceful complicity of much of the medical profession with the Nazi eugenics programme is now well known (see, in particular, Robert Jay Lifton's *The Nazi Doctors* [1986]), and went far beyond the twenty-three SS men arraigned at the 'Doctors' Trial' in Nuremberg. Such complicity certainly extended to working in the camps. As Rees puts it: "For the doctor ambitious to pursue a career in research and unencumbered by humanity or compassion, Auschwitz was a laboratory without parallel".[34] The most infamous experimenter was, of course, Dr Josef Mengele, who arrived in Auschwitz in March 1943. His work on twins was based on the desire to understand the role of genetic inheritance in development and behaviour, whilst Drs Clauberg and Schumann experimented with various forms of sterilisation, and Austria's chief medical officer, Dr Wirths, researched into the functions of the cervix, as part of the Nazi programme to banish all kinds of 'undesirables' from the Reich. Prisoners were also 'sold' to Bayer and other still-existing drug companies as guinea pigs for the testing of new products.

The way in which various aspects of the Third Reich are represented in the 'Nazi sadism' cycle do, then, have some basis in historical reality, even if a tenuous one. In this respect there is in fact a degree of truth in the prologue to *Ilsa*, which states that:

> The film you are about to see is based upon documented fact. The atrocities shown were conducted as medical experiments in special concentration camps in Hitler's Third Reich. Although these crimes against humanity are historically accurate, the characters depicted are composites of notorious Nazi personalities, and the events portrayed have been condensed into one locality for dramatic purposes.

However, taken as a whole, the cycle cannot really be regarded as anything other than a much mythologised mishmash of fact and fiction. Indeed, in terms of representations of Nazism (which are, of course, only one aspect of them) all of the films in this chapter serve to bear out Saul Friedlander's judgement that: "The terrain of the most extreme upheaval of our time, which remains a fixed point in the imagination of the epoch, provides us only with shadows and myths . . . The endless stream of words and images becomes an ever more effective screen hiding the past".[35]

The Blasphemous Reich

It could be argued that the films comprising the 'Nazi sadism' cycle carry within them, through their very excess, the possibility of breaking down some of the customary clichés about Nazism. However, although they do challenge certain taboos, they simply replace one set of clichés with another. As Jean-Pierre Geuens argues, the films "fail to break through the cultural defences, the *cordons sanitaires* that society erects to protect us from being soiled by the stench and the excrescence of the camps".[36] In particular, they do not go far enough "in transgressing the good conscience that permeates, for instance, the ending of *Schindler's List*, where the colourful closure of the 'good' people alive today permits us to relegate the darkness that preceded to an aberration of history".[37]

In my view, the only works of popular culture to have done this effectively are the novels and graphic works constituting the Lord Horror mythos,[38] which, as Benjamin Noys puts it:

> Force us to confront the question of fascinating fascism without any possibility of evasion, a confrontation that is avoided in other, more 'respectable' treatments of fascism . . . By choosing to represent fascism in complex, satirical and reflexive ways these comics raise complex problems of how we 'good Europeans', as Nietzsche put it, are to come to terms with the legacy of fascism.[39]

In particular, the graphic works of the cycle illustrated by Kris Guidio utilise the imagery and signifiers associated with 'fascinating fascism' in a way that is extremely disturbing in its ambiguity and its lack of any clearly signalled intention or authorial point of view. To quote Noys:

> In particular the desire to identify them as examples of a self-conscious or reflexive fascinating fascism becomes problematic. What is seductive about the concept of fascinating fascism is that it offers us a secure political position on ambiguous works that engage with fascism. It offers to resolve

that ambiguity for us and so allows us to take a critical distance from fascism and its representations. What we find in the world of Lord Horror is an ambiguity that never reaches closure, an undecidable effect that refuses us the comfort of detachment.[40]

Noys concludes, correctly in my view, that the anxiety which the Lord Horror mythos provokes is a sign that the thinking of fascism has still hardly begun. Indeed, I would argue that using the iconography of Nazism and the Holocaust in ways deemed culturally or politically 'inappropriate' constitutes the nearest that our secular society can get to a form of blasphemy – witness the fury which greeted Prince Harry wearing an Afrika Korps uniform, complete with swastika armband, to a fancy dress party in 2005. It also explains why none of the 'Nazi sadism' cycle has ever been passed by the BBFC, why the distributors of *Lager SSadis kastrat kommandantur* repeatedly landed in court, and why the publishers of the Lord Horror mythos were, for their pains, prosecuted and imprisoned under the Obscene Publications Act.[41] Little wonder, then, that it is so hard to move beyond the clichés explored in this chapter.

Notes

1. Alvin Rosenfeld, *Imagining Hitler*, Bloomington: Indiana University Press, 1985, p. 43.
2. Steve Neale, *Genre*, London: British Film Institute, 1980, p. 21.
3. Saul Friedlander, *Reflections on Nazism: An Essay on Kitsch and Death*, Bloomington: Indiana University Press, 1993, p. 19.
4. Norman Davies, *Europe: A History*, London: Pimlico, 1997, p. 40.
5. Nicholas Goodrick-Clarke, *The Occult Roots of Nazism*, London: Tauris Parke Paperbacks, 2004, p. 217.
6. Alan Baker, *Invisible Eagle: The History of Nazi Occultism*, London: Virgin Publishing, 2000, p. 295.
7. Neale, p. 22.
8. David Britton, *Motherfuckers: The Auschwitz of Oz*, Manchester: Savoy, 1996, p. 195.
9. Ibid., p. 83.
10. Quoted in Paul Taylor, 'Castles in Romania', *Monthly Film Bulletin*, vol. 52, no. 615, April 1985, p. 129.
11. The most comprehensive accounts of the cycle are to be found in Manlio Gomarasca, 'Schindler's Lust', *Nocturno* 4 (old series), pp. 12–23; and *Nocturno Book: Speciale Erossvastika*, pp. 7–51. The most interesting account of *Ilsa* is Lynn Rapaport, 'Profaning the Sacred in *Ilsa She Wolf of the SS*', *Shofar: An Interdisciplinary Journal of Jewish Studies*, vol. 22, no. 1, 2003, pp. 53–79. *Ilsa* is also featured at some length in Darrin Venticinque

and Tristan Thompson, *The Ilsa Chrónicles*, Huntingdon: Midnight Media, 2000. The Anchor Bay DVD of *Ilsa* has an informative commentary by the film's star, director and producer.

12. Adrian Luther-Smith, ed., *Delirium: A Guide to Italian Exploitation Cinema 1975–1979*, London: Media Publications, 1979, p. 39.

13. Jean-Louis Comolli and François Géré, 'Two Fictions Concerning Hate', in Stephen Jenkins, ed., *Fritz Lang: The Image and the Look*, London: British Film Institute, 1981, p. 130.

14. Susan Sontag, *Under the Sign of Saturn*, New York: Vintage Books, 1981, p. 102.

15. Ibid., p. 103.

16. Ibid., p. 101.

17. Klaus Theweleit, *Male Fantasies*, Vol. 1, Cambridge: Polity Press, 1987, p. 189.

18. George Mosse, *Nationalism and Sexuality: Middle-Class Morality and Sexual Norms in Modern Europe*, Madison: University of Wisconsin Press, 1985, p. 160.

19. Michel Foucault, 'Film and Popular Memory', *Radical Philosophy*, no. 11, Summer 1975, p. 27.

20. Laura Frost, *Sex Drives: Fantasies of Fascism in Literary Modernism*, New York: Cornell University Press, 2002, p. 20.

21. Ibid., p. 24.

22. Quoted in Hans Peter Bleuel, *Sex and Society in Nazi Germany*, Philadelphia and New York: J.B. Lippincott Company, 1973, p. 100. This lucid and cool-headed book remains the best study of this much-mythologised subject.

23. Quoted in ibid., p. 101.

24. Quoted in ibid., p. 118.

25. Ibid., p. 161.

26. Quoted in ibid., p. 162.

27. Quoted in Cate Haste, *Nazi Women*, London: Channel 4 Books, 2001, p. 116.

28. Hugh Trevor-Roper, *Hitler's Table Talk 1941–1944: His Private Conversations*, London: Phoenix Press, 2000, pp. 91–2.

29. Quoted in Haste, pp. 118–9.

30. Rapaport, pp. 60–1.

31. Laurence Rees, *Auschwitz: The Nazis and the 'Final Solution'*, London: BBC Books, 2005, pp. 190–205.

32. Quoted in Louis L. Snyder, *Encyclopedia of the Third Reich*, London: Robert Hale, 1995, p. 198.

33. Alison Owings, *Frauen: German Women Recall the Third Reich*, London: Penguin, 1995, p. 164.

34. Rees, p. 186.

35. Friedlander, p. 95, p. 97.

36. Jean-Pierre Geuens, 'Pornography and the Holocaust: The Last Transgression', *Film Criticism*, vol. 20, nos. 1–2, 1996, p. 127.

37. Ibid., p. 126.

38. This constitutes David Britton, *Lord Horror*, Manchester: Savoy, 1990; David Britton, *Motherfuckers: The Auschwitz of Oz*, Manchester: Savoy, 1996; David Britton, *Baptised in the Blood of Millions: A Novel of Fucking Holocaust Terror*, Manchester: Savoy, 2000; and the graphic series *Hard Core Horror*, *Meng & Ecker* and *Reverbstorm* (all published by Savoy).
39. Benjamin Noys, 'Fascinating (British) Fascism: *Lord Horror* to *Meng & Ecker*', in David Britton and Kris Guidio, *Fuck Off and Die*, Manchester: Savoy 2005. No pagination.
40. Ibid.
41. For a detailed account of what can only be described as the systematic persecution of Savoy by the Greater Manchester police and courts see Julian Petley, 'Savoy Scrapbook', in D.M. Mitchell, ed., *A Serious Life*, Manchester: Savoy, 2004, pp. 395–402.

13

Better the Devil You Know
Film Antichrists at the Millennium

This essay seeks to explore a small but significant subgenre of horror films that peaked during the lead-up to the millennium's passing. As a cultural phenomenon 'the year 2000' paradoxically evoked both considerable dread and excitement. No mere temporal node, this passage from second to third millennia AD was steeped in Judeo-Christian (as well as secular) apocalyptic anticipation and anxiety. Hence, something odd – but strangely predictable – began to manifest in contemporary cinema and the horror genre. After the mid 1990s apocalyptic alien invasion films (*Independence Day* [1995], *Mars Attacks* [1996]) and annihilating cosmic catastrophes (*Deep Impact, Armageddon* [both 1998]), a wave of supernatural films emerged at the decade's end also depicting the end of the world. For an increasingly fundamentalist America the millennium also witnessed a new phenomenon in cinema that can rightly be identified as operating at the boundaries of horror, namely, the cross-over to a mainstream mass-audience of religious dramas depicting the Antichrist, the battle of Armageddon and end-times.

But these are no ordinary spectacles of oblivion as a brief, historical overview of such movies will suggest. The dominant mass media form of the twentieth century had been long in depicting big screen collective and individual finitude. Pompeii and its countless Biblical simulacra were destroyed in numerous early silent films. Tempests and comets brought about global catastrophe in the teens and 1920s. Earthquakes and volcanic mayhem were frequently the perilous stuff of pre-war and mid-century film serials. Such 'acts of God' were the incessant cinematic disaster *du jour*. But after World War II, with its industrially perfected mechanisms of state-sanctioned genocide and the instantaneous atomic megadeath that vapourised tens of thousands in seconds, horror films took a decidedly secular turn.

While the mad scientist had been both a literary and cinematic staple of the horror genre, in the Cold War 1950s and 1960s, the convergence of the military-industrial complex and state security apparatus provided a compelling context for catastrophic horror on either an individual or national scale, something previously considered beyond human agency. The 1970s witnessed what Robin Wood has called 'the American nightmare', with Hollywood reflecting the political malaise of the Vietnam imbroglio and the systemic corruption of Watergate.[1] It was a time of zombies and antichrists as well as the peak of blockbuster A-list disaster films. As Wood suggests, during these decades the horror genre entered its "apocalyptic phase".[2] Concerns over superpower antagonism throughout most of the 1980s were reflected in a spate of films anticipating global war as well as survivalism where the holocaust is a narrative *fait accompli* relegated to either the opening titles or a distant past.[3]

In contrast, the 1990s was heralded as a period of respite despite war in the Gulf, genocide in Rwanda and ethnic cleansing in the Balkans. President Bush Snr declared the Cold War was won in 1991. The Berlin Wall had fallen and the previously monolithic Soviet Union disintegrated into autonomous 'democratic' republics. The threat of global extinction via thermonuclear war, so evident in the previous decade's East–West brinkmanship and strategic policy, seemingly receded with arms reductions and less bellicosity between the White House and the Kremlin.

The Millennial Context

As Jean Baudrillard reminds us, key future dates like the year 2000 are anticipated and experienced in advance through (media) simulation and simulacra, so much so that their power and influence is already drained of signification by the time such events pass chronologically into history.[4] In the lead-up to 1984, for example, the year became synonymous with George Orwell's dystopian literary vision of totalitarian states, omniscient surveillance and permanent propaganda (if not geopolitical) wars. But the signifying status of '1984' essentially vanished during the year itself, and has remained so since. Few refer to this previously auspicious date now as anything more than just another twelve months in the mid 1980s.

Yet few dates in history have been anticipated, analysed and argued about as much as the millennium's passing. Even secular society watched on with dread – remember the global Y2K scare? For the Christian West, the year 1,000 was also auspicious.[5] Many considered it to fulfil the Biblical prophecy of St. John's Revelation – Christ would return and battle the Devil that assumes the form of Antichrist.[6] A final conflict would occur, the righteous dead would be resurrected and the Antichrist defeated. Norman Cohn and others have demonstrated that the appeal of apocalyptic narrative and myth dates back to, surprisingly, well before it came to dominate Judeo-Christian monotheism.[7] The tale of a messianic deliver-hero who rids the world of an oppressive tyranny in an apocalyptic battle has its origins in ancient Persia through the prophet Zoroaster. Before Enoch, Daniel and Ezekiel, and well prior to St. John's revelatory book, a new messianic narrative template was forged. It is one that continues to inform the historical and political outlook of contemporary evangelical, neo-conservative Christians and dominates the way they interpret world affairs and shape public policy.[8] These 'true believers' go all the way to the top of the White House and include George W. Bush and former President Ronald Reagan.[9]

Belief in an apocalyptic scheme and interpretation of history is most attractive for people who feel oppressed.[10] It is through apocalyptic eschatology (the study of the end of things) that the underclasses, the marginalised and dispossessed find promises of a reward in an eternal afterlife while their foes are ruthlessly destroyed and damned for all time.[11] What is more, in this theology those events are predetermined and immutable. It is God's plan.[12] Human intervention can do nothing to alter the prophesied course of events, even though the inscrutable actions have been revealed to select prophets whose textual descriptions (like the book of Revelation) are dream-like descriptions of future events related, *post hoc*, as 'history'.

Apocalyptic eschatology is so enticing an ideology that its broad appeal ranges from socialist revolutionaries, and fascist dictators through to rightwing American neocon capitalists.[13] This vast political and social spectrum has its commonality in the apocalyptic interpretation of contemporary events as indicators of catastrophic change, where the perceived decadence of the prevailing, oppressive hegemony is violently overturned. The ambiguity of apocalyptic prophecy enables it to be read fluidly anywhere at anytime.[14] Contemporary events are interpreted – retrospectively – as portents of a predetermined, immutable fate foreseen in antiquity.

The Devil Inside

By now we should all know what the Antichrist looks like. We have seen him on countless occasions across the millennia rendered in multiple media, from parchment, mosaic, painting and sculpture through to theatre, song, film and television. Most recently the Prince of Darkness has been played by Sam Neill, Julian Sands, Gabriel Byrne and John Cassavettes, to name a few. However, the generic conventions of demonic representation in cinema oscillate between the Antichrist as a charming, suave confidence trickster who deceives all as false prophet/messiah, and the loathsome horned beast with cloven feet and other supernatural manifestations. Arresting cinematic depictions of the Devil have been a constant element in the horror genre, dating back at least to the silent 1922 Danish production *Häxan* (aka *Witchcraft Throughout the Ages*) with its horned, bat-eared, clawed and naked Lucifer. One of the most impressive examples of satanic imagery can be found at the end of Jacques Tourneur's *Night of the Demon* (1957), which envisions a snarling, drooling, horned beast with rows of razor-sharp teeth. This twentieth-century film iconography is chiefly drawn from the symbolism of religious art that reached its now stereotypical form around the twelfth-century.[15]

Historically, film scenarists have chosen the milieu of devil worship in order to craft a plausible and secular rationale for the apparition of His Infernal Majesty, rather than look to biblical sources such as Revelation for scriptural *bone fides*. The 1943 Mark Robson–Val Lewton production *The Seventh Victim* refreshingly eschewed the formulaic Middle Ages or witch-hunting New Englanders to create a chillingly understated drama centred around a sect of Satanists covertly operating in New York's Greenwich Village. The banality of everyday life in New York masking such demonic ritual was skilfully deployed later by Roman Polanski in *Rosemary's Baby* (1968). Indeed, the Big Apple is a favourite site for rendering satanic and apocalyptic end-time scenarios, such as *The Sentinel* (1976), both *Ghostbusters* movies (1984 and 1987), *Prince of Darkness* (1987) and more recently Hal Hartly's mini-feature *The Book of Life* (1998), *End of Days* (1999) and *Bless the Child* (2000). That the gates of hell erupt from the bowels of NYC, or that 'the city that never sleeps' is notionally rendered as the logical location for a final conflict between good and evil, attests to the conflicting semiotics the metropolis engenders in audiences world-wide. New York can be read as either the pinnacle of human civilisation and free enterprise capital, or a moribund and degenerate city worthy of divine wrath.

In his overview of 'Devil Movies', Kim Newman muses that in the wake of *The Exorcist* (1973) and *The Omen* trilogy (1977–81) such cinematic fare peaked in the 1970s, but notes significant Antichrist productions were still made throughout the 1980s.[16] Newman recognises that "during the postmodernist confusion" of the decade "as genre barriers fell apart, the Devil made something of a comeback" in the personae of Tim Curry (*Legend*, 1985), Robert De Niro (*Angel Heart*, 1987) and Jack Nicholson (*Witches of Eastwick*, 1988).[17]

In the 1990s a further blurring of generic boundaries witnessed hybrid, intertextual forms emerging, sometimes cutting across media. Chris Carter's highly popular *X-Files* television series spawned the darker, deeply apocalyptic companion series *Millennium,* as well as the feature film *Fight the Future* (1998). These programmes tapped into the millennial zeitgeist of the decade, as did the conspiratorial *Dark Skies, Roswell,* and Jim Cameron's post-catastrophe series *Dark Angel.*

Perhaps a useful way to distinguishing cinematic approaches to Antichrist representation amid this po-mo hybridity and intertextuality can come as an extension of Peter Malone's thesis in *Movie Christs and Antichrists.* Malone makes the important distinction between 'Jesus' films and 'Christ' movies, where the former encompasses specific portrayals of the Jesus figure, whereas the latter Christ-figure is generically broader and related to allegorical or thematic aspects of the Christ-ideal such as a saviour or redeemer.[18] This is an effective means to delineate the horror and supernatural genre depictions of demon and Antichrist. Hence, not all devils are the Antichrist, and following this schema, specifically Antichrist movies can be separated into literalist and allegorical 'types' of representation. For example, when screen character Donnie Darko in the eponymous film spontaneously screams at a self-help guru (whimsically played by Patrick Swayze), "You're the fuckin' Antichrist!", it is clear the allusion is figurative, not literal, whereas the Beast confronting Arnold Schwarzenegger in *End of Days* is clearly meant to be read semiotically as the actual Antichrist (in both its human or demonic form).

Fallen Angels

In Christian theology, based on older Hebrew scripture, Satan is a fallen angel.[19] Like a prodigal son, he has left the fold. Once trusted, Lucifer is cast out of heaven by archangel Michael after a war between competing angelic factions. The coup fails and Satan is cast out into Hades for eternity, forever scheming his return and the corruption of innocents.[20] Representations of fallen angels also emerged around the millennial cusp, notably in the *Prophecy* trilogy (1995–2000), Kevin Smith's *Dogma* (1999) and *Little Nicky* (2000). While not explicitly engaged in depicting the activities of the Antichrist, these films entertain narratives of apocalyptic endings and the struggle between angels and humans to prevent a holocaust or deliberately precipitate it. The apocalyptic theology is portrayed from the vantage point of angels, often satirically, where both a returning messiah and antichrist are significantly *absent* players. There is no need to invoke Jesus of Nazareth or his evil nemesis in these narratives of end-times.

In *Dogma* two renegade angels (Matt Damon and Ben Affleck) find a loophole in Vatican law that enables them to re-enter heaven and bring about the end of humanity. They are helped by a minor devil (Azrael, played by Jason Lee), who was sidelined in prehistory when the righteous archangels overthrew Lucifer's challenge to Yahweh. Azrael's plot enlists the pair of avenging angels to overthrow God and create a new order. Similarly, *Little Nicky* comically presented Satan's favourite son (Adam Sandler) competing against his two evil brothers in order to usurp their retiring paternal overfiend (Harvey Keitel) and literally make hell on earth. Although the film's scatological humour may seem course and lowbrow, it is entirely consistent with centuries of demonic imagery (especially from the Middle Ages) depicting demons engaged in puerile antics and anal humour.[21]

The *Prophecy* trilogy (1995, 1998, 2000) extended its apocalyptic tale across these films' lead-up to the millennial year. The trilogy began as a straight supernatural, quasi-religious thriller about a second war being waged in heaven. This time it is the trumpeting archangel Gabriel (Christopher Walken) who challenges the divine order, jealous over the lavish attention God showers on humans ('monkeys' the angels derisively call men), by stealing human souls in order to disrupt the balance between good and evil. In the sequel, Gabriel returns to Earth to prevent the birth of a messianic child, prophesied by a monk, that comes about from the union of an angel (Danyael) and a human mother, and culminates in a battle between opposing angelic forces in Eden. The final film presents a world-weary Gabriel, now demoted and damned to walk the Earth, becoming an unlikely ally of the human/angel hybrid in a final battle with Beelzebub.

The potency of millennial angel narratives can be found in their strong cross-cultural appeal amongst non-Western audiences. One of the decade's most impressive anime series from Japan, *Neon Genesis Evangelion* (1995–98), draws from Jewish and Christian apocrypha, biblical apocalypses and Gnostic gospels in its globalised postmodern fusion of *mecha* battles and post-holocaust science-fiction.[22] The remnants of a future human society battle 'angels', first thought to be extraterrestrials, in a fight for species dominance on earth. Similarly, in its hybrid tale of end-times the Japanese anime feature *Spriggan* (1998) conflated ancient civilisations, the Ark of the Covenant and a clandestine international force created to prevent the destruction of all life on Earth. Proximity to the millennium also informed the Hong Kong supernatural actioner *666 Satan Returns* (1996). Set just prior to the 1997 handover of Hong Kong to China, the context for this narrative's millennial anxiety is not predicated on Christian theology but geopolitical succession and a subtextual, apocalyptic fear of the mainland communist other.

Evangelical Apocalypse

To coincide with the coming millennium a wave of evangelical films were made as predominantly direct-to-video release features, chiefly for a Christian direct-market clientele. The Apocalypse Trilogy (*Apocalypse* [1998], *Revelation* [1999], *Tribulation* [2000]) and the follow-up video *Judgement* (2001) are all small-budget, independent productions that have turned a handsome profit drawing on a large, devout Christian audience while employing some former A-list film and television stars such as Margot Kidder, Gary Busey and Mr T.[23]

Most of these films deal with the post-rapture interregnum – the apocalyptic period of seven years commencing immediately after the point at which millions of the Christian faithful instantaneously ascended (raptured) to heaven, leaving the rest of humanity to face horrible tribulations before a final battle between Christ and Satan. Following the ultimate defeat of the Antichrist it is prophesied that a millennial reign of peace on Earth will last for 1,000 years. Interestingly, each of these evangelical films to date concentrates on the build up to the apocalypse or the pre-millennial trials and tribulations befalling the post-rapture society. Predictably, none of these dramas attempt to envision the promised Edenic millennium of harmony and bliss. The appeal of such features is intrinsically about portraying conflict, chaos, wrathful vengeance and the ultimate vindication of the righteous at the expense of an oppressive tyranny. An eternity of peace and cosmic order just does not cut it at the box office or the video rental store.

These films, usually based on successful best-selling evangelical novels, have gained wide audiences in the US, with some books outselling Stephen King and other literary genre dynamos.[24] As filmmaker André van Heerden (*Left Behind: The Movie* [2000]) suggests, apart from these films' obvious chronological proximity to the second millennium the apocalyptic fascination and foreboding stems also from current events which he finds are reflected in scripture:

> The times are biblically ripe . . . the attack on Manhattan's twin towers, the war in Iraq, and the constant threat of terrorism have made people fearful of the future.[25]

There is no shortage of doomsayers looking to global events as signs of impending holocaust and catastrophe. Unlike the scholarly hermeneutics and biblical exegeses of Paul Ricoeur, Northrop Frye and Frank Kermode, chart-busting author Michael Drosnin (*The Bible Code* and *Bible Code II: The Countdown*) follows the familiar path trod by passé prophets such as Hal Lindsay (*The Late Great Planet Earth*) whose mid 1970s pontification about the Arab-Israeli war, oil crises and godless Soviets with nukes conforming to Revelation's signs of imminent end-times make refreshingly amusing reading today.[26] It seems any spurious and *post hoc* sociological entrail-reading or examination of textual tea-leaves will appeal to a mass audience that strives to make sense of the (end)times, believing that the apocalypse may always be nigh. Drosnin, for instance, claims to have found in the Bible the words 'twin', 'towers', 'airplane', 'it knocked down' and 'crime of bin Laden'.[27]

   Given the audience profile it should be of little surprise that these evangelical films display evidence of the Christian right's hostility towards its ideological others. According to Morgan Strong, former Professor of Middle East History at State University of New York, the strengthening influence of American evangelists cannot be underestimated:

> Rev. Jerry Falwell believes fully, and unequivocally that we must go to war with Iraq to set in motion the cataclysmic events that will ensure the second coming of Jesus Christ . . . War with Iraq will lead to the end of the World, as we know it . . . Israel will be no more. Israel will be destroyed during the apocalypse. Any Jews that survive anywhere will be converted to Christianity.[28]

Hence, such popular filmic texts provide evidence of the political unconscious operating in the mindset of neocon advisors to government. In *Apocalypse* a potential global nuclear war is averted by a charismatic President of the European Union, Franco Macalousso. But a pair of American news anchors suspect Macalousso is actually the Great Deceiver and False Prophet of the apocalypse – the Antichrist. Such a simplistic dichotomy of good and evil, America and Europe, greenback versus Euro evokes the rhetorical stoushes over the geopolitical irrelevance of 'old Europe' during the invasion of Iraq, single currency reforms and the unilateralism of *pax Americana*. In the sequel, *Revelation*, 200 million people inexplicably vanish from the face of the Earth. It is the end of days, the rapture. The chosen elect have ascended into heaven. The vast majority of those left behind are left to ponder what happened while facing the horrors of tribulation. Their choice is stark – whether atheist, Jew, Muslim, Buddhist, Hindi – convert to Christianity or face the Day of Wrath with oblivion in eternal damnation. No room for pluralism here. No Christian tolerance for loving and forgiving thy neighbour. Hence, traditional conservative American suspicions and conspiracies are latent in this film's depiction of a Christian underground resistance movement fighting against the new World Government, One Nation Earth (ONE). Certainly the George W. Bush administration's public disdain for, and derision of, the United Nations and its agencies confirms the political currency of such sentiments.

A later addition to the series, *Judgement*, evokes US policy concerns over international conventions and jurisdiction of American citizens. With the One World leader succeeding in branding most of the world's population with his mark (666), the Antichrist arranges for the head of the Christian resistance to be tried by the One Nation Earth Court of Justice. These fictitious narratives play on widely held fears of American appeasement and internationalism. Increasingly conservative US politicians and their allies have railed against multilateral or international peer treaties if deemed against American commercial or strategic interests. Significantly, the US refuses to sign up for the International Criminal Court, it has ignored World Court decisions in the Hague, and it has failed to ratify key international treaties such as the Kyoto Protocol.

One of the biggest film industry surprises at the turn of the millennium was the breakthrough, cross-over movie *The Omega Code* (1999) which gained a broad international theatrical release. As in the Apocalypse trilogy, this literalist evangelical narrative features a charismatic Italian tycoon, Stone Alexander (Michael York), who rapidly advances from Chairman of the European Union, after signing a global seven-year peace treaty, to become self-proclaimed World Emperor. Antichrist Stone unleashes a nuclear strike on Israel in order to destroy the temple and bring about Armageddon but is thwarted by a pair of angels who turn the ICBM back on the devil, which explodes above his Roman lair. The blast and electromagnetic pulse kills the human host and the demon within is thrust out in ectoplasmic form and banished.

Only Michael Tolkien's vastly underrated *The Rapture* (1995) came close to a mainstream Hollywood evangelical vision with its literalist view of end times. Yet *The Rapture* totally eschews Antichrist or messiah imagery, although it does gesture to Revelation's seven seals and four horsemen. Tolkien's narrative is a rich tapestry of Christian ideals of self-sacrifice, redemption and human choice in a peculiarly moribund and predetermined cosmos. As such it prefigures *Stigmata*'s (1999) Gnostic theology, which disregards institutional religion by suggesting divinity and the kingdom of heaven can be found 'within'. For *The Rapture*'s protagonists the apocalyptic and millennial stakes are individual and personal, not global and universal.

Secular Apocalypse

As discussed above, evangelical apocalypse *embraces* chaos and tribulation since that theology recognises such actions are merely the necessary transitional phase immediately prior to the prophesied millennium

21. Self-proclaimed World Emperor: Michael York in *The Omega Code* as the antichrist, Stone Alexander

and the final defeat of tyranny. However, the *secular* interpretations of apocalypse are about finitude and/or its prevention. They are not religious. In mainstream Western society 'apocalypse' usually connotes a catastrophic period or single disastrous event of epic proportions – one that ushers in the end of humanity.[29] For example, the secular view of apocalypse in *Strange Days* (1995) unfolds during the social chaos at millennium's end where the invention of a revolutionary technology may change the nature of human society. *The Matrix* (1999) depicts an illusory future world revealed by a reluctant messiah, and although the narrative tropes are similar to archaic apocalypses, no literal Antichrist or Christian theology is espoused.[30] Similarly *Terminator 3: Rise of the Machines* (2002) continues the trilogy's messianic narrative from a decidedly secular perspective, albeit one which obliquely references Revelation (a global holocaust, terminators as deceivers). The Canadian production *Last Night* (1998) is perhaps the most unrelenting in its bleak vision of absolute finitude and the extinction of *homo sapiens*. There is no hint of salvation/redemption here as a massive solar flare razes all life on Earth during its 24-hour diurnal rotation.

Those popular film expressions of the apocalypse that do incorporate literalist renderings of the Antichrist are also essentially secular interpretations of Judeo-Christian theology. Unlike the examples of non-religious movies mentioned above, these films conform closely to the archetypal religious narrative by drawing *typologically* on earlier, well-known apocalyptic and biblical references. Northrop Frye has noted that typology is essential to the structure of the Bible; it is its fundamental 'code'.[31] Primarily this code is the structural repetition of tropes, motifs and themes across differing books and periods, where key elements are recast into types and anti-types to ease comprehension by evoking reader familiarity with extant concepts in unfamiliar and new contexts. According to Frye: "In the Old Testament the New Testament is concealed; in the New Testament the Old is revealed". Events manifest in the New Testament become an 'antitype', a form of something presaged as 'type' in the Old Testament.[32] Hence, the Book of Revelation is replete with narrative typologies from the older scripture (Genesis, Daniel, Enoch etc). Since apocalypse is to be read as a prophecy which confirms an historical trajectory as planned and immutable, each new writing strives – often obliquely – to reference past events from the perspective of a current, or future, vision where the (traumatic) events of the past only make sense at the anticipated ending. The rich literary symbolism in such writing resonates in its association with prior testaments. It simultaneously reconfirms this scriptural tradition, effectively becoming intertextual cross-referencing.

Hence, secular film versions of the apocalypse also exhibit this typological tradition. In something akin to generic evolution and renegotiation, where audiences expect a combination of *both* convention and departure from formulae to engender narrative pleasure, Antichrist movies build on the subgenre that has preceded it, while consciously referencing the biblical typologies and the cinematic genre traditions. These include iconography, decor, characterisation, mise-en-scène and special effects. Similarly, revelatory dreams, demonic possession, arcane or secret/hidden texts, insanity, menacing animals (often hounds or ravens), childbirth, devil worship, sexual 'depravity', celestial convergences, miracles or supernatural occurrences, seals broken, trumpets sounding, inverted crucifixes, levitation, stigmata, ceremonial daggers and suicide all become the typological stuff of secular Antichrist films.

As the millennium approached the number of screen presentations of apocalyptic themes increased. The 1980s and 1990s were widely considered a postmodern era – one where the grand narratives of legitimacy from our Enlightenment past were increasingly irrelevant or breaking down.[33] It was a time of perpetual crisis (patriarchy, sexuality, family) and one informed by either hyperreality or simulation, where signification no longer had certainty or constancy.[34] It was the end of history.

Yet secular apocalyptic films made in these decades challenged these assumptions by (mostly) conservatively reinforcing one of the oldest grand narratives of legitimation – Judeo-Christian apocalypse. Made for television, *Omen IV: The Awakening* (1991) reinterpreted the Damien Thorn Antichrist mythology by initially switching the demon child from boy to girl and centring on New Age mysticism (psychic fairs, amulets, auras) as opposed to the genre clichés of Christian paraphernalia. Like its predecessors, the production drew from the cinematic tradition of its genre while advancing the pre-apocalyptic narrative along an unconventional and inventive plot before returning at the conclusion to the preordained gender outcome nevertheless demanded by tradition. A decade later, *Lost Souls* (2000) provided a stark opportunity for salvation or damnation. In this case a former psychiatric patient (Winona Ryder), who was demonically possessed and successfully exorcised, uncovers Satanists conspiring to groom an unwitting criminologist-author into becoming the Antichrist symbolically on his 33rd birthday. Good triumphs over evil unconvincingly at the conclusion when the transformed Antichrist is perfunctorily shot by Ryder. A single bullet does the trick, and not even a silver one at that. That a simple handgun could so readily dispatch the universal overfiend and thwart his eternal damnation of the planet delivers an underwhelming denouement.

Unlike *Lost Souls*, the secular Antichrist blockbuster movie for the millennium was Peter Hyams' *End of Days* (1999) starring Arnold Schwarzenegger as a suicidal ex-cop (Jericho Cane), now a celebrity

22. Challenged by the forces of Satan and the apocalypse: Arnold Schwarzenegger in *End of Days*

bodyguard caught up in an assassination plot. Like many films of the genre it opens with a title sequence quoting scripture (Revelation 20:7) "And when the thousand years are expired Satan shall be loosed from his prison", and is followed by a credit sequence with overlapping images referencing the iconography of apocalypse: biblical texts, burning crucifixes, demons, rosary beads, pentagrams, eclipses. A celestial apparition is considered a portent (a comet above a full moon is described as "opus dei – God's work") signalling the birth of a child destined to bear the seed of Lucifer. The woman predestined to be the mother of Satan's child – who can only be conceived in the minutes just prior to the millennial transition (midnight on 31 December 1999) – is secretly abducted and raised by Satanists. Thirty years on, Christine York (Robin Tunny) is troubled by disturbing visions and dreams which have haunted her throughout her life, particularly one which repeatedly involves a man coming to impregnate her. When the Devil finally arrives in Manhattan he is indeed horny. After a pyrotechnic supernatural entrance through Manhattan's sewers, Satan undertakes human form (invisibly assaulting/possessing the body of Gabriel Byrne in a restaurant toilet) and then proceeds to spontaneously seduce and lustily grope a female business associate before destroying all the occupants of the diner in a supernatural inferno.

Sexual decadence and 'depravity' is a frequent thematic indicator of the Antichrist's corruption. Byrne soon calls on the Satanist doctor (Udo Kier) of his betrothed and immediately seduces the man's wife and daughter. In an arresting and surreal CGI sequence, this demonic *ménage a trois* corporeally merges the three writhing participants into two, then morphing to become Antichrist and Christine York (the latter awakes screaming from this experience as a vision/dream). Similarly, Julian Sands, in *Warlock: The Armageddon* (1993), digitally penetrates his human mother's abdomen in order to bizarrely communicate with his satanic father. Incest is a frequent sign of demonic corruption. The soon-to-be Antichrist of *Lost Souls* is sired from his devil-worshipping 'uncle' and mother, while a key subplot of *The Seventh Sign* (1988) concerns the execution of a Downs syndrome killer who murdered his incestuous parents, justifying his action by quoting Leviticus that his action was the "law of God".

Another key genre indicator of end-times is images of natural and physical laws in flux, where such imagery is often deployed as an iconic means of forewarning of the Antichrist's approach or proximity. A favourite sequence referenced typologically is the reversed motion of water or some other liquid, seemingly defying gravity in its supernatural betrayal of fluid dynamics. Such imagery is evident in *Prince of Darkness, Stigmata, Lost Souls* and *Prophecy*. Similarly, the iconic use of daggers and blades as both instrument of satanic rite and means to dispatch the Antichrist is generically transposed across films. Borrowing from Revelation's seven swords, *The Omen*'s seven daggers of Meggido are deployed throughout the series as the sole means to prevent the Antichrist's final conquest. In Antichrist movies, secular or otherwise, blades are now generically and typologically ingrained culturally, like wooden stakes for vampires, as an iconographic signifier. In *End of Days*, after shooting a dagger-wielding renegade Vatican hit squad (one shot breaks the blade) that is attempting to kill Christine, Cane ultimately defeats Satan (who has now possessed *him* after leaving Byrne's defeated and dismembered corpse). As an act of self-sacrifice/suicide Cane then impales himself on an angelic sword felled from a church statue, which instantly dispatches the Antichrist back to Hades. Having saved Christine from demonic rape and denied Satan his millennial chance, Cane is rewarded in his dying moments by a heavenly vision that reunites him with his dead wife and daughter.

Schwarzenegger, who admits to believing "in God, and evil", suggested somewhat disingenuously at the time of the film's release that his motivation for participating in *End of Days* reinforced his personal philosophy of:

> resolving conflicts without resorting to violence. I think that's one of the reasons why I enjoyed doing this film. I was happy with the ending with message [sic]: you can't confront evil with evil but use a dialogue, other means to solve problems.[35]

Given the enormous body count, gunplay and eviscerating violence (supernatural and otherwise), this finale is merely a redemptive coda, like the conventional Hollywood studio 'happy ending', that fails to diminish the spectacular mayhem, righteous bloodlust and ideology of vengeance that precedes it.

As the plot-lines and narrative typologies described above indicate, like their evangelical contemporaries, secular Antichrist films are fundamentally conservative in world-view. Their narratives serve to unproblematically reinforce traditional values of patriarchy, heterosexual monogamy, predeterminism, divine agency, might equating right, and simplistic binary ethical and moral oppositions devoid of gradation and nuance.

This article has suggested the recent historical convergence of secular studio films of end-times with independent conservative Christian religious dramas has created a unique merging and overlap of horror tropes, iconography, motifs and characters to entertain audiences world-wide. The cultural implications of such a convergence seem troubling, apparently reinforcing age-old beliefs in prophecy, fate and the irrelevance of human agency.

In periods of uncertainty and anxiety film narratives of apocalypse that represent a literal and identifiable Antichrist provide an historically mythic template for action and drama that simplifies complex relations into alliances of either good or bad, or right and wrong, which unfolds according to a predestined cosmic plan. Into this new century and new millennium as we encounter the rhetoric of waging a 'crusade' against a 'barbaric' foe, or an 'axis of evil', it is worth reflecting, as Cohn and Kermode have repeatedly demonstrated, that virtually every generation considers itself the one facing end-times.[36] But unlike previous millennia where a divine, cosmic wrath was both feared and anticipated, humankind now possesses the technological capacity to bring that apocalypse down upon itself.

Notes

1. Robin Wood, *Hollywood, from Vietnam to Reagan*, New York: Columbia University Press, 1986.
2. Ibid., p. 84.
3. See Mick Broderick, *Nuclear Movies*, Jefferson North Carolina: McFarland, 1991.
4. Jean Baudrillard, *The Illusion of the End*, trans. Chris Turner, Cambridge: Polity Press, 1994.
5. See Damian Thompson, *The End of Time: faith and fear in the shadow of the millennium*, London: Minerva, 1996.
6. See Bernard McGinn, *Anti-christ: Two Thousand Years of the Human Fascination with Evil*, New York: Columbia University Press, 2000.
7. Norman Cohn, *Cosmos, Chaos and the World to Come: the ancient roots of apocalyptic faith*, New Haven: Yale University Press, 1993.
8. See Stephen D. O'Leary, *Arguing the Apocalypse: A Theory of Millennial Rhetoric*, New York: Oxford University Press, 1994; and Paul Boyer, *When Time Shall Be No More: Prophetic Belief In Modern American Culture*, Cambridge Massachusetts: Belnap Press, 1992.
9. See Gore Vidal, *Armageddon? Essays, 1983–1987*, New York: Penguin, 1987; Jeff Smith, 'Reagan, Star Wars, and American Culture', *Bulletin of the Atomic Scientists*, January/February 1987; and Michael Rogin, *Ronald Reagan: The Movie – and Other Episodes in Political Demonology*, Berkeley: University of California Press, 1988.
10. See Norman Cohn, *The Pursuit of the Millennium*, Fairlawn, New Jersey: Essential Books, 1957.
11. See Jon R. Stone, *Expecting Armageddon: Essential Readings in Failed Prophecy*, New York: Routledge, 2000.
12. See McGinn.
13. See John R. Hall and Sylvaine Trinh, *Apocalypse Observed: Religious Movements and Violence in North America, Europe and Japan*, New York: Routledge, 2000.
14. See Lois Parkinson Zamora, *Writing the Apocalypse*, New York: Cambridge University Press, 1991.
15. See Nancy Grubb, *Revelations: The Art of the Apocalypse*, New York: Abbeville Press, 1998; Frederick Van der Meer, *Apocalypse: Visions from the Book of Revelation in Western Art*. New York: Alpine Press, 1977; and Gilles Néret, *Devils*, Köln: Taschen, 2003.
16. Kim Newman, *Nightmare Movies*, London: Bloomsbury, 1993.
17. Ibid., p. 49.
18. Peter Malone, *Movie Christs and Antichrists*, Eastwood, NSW: Parish

Ministry Publications, 1988, p. 17.

19. See McGinn.

20. In terms of Biblical typology, the 'fall of Man' in Genesis, where Adam and Eve are banished from Eden and inherit 'original sin', reprises the exclusion of Lucifer and his forces.

21. The notorious torments and tortures of the damned were frequently presented pictorially by the likes of artists such as Brueghel the Younger, Bosch and Dürer, with imps, harpies, goblins and devils gleefully inserting all manner of implements into the orifices of naked humans, or urinating and defecating on their hapless prey, during the Day of Wrath and Last Judgement. See Néret, pp. 117–59. In *Little Nikki*, Satan (Harvey Keitel) perfunctorily shoves a large pineapple up the rear end of Adolf Hitler, dressed as an *au pair*, presumably as part of the former dictator's daily punishment into eternity.

22. See Mick Broderick, 'Anime's Apocalypse: *Neon Genesis Evangelion* as Millenarian Mecha', *Intersections*, no. 7, 2002.

23. Gayle MacDonald, 'Lights, Camera, Apocalypse!', Bell Globemedia interactive. 19 July 2003, <www.globeandmail.com/servlet/ArticleNews/ TPPrint/LAC/20030719/APOCALYPSE19/TPEntertainment/>.

24. Ibid.

25. Ibid.

26. See O'Leary.

27. See MacDonald.

28. Morgan Strong, quoted in 'Apocalypse Soon: Iraq War Fuels Visions Of Armageddon End Times', 8 April 2003, <http://www.atheists.org/flash.line/ iraq2.htm>.

29. See Debra Bergoffen, 'The Apocalyptic Meaning of History', in Lois Zamora Parkinson, ed., *The Apocalyptic Vision in America*, Bowling Green: Bowling Green University Press, 1982, pp. 11–35.

30. See Mick Broderick, '*The Matrix* and the Millennium', *Millennial Stew*. Summer 1999, pp. 11–12.

31. Nothrop Frye, *The Great Code: The Bible and Literature*, London: Routledge & Kegan Paul 1982.

32. Ibid., p. 79.

33. See François Lyotard, *The Postmodern Condition: A Report on Knowledge*, trans. Geoff Bennington and Brian Massumi, Manchester: Manchester University Press, 1984; and Fredric Jameson, 'Postmodernism, or The Cultural Logic of Late Capitalism', *New Left Review*, vol. 146, 1984, pp. 53–92.

34. See Umberto Eco, *Apocalypse Postponed*, London: BFI, 1994; and Jean Baudrillard, 'The Anorexic Ruins', trans. David Antil, in Dietmar Kemper and Christoph Wulf, eds, *Looking Back on the End of the World*, New York: Semiotext(e), 1987.

35. Arnold Schwarzenegger, 'The good, the bad and the satanic', *Empire online*, 1999, interviewed at <www.empireonline.co.uk/features/interviews/arnie/>.

36. See Cohn, *The Pursuit of the Millennium*; and Frank Kermode, *The Sense of an Ending: Studies in the Theory of Fiction*, London: Oxford University Press, 1967.

14

Feminine Boundaries
Adolescence, Witchcraft, and the Supernatural in New Gothic Cinema and Television

ESTELLA TINCKNELL

The institutional and generic relationships between television and cinema have always been more fluid and interdependent than some disciplinary conventions – and media commonsense – allow. One of the most significant emergent genres of the 1990s, the 'new Gothic', was, for instance, found in both television and film forms. *The Craft* (1996), *The Faculty* (1998), *Practical Magic* (1998), *Ginger Snaps* (2000) and *Twilight* (2008) were all successful cinematic examples of the genre, while *Buffy the Vampire Slayer* began life as a feature film in 1992 before becoming an iconic television text for the late 1990s, a status it retained up to and throughout the final series in 2003. Variations on the genre, such as *Sabrina the Teenage Witch* (1996–2003) and *Charmed* (1998–2006), have offered a domesticated hybrid version of the Gothic which integrates elements found in soap opera, such as strong female characters and a focus on personal relationships, with plots based around the supernatural. This hybridity, together with the range of media influences that many such texts display, including the use of a style-driven visual aesthetic informed by music video, means that they challenge a number of generic and conceptual boundaries. Furthermore, while clearly acting as a space for the articulation of adolescent pathologies they do not seem to be narrowly addressed to a teenage audience.

This chapter will consider the contradictions and problematic dimensions to this as well as the continuities between cinema and television versions of the genre. It will do so by exploring three of the boundaries that are disrupted by the genre: the liminal boundary between teenagerhood and adulthood that the central protagonists occupy in these stories; the boundary between the 'special powers' of the supernatural that the teenage heroines possess and their 'ordinary' female selves; and the aesthetic boundaries between television, music video and cinema conventions that these texts reconfigure. The chapter argues that there is a powerful and ongoing discursive relationship between television and cinema genres, partly produced out of significant shifts in the cultural identity of adolescence. It also considers the extent to which such narratives stage, subvert or recuperate a 'new' femininity.

Liminal Boundaries: Adolescence and Adulthood Rethought

Special effects dominated 'blockbuster' movies such as *Titanic* (1997), the *Lord of the Rings* trilogy (2001–03) or animated films such as *The Lion King* (1994) and *Finding Nemo* (2003) have become increasingly central to contemporary mainstream popular cinema since the late 1970s, as the major studios and media conglomerates have sought to maximise audiences through cross-promotional marketing and the development of films that can be simultaneously offered to a range of audience constituencies. Such movies frequently combine the visceral and visual pleasures of choreographed action with ironic dialogue or knowing references that speak simultaneously – albeit in different registers – to both adults and children without automatically excluding the other. In a discussion of this phenomenon, Robin Wood has argued that the legacy of the success of such blockbuster movies in the 1970s and 1980s has been the development of what he calls "children's films conceived and marketed largely for adults – films that construct the adult spectator as a child, or, more precisely, as a childish adult, an adult who would like to be a child".[1] In other words, for Wood, the blurring of boundaries between the specific audiences being addressed by such films also marks a regressive step for popular cinema itself. However, it may be more useful to situate these changes in film style and address within larger and continuing transformations in the relationship between adulthood and adolescence over the last fifty years, transformations which intensified during the last two decades of the twentieth-century.

Prefigured by the novel *The Catcher in the Rye* (1951), which gave its teenage narrator moral authority, and by 'social problem' films such as *Rebel Without a Cause* and *Blackboard Jungle* (both 1955), which took teenage experience relatively seriously, popular cinema in the 1950s was already becoming a site for the exploration and testing out of new discourses around youth, masculinity, individualism and social rebellion in the post-war period. Throughout the 1950s and 1960s, however, confused or angst-ridden teenage characters and the cultural sensibility of adolescence were largely cast against an apparently stable adult world embodied by stars such as Glenn Ford. 'Teenagerhood', articulated in the troubled figures of James Dean or Vic Morrow, was explicitly represented as a temporary stage in life, soon to be relinquished for the safety of adult maturity and the certainty of work and marriage. Yet, rather than marking the emergence of a novel and temporary set of cultural practices and identifications, the development of the teen film in the 1950s actually pointed to a much larger emergent shift in which adulthood itself would become more culturally marginal.

By the 1970s, youth culture had assumed an increasingly powerful social role, and the teenager had become pivotal in many conventional media representations of family life, particularly in television sitcoms such as *The Brady Bunch* (1969–74) and the musical family drama, *The Partridge Family* (1970–74). In these shows – nostalgically invoked by the retro sitcom, *That '70s Show* (1998–2006) – adolescent masculine subjectivity is privileged but it is also problematic. Indeed, the adult-adolescent male typified by the character of the Fonz (Henry Winkler) in the 1950s-set sitcom, *Happy Days*, (1974–84), seems forever poised in the act of *becoming* adult while never being required to take on adult responsibilities. The further development and refinement of the teen movie into various subgenres, such as the romantic melodrama (*The Breakfast Club*, 1985), the gross-out comedy (*Dumb and Dumber*, 1994) and the retro soundtrack movie (*Dazed and Confused*, 1994), with their foregrounding of childlike adults and 'adult' children in the 1980s and 1990s, also marked an increasing blurring of boundaries around narratives and their audiences. Often, such films mobilised a rich mix of nostalgia for an idealised past together with the suggestion that growing older was something that could be resisted at the level of cultural affiliation. At the same time, far from offering the simple regressive pleasures problematised by Wood, they were marked by a degree of cultural anxiety about adulthood that has become pervasive in popular culture and which has contributed to the changing status of other texts.

For example, by the 1990s the cultural hegemony of youth culture had also helped to transform the status of and audiences for literary genres cognate to Gothic horror, such as fantasy fiction, which is no longer defined in terms of an 'adult' or 'youth' audience, but is instead complexly related to the cultural revision of taste and the extension of youth discussed above. This shift towards a crossover audience has also been taken up in the marketing of the Harry Potter novels and Philip Pullman's *His Dark Materials* stories, which have been expressly sold to both adults and children. In this respect, the new Gothic is both symptomatic of the cultural shifts around adulthood and adolescence being articulated elsewhere and a peculiarly apt location for the cultural expression of these changes because of its fantasy elements, as I discuss below.

The generic and textual differences between popular narratives addressed to adults or to young people are, then, much less clearly delineated than 30 years ago, while the audiences they seem to speak to and for are defined less in terms of generation than in constituencies of interest which may transcend age in significant ways. These social changes were central to the development of hybrid television dramas during the 1990s such as *Buffy the Vampire Slayer*, *Angel* (1999–2004) and *Smallville* (2001–), which drew on the generic traditions of horror and those of melodrama and soap opera in equal measure. Such dramas focused upon the social relationships of teenage characters and the affective sensibility of teenagerdom, but did so for audiences that were often socially and economically adult, but culturally attached to youth cultures and identities. They also used the tropes of Gothic horror, with its emphasis on bodily transformation and transgression in the form of the vampire, the zombie or the mutant, to articulate and reflect on contemporary anxieties about the development of an adult 'self'.

As Zoe Williams has pointed out, *Buffy the Vampire Slayer* in particular had such a broad audience appeal that an appropriate location within the television schedules was especially difficult to identify for a BBC accustomed to strict segmentation between the 'pre' and 'post watershed' time zones.[2] WB, the producers of the show (and the television arm of Warner Brothers), insisted that it was intended to have 'multi-generational' appeal, according to Lisa Parks.[3] Yet such appeal is hardly akin to that of the family orientated entertainment offered by the sitcom or family musical of television or cinema in the 1960s. Indeed, rather than appealing 'multi-generationally', it seems more likely that *Buffy*, like other teen soaps and new Gothic texts, appeals *cross*-generationally, to an audience which inhabits the cultural space of extended adolescence. This might well include sophisticated eight-year-olds whose access to the appropriate cultural capital has been developed, but it is unlikely to incorporate those claiming a pension.

The emphasis of these shows on adolescence as the appropriately liminal space through which desires, fears or anxieties which are otherwise unrepresentable can be articulated is crucial. In contrast to the 1970s teen-orientated soaps and comedies discussed above, however, the new Gothic tends to focus on the teenage *girl* as its locus of interest. The specific way in which the genre expresses the complex relationship between adolescence and adulthood is therefore through the exploration and testing out of boundaries and transgressions around the contemporary norms of femininity. If the way in which adolescence was conventionally represented in cinema and television during the late 1990s was to position its main characters always on the cusp of adulthood yet never quite reaching maturity, it is therefore interesting to consider how this has informed the recent cycle of new Gothic horror films and television shows with their foregrounding of female characters, feminine cultures and the female body.

Boundaries of Self: The New Gothic, Femininity, Witchcraft and the Supernatural

Alongside the appearance of the new Gothic, an apparently newly active femininity, physically assertive, and offering the female body as a site of resistance and control rather than sexual passivity has been an important feature of a range of major feature films in the early 2000s. Releases such as *Charlie's Angels* (2000) or *Kill Bill* (2003) seemed to offer an emancipated, pleasurably 'post-feminist' femininity, in which physical action and social autonomy for women were, for the first time, celebrated. These films were important because of their mass appeal and mainstream status. Rather than being defined in terms of a niche or 'feminist' audience base, they were presented as big-budget offerings that, like the television teen dramas, were intended to appeal to a range of viewing constituencies. Their emphasis on active female bodies and on women's narrative agency was central to this and seemed also to mark an important cultural shift in which feminist resistance was part of the representation of a new femininity.[4]

The new Gothic films and television shows also made considerable space for female characters and, perhaps more unexpectedly, for the testing out of tropes around ideas of community, female independence and self-reliance. In these texts relationships between mothers and daughters, sisters and friends were both narratively central and accorded a degree of emotional complexity and seriousness that was relatively unprecedented. The relationship between Buffy (Sarah Michelle Gellar) and her mother in the television series is crucial to the former's sense of self, for example, while Carrie and Sally Owen (Nicole Kidman and Sandra Bullock) the sisters in *Practical Magic*, are friends not rivals. In *Charmed*, the three Halliwell sisters, Phoebe (Alyssa Milano), Prue (Shannen Doherty) and Piper (Holly Marie Combs) are bound together by their supernatural powers, despite profound differences of character. In each of these cases, femininity is represented as a form of cultural bonding, not simply a matter of blood ties.

However, the genre's emphasis on central female characters and on the mise-en-scene of teenage culture, including the high school, suburban streets and houses, the coffee bar and shopping mall, is interestingly reminiscent of the textual style and narrative approach of another horror subgenre in which female characters were foregrounded, the slasher movie, so-named because of its particularly graphic use of scenes of bodily harm and physical dismemberment and its frequent representation of the point of view of the stalker villain in its build-up of suspense. Appearing from the late 1970s through to the mid 1980s, films such as *Halloween* (1978), *Friday the 13th* (1980), *Prom Night* (1980) and *Graduation Day* (1981) expressly positioned themselves within the market as 'teen horror' through their teenage protagonists and their self-conscious use of the tropes of teenage culture (the prom night, 'making out', babysitting) which were graphically and systematically turned into murder scenes so viscerally unpleasant they verged on the comic. The genre was revived in a postmodern ironic form in the mid-1990s in the *Scream* series (1996–2000), in a move that was also clearly related to the emergence of the new Gothic as a popular genre.

The slasher's narrative focus on a key female character, whose studiousness and moral probity seemed to guarantee her survival despite the killer's repeated attempts to track her down, was both novel and crucial to the genre's impact. Carol J. Clover's now seminal analysis identifies this character as a kind of female hero, the 'final girl' whose relative lack of excessively 'feminine' characteristics and virginal asexuality enables her to survive. For Clover, the final girl is "feminine enough to act out in a gratifying way, a way unapproved for adult males, the terrors and masochistic pleasures of the underlying fantasy, but not so feminine as to disturb the structures of male competence and sexuality".[5] Moreover, it is her apparently asexual sensibility that protects her and legitimates her heroism, allowing her to escape the horrific end meted out to her fellow teens, whose often overtly sexual behaviour is grotesquely punished by the killer. For more recent horror movies which have deployed a final girl figure, the requirement that she remains virginal seems to have retained its importance. In *Ginger Snaps*, for example, it is Ginger Fitzgerald's (Katharine Isabelle) plain and pre-menstrual younger sister, Brigitte (Emily Perkins), bright enough to have 'skipped a year' at school and to share classes with Ginger yet also quiet and self effacing, who is the only person capable of overcoming Ginger's terrifying violence.

Buffy too partly recasts, partly reworks the figure of the final girl of the slasher movie, and makes her more complex. First, Buffy is empowered to protect not only herself but the whole community, and does so through a combination of physical power and special knowledge – it is only by using both her intelligence and her martial skills that she can defeat her enemies. Her response to the threat of the vampire killers is therefore overtly active and physical rather than reactive and moral. Buffy, after all, is a vampire *slayer*, not a passive victim. In this respect, she is accorded a much greater

23. Buffy (Sarah Michelle Gellar), the new Gothic active female with special powers

degree of social and sexual agency than her predecessors. Resourceful, independent and knowledgeable, she is a complex development of the final girl for not only does she move beyond defence and escape towards an active and spectacular battle with the forces of evil, she also expresses a sexual awareness and autonomy that was a noted feature of the 'new' femininity.[6] For Rachel Moseley, the figure of the female teen with special powers that is so central to many of these new Gothic film and television texts is one "through which the articulation in popular culture of the shifting relationship between 1970s second-wave feminism, postfeminism in the 1990s and femininity ...[can] be traced".[7]

In this way, supernatural powers of various kinds also offer access to a form of post-feminist sisterhood through which women can deal with the threat posed by excessive forms of male behaviour such as physical violence while also defending a wider community. In *The Craft*, for example, Nancy (Fairuza Balk) is able to use her supernatural powers to prevent her stepfather from attacking her mother. Buffy's friendship with Willow (Alyson Hannigan) and Cordelia (Charisma Carpenter) in the television version is also crucial to her legitimacy in acting on behalf of the community. The new witchcraft may then be seen as a form of 'new femininity' that has successfully incorporated feminist resistance – to male violence or excessive patriarchal control – into a modernised subjectivity.

Yet both Buffy herself and the other main characters in the texts discussed here are remarkably conservative in their affiliations. Buffy, after all, acts to defend the status quo of white, small-town America, and even where differences of sexuality, cultural identity or ethnicity are acknowledged, they tend to be incorporated back into the textual and narrative structures of teenage drama. In contrast to the original slasher heroines, Buffy is represented as conventionally 'feminine', even 'girly', in her interests and cultural identity, even though she is allowed to be sexually desiring as well as sexually desirable. Above all, Buffy's status as a heroine seems partly to depend on a highly conventionalised model of femininity, signified perhaps especially by her blondeness, rather than a meaningful challenge to its norms. It is this tendency in these texts that helps to problematise them as radical.

Moseley goes on to argue – convincingly – that the double-edged meaning of 'glamour' as both a term describing feminine allure and sexual power and as a word to describe witchcraft has been important. In most of these films and shows, a benign version of magical powers is not only wholly bound up with youthful female sexual desirability, it is taken to be central to femininity itself, an essential – and essentialised – component of the human female character. The idea that female sexuality has a supernatural dimension has been regularly articulated in the lyrics of popular song.[8] It is also present in the convention of the 'magical' transformation from invisible woman to desirable (and marriageable) love object with the help of the feminine props of clothing and make-up that is an important trope in numerous popular mythical accounts of feminine identity from Cinderella to *Pretty Woman* (1990) and television make-over shows such as *What Not To Wear* (2001-).

Indeed, the traditional female domestic activities of cooking, cleaning and housekeeping have also sometimes been represented in popular texts as diverse as *Calamity Jane* (1953) and *Bewitched* (2004) as requiring little more than a bit of magic dust – and a montage sequence – to achieve, rather than heavy duty manual labour. Both witchcraft and slayercraft in these accounts therefore seem to offer an apprenticeship into a socially sanctioned model of gender, even if it is one that has the added attraction of martial arts skills. The practices and range of knowledges legitimately available to the teenage apprentice remain remarkably narrow in focus, firmly linked to domestic labour, the culture of femininity or to individual (physical) transformation rather than any wider social change. As Moseley herself points out, *Charmed* tends to privilege the domestic realm as well as articulating "the postfeminist difficulties of 'having it all' when it represents deciding between career and motherhood as a (necessary) choice for one of its characters".[9] If the skills of a benign witchcraft are available only to the young, the nubile, the blonde (and white) and are primarily linked to an individualised form of personal transformation, then, it is worth asking to what extent they may be seen to be feminist or even particularly new.

For, while these versions of female magic represent it in relatively benign terms, other representations make a more explicitly mystified link between menstrual cycles and a monstrously uncontainable supernatural power. Even more troublingly, when the powers in question are malign, these texts fall back into conventional prescriptions: menstruation as the catalyst for hysteria or spite, female friendship as a coven of conspiracy against men. In *Ginger Snaps*, for example, it is the onset of menstruation as well as a brutal encounter with the 'beast' stalking Baileysville which – predictably – induces Ginger's transformation into a werewolf. Like the central character of Stephen King and Brian de Palma's *Carrie* (novel [1974] and film [1976]), the eponymous Ginger is empowered by becoming physically mature, but is also turned into a destructive force who contaminates the men she sleeps with and must, ultimately, be destroyed. Unlike the passive and initially weak Carrie, however, Ginger is much more overtly, threateningly sexual. The phallic tail which she grows, and which is one of the markers of her lycanthropy, signifies her increasingly untameable desire for flesh – her beastliness – and her sexual predatoriness, which threatens the whole community.

Of course, it is possible to read such texts as celebrations of women's fecundity and reproductive potential – or it would be if the menstrual cycle were not so readily represented in terms of disgust and fear, and if Ginger's powers were not cast as profoundly destructive as well as sexual. Her transformation into a werewolf is explicitly linked to her burgeoning sexuality, since it is prefigured by her temporary change into a vulpinely attractive (perhaps 'foxy' to pursue the canine link) young woman whose sexual voraciousness makes her an object of desire to her male peers. By the end of the film, however, she has become a fully-fledged and hideously carnal monster whose destruction is legitimated by the narrative.

Yet *Ginger Snaps*, in the tradition of the slasher movie, hardly represents Baileysville as a place worth saving, nor does it uncritically endorse the values of small-town life. Both Ginger and her sister, Brigitte, begin the film as stroppy outsiders in their parochial community, held together by a mutual interest in the sub-cultural pleasures of a Gothic obsession with death and self-mutilation. The film, like *Carrie,* also presents the high school as a place in which teenage femininity is a condition marked in turns by emotional insecurity, vacillating superficiality and stupefying conventionality in which casual viciousness is a given. In this way,

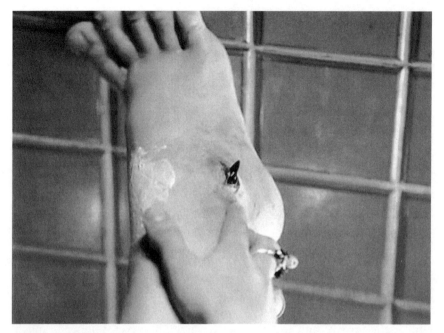

24. A time of change. The adolescent Ginger shows signs of the beast within in *Ginger Snaps*

the violence wreaked by Ginger, including the murder of the town's top cheerleader, may be read as a form of social critique. Yet Ginger's temporary physical change is also closely shadowed by the film's tropes of self-mutilation, which feature both in Ginger's earlier role as a teenage 'goth' whose death-fixation involves regular cutting, and in her increasingly desperate attempts to rid herself of the physical signs of her lycanthropy. In this way, the film's violent narrative closure in which Ginger herself is hunted down seems also to mark off a degree of ideological closure around the possibilities that have been opened up. Teenage femininity, it seems, must still conform to survive. Furthermore, there are two versions of femininity in these texts: one is the contained and unchallenging neo-femininity represented by Buffy, whose agency is acceptable; the other the disturbingly visceral femaleness of Ginger, who is destroyed.

Femininity as a cultural identity has, of course, been repeatedly cast as contingent - always in the process of becoming, of being transformed, improved, modified and modernised. It is not conceived of as a finished state but rather a condition which requires regular monitoring and management. Anxiety about this is most clearly articulated in the self-help articles and advice columns in women's and teenage magazines, as Angela McRobbie, Joke Hermes and I have argued elsewhere.[10] It is also central to the increasingly physically invasive 'reality' make-over television shows such as *The Swan* (2001–02) or *10 Years Younger* (2004–) which have become a distinctive feature of contemporary culture, and which routinely feature cosmetic surgery as the solution to women's social and psychological insecurities. In each case, femininity is cast as an unstable category in which full subjectivity can never be achieved, only aspired to. Perhaps it is this instability, this openness to change and to invasion, which renders the teen witch figure, the werewolf and the vampire slayer convincingly available to transformation; because femininity is more problematically understood in terms of a 'finished', fully adult human subject, female adolescence has become an 'obvious' site for new cultural articulations around identity.

Of course, the condition of contingency is neither straightforwardly negative nor entirely confined to femininity. The cultural changes in perceptions of adult masculinity have also contributed to the way in which 'being a man' is no longer achieved through specific social rituals or rites of passage. These perennially adolescent heroines, rather like the original final girl, therefore have the potential to become identificatory figures for both men and women. But this also presents problems for the idea that these heroines are meaningfully subversive of conventional femininity, since the magical powers they possess are either innately female or tied into their positioning between adolescence and adulthood. These texts articulate some interesting contradictions, then. On the one hand they offer a space for the testing out of uncertainties about contemporary productions of the 'self' as adult, as responsible, as located within a defined community; and in this respect they also offer a much greater narrative opportunity for female characters. On the other, when a female character's reproductive cycle is more fully foregrounded rather than evaded, it frequently becomes a site of tension and reductionism: woman *is* her body after all.

Boundaries of Form: Disrupting Institutional Conventions

In these texts the spectacularisation and aestheticisation of violence also recalls and reworks the 1980s slasher movie's use of a grotesque choreography of death. In *Ginger Snaps*, for example, Ginger's eventual demise takes place throughout a long, bloody and highly graphic sequence in which she and Brigitte are both wounded and Ginger's final transformation into a wolf marks her death. The prolonged nature of this sequence is both reminiscent of and a neat reversal of the lengthy stalk and slash scenes that constituted the culmination of many of the slasher films: the main difference is that here it is the werewolf who is the hunted not the hunter from the start of the sequence, rather than her nemesis, the final girl.

Crucially, however, the new Gothic also draws on a range of other media forms and genres for its style. An aesthetic directly derived from the conventions of music video is an important factor in the way in which these texts disrupt the boundaries of media form. Kay Dickinson, drawing on E. Ann Kaplan's earlier formulation of the 'MTV aesthetic', explores the ways in which teen movies have increasingly deployed the conventions of music video at moments of dramatic or emotional intensity, by their use of a foregrounded soundtrack and a distinctive visual style. As Dickinson points out, speed is a central organising idea to both the music video and to other contemporary youth cultural formations and identities, with the ingestion of fast food and fast drugs (amphetamines) part of the mix.[11] Indeed, the idea of speed as the defining trope of youth is vital: "Speed in most of these forms works within a system of relatives in which it assumes superiority...Speed eliminates those who cannot keep up: weeds the weak from the strong in youth fashion terms".[12] The combination of rapid-paced editing, a pounding rock soundtrack and dramatic imagery in these scenes of violent action thus produces a powerful sense of immediacy and packs a strong emotional punch.

Such conventions are perhaps particularly suited to the new Gothic's bursts of intense and terrifying drama. Stylised action is choreographed to a rock score, with the trope of the newly empowered kick-ass female martial arts expert underlined by a soundtrack that is aurally foregrounded. In the original film version of *Buffy the Vampire Slayer*, for example, a choreographed montage sequence intercuts Buffy's (Kristy Swanson) rigorous training schedule supervised by Marek (Donald Sutherland) with moments from her everyday life accompanied by a rock song, while the sequences of slaying are also choreographed to a rock score. In the television version, the relationship between music video and the dramatic enactment of Buffy's slayings is even more central to textual meaning, since the theme music that signals the start of each episode is a piece of pounding heavy rock that accompanies a montage of swiftly edited moments of shock, horror or comedy that is intended to summarise the pleasures offered by this particular text. *Buffy* thus explicitly allies itself to the MTV text, both in its deployment of video conventions and also in its address to an audience for whom the music video is an entirely familiar form of popular culture.

However, it is important to note that these conventions are not always about the speeding up of images. Indeed, in both *Buffy* and in *Ginger Snaps* it is the deliberate and artificial *slowing down* of the action achieved through the use of slow-motion camerawork, accompanied by a lusher, more ballad-like musical soundtrack, that marks moments of profound sorrow or emotional intensity. The final scenes of the latter, for example, use slow motion to emphasise the potentially tragic dimensions to Ginger's death. In these instances, speed is indeed important – but not in the sense of a quickening of action or experience. Perhaps even more interesting is the way in which slow-motion is used to suggest its opposite – impossibly fast action – in these sequences, in a clear borrowing from the conventions of the Hong Kong action movie. In such instances the slowing down of a visual sequence not only indicates that the 'real' action is too fast to be captured by the eye in real time but also tells the viewer that it is a moment of aesthetic pleasure too.

In this respect, the new Gothic also draws on some of the stylistic modes of the music video, but in its less overtly rock-orientated modes. It is notable that such scenes offer space for a more 'feminine' set of musical and cultural articulations in which romance or regret may be important.

The presence of a female protagonist in such sequences therefore seems to have precipitated a change in the mode of representation being used. It has also been part of a dramatic shift in the audience constituencies being addressed. By foregrounding female characters and the female body as active rather than passive the new Gothic also seems to have been engaged in a reworking of cultural expectations around the idea of agency itself that is most effectively expressed through the device of the choreographed action montage.

Conclusion

Having said this, however, it is also important to retain some scepticism about the extent to which these texts offer a genuine challenge to or transformation of conventional representations of femininity, as I have suggested. These narratives quite successfully stage some aspects of a 'new' femininity, but they are also recuperative texts in which the potential for transgression is managed and almost inevitably closed off. It may therefore be useful to contrast these representations of feminine magic with Neil Jordan's 1984 film of Angela Carter's collection of reworked fairy tales, *The Company of Wolves*.[13] Like *Ginger Snaps*, Jordan's film also identifies the onset of menstruation as the site of female power, yet it offers a more radical representation of female adolescence and desire. In Jordan's wonderfully dreamlike movie sex and death are profoundly (and overtly) intertwined and are indeed fearsome, but they are also embraced not defeated. Here, the teenage heroine, Rosaleen (Sarah Patterson), *chooses* to become a wolf because this offers sexual and personal freedom, but she is also guided in her choice by a wise woman, her 'granny' (Angela Lansbury), a figure who is conspicuously absent from any of the texts explored above, perhaps because such women are neither conventionally sexy nor particularly interesting to an audience accustomed to the marginalisation of older women in popular culture. Yet a story that focuses on the figure of an old woman as the keeper of a magic that is both powerful and benign is, I would argue, the only one that can be called genuinely culturally provocative – and perhaps transforming too.

Notes

1. Robin Wood, *Hollywood from Vietnam to Reagan*, New York: Columbia University Press, 1986, pp. 162–3.
2. Zoe Williams, 'The Lady and the Vamp', *Guardian Weekend*, 17 November 2001, pp. 35–6.
3. Lisa Parks, 'Brave New Buffy: Rethinking TV Violence' in Mark Jancovich and James Lyons, eds, *Quality Popular Television: Cult TV, the Industry and Fans*, London: BFI, 2003, p. 119.
4. See Angela McRobbie, 'More! New sexualities in girls' and women's magazines' in Angela McRobbie, ed., *Back to Reality? Social Experience and Cultural Studies*, Manchester and New York: Manchester University Press, 1997, pp. 190–209.
5. Carol J. Clover, *Men, Women and Chain Saws*, London: BFI, 1992, p. 51.
6. See McRobbie, pp. 196–7.
7. Rachel Moseley, 'Glamorous witchcraft: gender and magic in teen film and television', *Screen*, vol. 43, no. 4, 2002, p. 403.
8. Moseley identifies 'That Old Black Magic' and 'Witchcraft' as examples of this tendency from the tradition of romantic ballads. We can also include 'Black Magic Woman', 'Witchy Woman' and 'Devil Woman' amongst numerous others from the pop canon.
9. Moseley, p. 421.
10. See McRobbie; Joke Hermes, *Reading Women's Magazines: an Analysis of Everyday Media Use*, London: Polity, 1995; and Estella Tincknell et al, 'Begging For It: "New Femininities", Social Agency and Moral Discourse in Contemporary Teenage and Men's Magazines', *Feminist Media Studies*, vol. 3, no. 1, 2003 pp. 47–64.
11. Kay Dickinson, 'Pop, Speed, Teenagers and the "MTV Aesthetic"' in Kay Dickinson, ed., *Movie Music: The Film Reader*, London and New York: Routledge, 2003, pp. 147–8.
12. Ibid.
13. Published in 1979 by Virago Press.

15

Impaired Visions
The Cultural and Cinematic Politics of Blindness in the Horror Film

Angela Marie Smith

When exploring horror film's preoccupation with the deformation and transgression of bodily boundaries, few scholarly analyses consider the genre in relation to disability as a material, political or cultural category. Fewer still examine what horror films can tell us about their disability context – the political and cultural discourses around disability that underwrite horror films. Yet careful attention to the representation and use of disability in horror, shows the genre's dependence upon disability for its spectatorial effects, and reveals horror films as maps of the cultural imagination of disability.

At the centre of the classic horror film is the encounter between the (often physically deformed) monster and the (usually female) victim. On the one hand, this encounter, as in the horrified response of Christine Daae (Mary Philbin) to the disfigured face of the Phantom (Lon Chaney) in *The Phantom of the Opera* (1925), sensationalises the monster's physical deviance, rendering him an object for the gaze of characters and spectators who reassure themselves of their own normalcy by demonising the physical difference on display. This tendency has led disability scholar Lennard Davis to characterise horror films as 'racist' in their depiction of disabled people.[1] On the other hand, the self-conscious emphasis on framing and gazing in such scenes also undermines the idea that deviance inheres only in the monster's body. Christine's pained gesture of self-defence, one arm raised to shield her eyes, suggests a dis-abling of 'normal' vision and presents disability as something constructed – and potentially passed on – through an exchange of looks.[2] Indeed, an attentive reading of horror's disability politics suggests that the genre can realise the most radical implications of Davis's definition of disability as "a disruption in the visual, auditory, or perceptual field as it relates to the power of the gaze".[3]

Contemporary horror films rework classic horror's disability politics through the dynamic of the gaze. Carol J. Clover notes that horror films often foreground the assaultive gaze of the killer, as in the opening scenes of *Halloween* (1978), through the 'I-camera', a cinematic technique which forces us to collude with the killer's perspective as he closes in on the object of his murderous intent.[4] But, Clover also emphasises, this 'phallic' masculine gaze of complete mastery is a fiction, and if the horror film exploits that gaze to effect, it also undermines it through the unsteadiness and unfocused attributes of the killer's camera perspective, which often "does not see well",[5] and through themes "of assaultive gazing that is foiled – thwarted, swallowed, turned back on itself – and of assaultive gazers who end up blinded or dead or both".[6] But counterpart to horror films' assaultive gaze is the 'reactive gaze', where eyes and vision are attacked both within the film and by the film.[7] The blurring of these gazes in horror shapes a genre which simultaneously exploits disability for shock effect, drawing on ancient myths and prejudice, and suggests that disability is constructed in the act of looking, indicating an affinity with late twentieth-century disability rights' movements.

Because visions of disability and the dis-abling of vision are central to horror film, films of the genre featuring blindness or impaired vision are particularly tied to contemporaneous disability politics. Contemporary horror films which employ blind characters testify to the interdependence of philosophies and fantasies about disability and the social and political realities of disabled people, both exploiting stereotypes and exploring issues of discrimination and self-determination. Simultaneously, in encoding impaired vision cinematically, through shot selection and editing, films such as *Manhunter* (1986), *Afraid of the Dark* (1991), *Jennifer 8* (1992), *Blink* (1994) and *Red Dragon* (2002) emphasise and question the visuality of our response to disability. Indeed, in employing impaired vision to physiologically startle, shock and confuse their spectators, these films demonstrate the contextual, and mutable nature of disability, and the ever-shifting boundaries of normalcy.

Horror's Cultural Politics of Disability

Disability activists have long argued that disability is not a pathology inherent in specific, dysfunctional bodies, but a product of "the interaction of physical differences with an environment".[8] In 1976, the Union of the Physically Impaired Against Segregation emphasised the distinction between 'impairment'– denoting a physical or sensory lack or dysfunction – and 'disability' – "the disadvantage or restriction of activity caused by a contemporary social organisation which takes no or little account of people who have physical impairments and thus excludes them from the mainstream of social activities".[9] The efforts of activists to disseminate such ideas, and to change the ways state organisations approach disability issues have only recently begun to bear substantial fruit. In particular, the early 1990s constituted a landmark moment for disability rights in the Western world, notably with the signing into law of the Americans with Disabilities Act (ADA) in 1990. The act legislated to prevent discrimination against disabled persons in the spheres of employment, public services, public accommodations and telecommunications. In so doing, it acknowledged that social infrastructure was conceived and designed only for certain kinds of bodies, and that environmental and legal changes could 're-enable' the disabled. Just as such social movements recast disability as a matter of inequitable practices and structures, a burgeoning field of scholarly texts explored historical, cultural and textual constructions of disability, challenging the medicalisation and pathologisation that "reinforc[ed] on to isolated, individual disabled people the idea that the problems they experience in everyday living are a direct result of their own personal inadequacies or functional limitations".[10]

These shifts in scholarly and legal understandings of disability are reflected in the use of disability within contemporary horror film. If early horrors toyed with the idea that disability might be culturally constructed, post-classical horror films, specifically those dating from the late 1960s, increasingly emphasise the social and cultural structures that determine and define disability. Horror's contemporary monsters are often less overtly disfigured, and apparently normal exteriors often hide psychological dysfunction.[11] Disability is further dispersed across the horror-film text in the slashing, dismemberment and destruction of previously unimpaired bodies. Thus, even as horror continues to pathologise deviance and rely on sensationalistic presentations of physical difference for horrific effect, it also indicts normative social systems as producers of monstrosity, undercuts a reliance on visual techniques for diagnosing pathology, and envisions the vulnerability of all bodies to disability.

Blindness in the Horror Film

Given the links between visuality and the mechanics of horror, horror films that depict blindness are doubly significant for understanding the genre's disability politics. Contemporary horror films featuring blind characters draw on centuries-old stereotypes which view blind people as either helpless, melancholy, and useless victims, or as insightful and spiritual visionaries, compensated for their loss of sight by heightened sensitivities and intuition. At the same time, such films also engage with the politicised disability context of the late twentieth century. Much disability activism has occurred around the needs and rights of the blind, particularly in the early 1990s. America's National Federation of the Blind (NFB), for instance, was an active participant in the drafting of the ADA, and, like other disability groups, hailed its advent as "the potential for the emancipation and productive independence of every person with a disability on earth".[12] Members of the NFB also addressed the cultural significance of media representations of blind people, picketing ABC network offices in regard to "a Mr Magoo-like character" on a new sitcom.[13] Meanwhile, in Britain, which would not witness its own major act of disability legislation until 1996, a well-publicised 1991 Royal National Institute for the Blind (RNIB) survey identified a large population of vision-impaired and blind adults who were isolated by physical and social barriers from the resources and information they required, as well as from the forms of expression and entertainment sighted people take for granted.[14]

Contemporary horror films representing blind characters thus emerge from a conflicted disability context, where the blind are outspoken activists about their needs and rights even as old prejudices persist, and disability is increasingly presented as a construct of environmental and political systems, rather than something that inheres only in safely marginalised bodies. We can trace these competing models of disability in horrors and horror-thrillers at the end of the twentieth-century such as *Manhunter, Jennifer 8, Blink,* and *Red Dragon,* which provide a late twentieth-century perspective upon horror's cultural politics of blindness.[15] The Thomas Harris novel *Red Dragon* (1981) has generated two cinematic adaptations: *Manhunter* (1986), directed by Michael Mann, and *Red Dragon* (2002), directed by Brett Ratner. Both films, like Harris's book, are concerned primarily with the effort of detective Will Graham (respectively, William Petersen and Edward Norton), 'assisted' by jailed psychopathic cannibal Dr Hannibal Lecter (respectively, Brian Cox and Anthony Hopkins), to track down another serial killer, nicknamed 'The Tooth Fairy'. The pathology of The Tooth Fairy, Francis Dolarhyde (respectively, Tom Noonan and Ralph Fiennes), is confirmed by his physical defect, a hare-lip and deformed soft palate, the overtness of which serves to compensate for the obscure nature of both Dolarhyde's and Lecter's mental dysfunctions.

In *Jennifer 8,* directed by Bruce Robinson, John Berlin (Andy Garcia), a burnt-out city cop, comes to small-town Eureka, Oregon, and soon embarks upon a search for a serial killer who, he believes, targets blind women. Eventually, Berlin discovers that his fellow officer, John Taylor

25. Horror's cultural politics of disability: The beautiful blind woman as victim and witness

(Graham Beckel), grew up with a blind mother and attended a school for blind girls. Taylor is ultimately caught, but not before Berlin himself is suspected as the murderer. Finally, in *Blink*, directed by Michael Apted, detective John Holstrom (Aidan Quinn) seeks a serial killer of young women. Late in the film, the killer is revealed as Neal Booker (Paul Dillon), a hospital janitor obsessed with a nurse who recently died in a car accident. The nurse's organs were given up for donation and, Holstrom comes to realise, Booker is tracking down the recipients, murdering and raping them, and slitting their wrists so that blood loss will make further organ donation impossible.

Each of these films introduces a blind woman endangered by the killer. In *Manhunter* and *Red Dragon*, Dolarhyde meets and is attracted to Reba McClane (respectively, Joan Allen and Emily Watson), a blind woman who works with infrared film. But believing that Reba has betrayed him with another man, Dolarhyde eventually holds her captive, torments her, and threatens to kill her. In *Jennifer 8*, Berlin seeks to protect – and begins a relationship with – Helena Robertson (Uma Thurman), a young music teacher at a local blind institute, who may have unwittingly met the killer, and who is thus Berlin's sole 'witness'. And in *Blink*, Emma Brody (Madeleine Stowe), a blind violinist, is the only witness to and the next target of the killer, having received the corneas of the object of his affection in a sight-restoring operation. Her continuing impaired and unreliable vision complicates her witness status.

These films grapple with competing models of disability primarily in three ways, each explored more fully below. First, in their pathologised killers and disabled victims they continue to exploit disability as a deviant physical or psychological defect, often falling back on stereotypes of blind characters. At the same time, they portray blind people, to varying extents, as complex, independent characters that challenge disability stereotypes. In particular, this ambivalence surfaces in depictions of blind victims who, despite their endangerment, use non-ocular senses to bear witness. Second, in the figure of the seeing detective who uses his vision to hunt down and identify the deviant killer, these films reconfirm the practice of the normative Enlightenment gaze. Nevertheless, in pathologising vision through the voyeuristic practices of the killer, and in likening those practices to the surveillant gaze of the protagonist, these films undermine the concept of an objective and objectifying gaze, suggesting that it is vision, rather than blindness, that dis-ables. Third, and relatedly, while these films sometimes exploit the spectacle of disability to further the sadistic and voyeuristic gaze, they also employ cinematic techniques in ways that undermine faith in vision. They are thus part of a postmodern and media-dominated world, in which, as Susan Crutchfield points out, "vision . . . is not considered a transcendental, clarity- and knowledge-producing sense".[16] The films are also, I argue, part of a world seeking to understand the implications of new perspectives on disability.

Blind Witnesses

The dominant image of blindness in horror-thrillers of the late 1980s and early 1990s is that of a young, attractive woman, whose blindness compounds her vulnerability as she is menaced by a (usually serial) killer.[17] Despite their emergence in a period of disability-rights activism, these movies draw to some extent upon disability stereotypes like those discussed by Martin Norden: the young 'Sweet Innocent' who is cured in a happy ending;[18] the Saintly Sage, "a pious older person . . . who serves as a voice of reason and conscience in a chaotic world";[19] and the Civilian Superstar, a noble individual whose selfless courage serves as an "inspiration to us all".[20]

In invoking the concept of the blind victim-witness, each of these films dwells upon both the incapacity often associated with the blind and the threat to identity and consciousness posed by blindness. In a culture in which visual observation is understood as the primary access to knowledge, the sighted person's encounter with a blind person symbolises "the loss of [the former's] own identity, of his sense of who and what he is; in short, the death of his consciousness".[21] The blind person is thus rendered invalid, but also poses the possibility of a knowledge-system not grounded in visuality.

A brief glance at representations of blind people in the news in 1991 demonstrates the persistence of blindness as a disability deemed invalidating, while hinting at the possibility of a non-ocular epistemology. In January, 1991, a young blind Chicago woman, raped in an apartment building's laundry room, "identified the youth arrested in connection with the crime by smelling his cologne and later feeling his hands in a police lineup". Declared the *Chicago Tribune*, "[t]here are no witnesses to the crime".[22] In Britain, in February 1991, under the headline "Bar Ends for Blind in Judiciary", *The Guardian* reported that John Wall would become the nation's first blind judge; the following month, a blind civil servant questioned Washington D.C.'s exclusion of the blind from serving on juries.[23] And in August, 1991, a New York man was arrested and charged with a 1989 string of rapes and stabbings of women in their Upper East Side apartments, and with the murder of a young, pregnant woman. Newspapers reported that Matias Reyes "slashed [two] victims around the eyes with a kitchen knife", threatened to "blind or kill [the women]

26. Reba (Emily Watson), the imperilled blind woman who senses the serial killer Dolarhyde's affliction in the film *Red Dragon*

to prevent their identifying him", and told one woman "Your eyes or your life", before killing her.[24] These texts indicate, certainly, that political and social changes were forcing reconsideration of the assumption that the blind cannot testify or bear witness. But the continuation of the D.C. ban on blind jurors and the brutal assault on vision explicit in the Reyes attacks convey a belief that, in matters of identification and witness, the blind are still in-valid. Moreover, the construction of blind women as helpless victims of male sexual violence gestures toward an enduring association of blindness with passivity and victimhood.

The conflict between passive victim stereotypes of the blind and contemporary assertions of blind self-determination surface in the character of Reba in *Manhunter* and *Red Dragon*. In many ways, Reba constitutes a modern disabled woman. She works as an infrared film specialist and is independent, humorous and assertive. In *Manhunter*, noting wryly that her employers "had to hire the handicapped, to shape up their employment practices to get this defense contract", she demonstrates a pragmatic awareness of the role of affirmative action quotas and corporate self-protection in career opportunities. Reba is also presented as sexually desiring; refusing the passive role, she initiates sex with Dolarhyde. To some extent, in presenting Reba, the films also follow the logic of their implication that disability is in the eye of the beholder. Like the blind hermit of *Bride of Frankenstein*, Reba cannot see the Monster's 'affliction', although she senses it, empathises with his marginal status, and offers him welcome and comfort. As someone who 'sees' differently, Reba thus offers Dolarhyde his only true chance at 'transformation'.

But, following Harris's novel, the two films' treatment of the imperiled blind woman reinstates disability stereotypes and the primacy of 'normal' vision as a prerequisite for valid knowledge, ultimately punishing Reba for both her sexual assertiveness and her blindness. In the scene in which Dolarhyde watches a video of his next intended victim, while Reba, blind to the television screen, approaches him sexually, Reba is rendered complicit in, willingly blind to, his pathology. Despite a brief interlude in which Dolarhyde attempts to give up his obsessive activities, the logic of *Manhunter* and *Red Dragon* moves inexorably towards the scene in which Dolarhyde spots Reba with another man and mistakenly assumes her unfaithfulness, and from there to the scene in which he torments her in his house, delighting in her blind vulnerability.

While *Manhunter* abbreviates the novel's narrative, concluding with Graham shooting Dolarhyde, helping Reba from the house, and reuniting with his family, *Red Dragon* follows the story to its conclusion in a manner that further in-validates the blind witness. Dolarhyde sets a fire in the mansion and apparently shoots himself. In a perfect example of horror's reactive gaze, our vision of Dolarhyde's suicide is limited to the splattering of blood across Reba's horrified face and wide-open eyes. Crawling across the floor, Reba touches the bloodied mess of Dolarhyde's body, before staggering out of the burning house and into Graham's arms. Reba tells Graham and the police that Dolarhyde is dead; she is the only witness to his death as the fire consumes the evidence. Belatedly, however, it becomes clear that Dolarhyde has staged his death, and Reba has misidentified as his the body of another victim. Reba's blindness thus enables Dolarhyde to pursue one last assault upon the family unit, leaving Graham shot and severely injured, his son hysterical, and Dolarhyde, finally, dead.

The scene in which Dolarhyde stages his death exemplifies the abjection of blind victims in slasher films discussed by Crutchfield. The role of blind victims, Crutchfield suggests, is both to heighten spectators' emotional response "by capitalising on cultural discourses encouraging sympathy and concern for the disabled" and to exploit their "objectified shockability": "Blind characters are deployed for their capacity to be shocked masochistically by an unexpected touch".[25] These concepts are borne out in *Red Dragon*: Reba's blindness intensifies the shock experienced by viewers as blood unexpectedly spatters across her face with its open eyes, and as she reaches out and touches a bloodied body. While, as noted below, Crutchfield believes slasher films somewhat counteract such abjection of the blind by portraying the capacity of touch to deconstruct the power of the purely visual, she concedes that such films seek "to protect against any potential damage to the hegemony of vision over tactility" by rendering blind touch 'taboo' or 'grotesque'.[26] Equally, I would argue, blind touch is invalidated by its depiction as fallible or wrong: Reba's misidentification of the body endangers our hero and his family, and leaves her a pale and shaken version of her former confident self.

Similar ambivalences characterise Uma Thurman's character, Helena, in *Jennifer 8*. Despite laughingly dismissing clichés such as blind people's alleged sixth sense, Helena largely conforms to the Sweet Innocent stereotype. She is consistently represented as isolated, passive and vulnerable. The film does make some effort to validate non-ocular knowledge, presenting the information Helena provides about the killer's voice and breathing as important clues, and showing the audience that she is not imagining the menacing visit by the killer that Berlin dismisses. Ultimately, however, while Helena participates in entrapping the killer, it is a sighted woman, the widow of Berlin's police partner, who shoots and kills him.

Of the four films, *Blink* offers the most complex portrait of a vision-impaired heroine. Emma has been blind since she was eight years old, and has adapted to her disability in a way that challenges the 'Sweet Innocent' stereotype: she lives independently with her dog, pursues her love of music, has held several jobs, and has had an active sexual life. A corneal transplant provides her with sight, but *Blink* shows a return to sight can be traumatic and unsatisfying for someone who is blind.[27] Emma's vision after the operation is extremely blurred and unreliable. Moreover, she has episodes of delayed vision, in which sights do not become clear to her until the next day, and of hallucination, in which she sees things that are not there. When she unknowingly witnesses the killer in her hallway, it is not until the following day that his face leaps distinctly to her eyes. Like Helena, Emma is viewed as a bad witness by the male cops who are working the serial-killer case. And like Helena, Emma is both championed and doubted by the lead detective on the case as he falls in love with her. Lured into a trap by the killer, Emma must fight him alone. Despite her blurred and shifting vision, like the 'Final Girls' of horror she triumphs after a violent struggle, shooting Booker dead as he lurches toward her.

Thus, of these four films, only *Blink* places the gun in the hands of the blind woman and does not in-validate the impaired gaze.[28] But in adopting these conflicting representations of blind characters, the films exemplify equally conflicting popular and political attitudes towards blindness. More radically, as discussed below, in their pathologisation of normative vision and their cinematic impairment of vision, the films adopt a contemporary approach suggesting that disability is constructed and disseminated through acts of assaultive gazing.

Pathological Vision

Despite dominant narratives in which deviance is pathologised, sought out, and shot down, each of these films to some extent also construes disability as a product of normative forces. If *Manhunter* and *Red Dragon* present blindness as a victimising condition, they also reveal normative vision as suspect and potentially pathological. Dolarhyde's smashing of mirrors and his desire for metaphysical transformation characterise his pathology as a product of others' responses to his disfigurement. His dysfunction is explicitly located in his efforts to wield the normative and assaultive gaze that has damaged him: a technician at a video laboratory, he chooses his victims from family home-videos, he films and rewatches his crimes, and he inserts pieces of mirror-glass into the eyes of the corpses, arranging the other family members as an audience for his final violation of the dead woman.

Insofar as Graham must imitate these viewing practices in order to catch Dolarhyde, striving to access the killer's 'point of view', he is complicit with this normative and assaultive gaze; he is simultaneously rendered vulnerable to the destructive gaze, tormented by 'ugly thoughts', and unwittingly subjected to the predatory photography of tabloid reporter Freddy Lounds (Stephen Lang in *Manhunter* and Philip Seymour Hoffman in *Red Dragon*). Lounds's own experience of 'hurtable vision' confirms the film's pathologisation of vision. Captured by Dolarhyde and glued into a wheelchair, he is forced to watch a slideshow of Dolarhyde's victims. Each slide is like a blow to Lounds; each is punctuated with Dolarhyde's manic 'Do you see? Do you see?' The dis-abling of Lounds that follows is only the physical correlate to his act of witnessing.

Jennifer 8 and *Blink* also complicate the horror genre's typical pathologisation of the serial killer, and locate pathology in 'normalcy', particularly normative vision. In *Jennifer 8*, Berlin finds the clue to the killer's identity in a photograph that reveals his fellow cop, John Taylor, as a sighted student in a school for the blind: a revelation conveyed by the sightless gazes of Taylor's blind classmates juxtaposed with his own sullen return of the camera's gaze. In this photograph and the film itself, Taylor is rendered aberrant by virtue of his ability to see. Certainly, the film might imply that Taylor is warped because he grows up surrounded by blindness. But Berlin's theory, which is all the film offers by way of explanation, asserts instead that Taylor could not bear the blind girls' romantic and sexual refusal of him, their assertions of independence which violate his normative construction of blind women as vulnerable and passive objects of his gaze. In this reading, Taylor's kidnappings and murders of blind women serve an ableist agenda. Even more explicitly, in *Blink*, Booker's pathology consists precisely in his desire to reconstitute a whole, ideal and 'normal' body. In concert with the partial acknowledgement of non-visual paths to knowledge provided by the blind witnesses, this pathologisation of normalcy and normative vision affirm disability as an element of the human condition, and as a potential path to less hegemonic means of perception.

Impaired Visions

Along with these thematic efforts to humanise and validate blind characters, and to problematise the assaultive gaze that renders disability monstrous, *Jennifer 8* and *Blink* also employ disability at a formal level, enacting the dis-abling of spectators through a cinematic impairment of vision. In this way, they participate in horror films' use of what Dennis Giles has termed the "delayed, blocked or partial vision"[29] that withholds or obscures the monster's appearance, or confuses audiences with apparently motivated camera movements that provides "a monstrous overtone".[30] While, for Giles, such impairment enacts a fetishisation of the monstrous and defends the viewer from the vision of the monstrous,[31] I contend, rather, that such cinematic conventions foreground the constructedness of disability, most obviously in films that link such cinematic impairment to actual visual impairment.[32]

As noted above, the vision of disability and dis-abling of vision central to horror is often revealed most fully in scenes of confrontation between monster and victim. *Jennifer 8* employs impairment of vision in depicting a voyeuristic attack on Helena. The scene engages the 'I-camera', leading us to believe that the viewpoint we are adopting belongs to the killer. The camera begins to exhibit the unsteady, erratic characteristics of a motivated shot as Helena prepares a bath and undresses. Suspenseful music and sudden shifts and zooms clue us to the presence of a killer in her room, confirmed as a camera-flash illuminates her naked body, and we finally see a photographic camera aimed at Helena. The movie camera again adopts the attributed perspective, which we now recognise as that of the voyeur's camera, and Helena's body is lit by more quiet flashes as she enters the bath, relaxing into a sitting posture, tilting her head back and turning her eyes upward, in a position that emphasises her physical vulnerability and blindness. When the voyeur leans too far over the bath, he sets off a sensor, alerting Helena. With a sudden, jarring burst of music, he grabs Helena's wrist with his gloved hand, she screams and leaps up, grabbing for a towel, and he makes his escape. Helena is left crouched on the floor, clutching a towel to her, and flailing her arm in the air in front of her.[33]

The scene is a prime example of how the horror film seeks to eat its cake and have it too. It delights in the prurient and violating objectification of the blind woman's naked body, even as it draws attention to our own pleasurable complicity with the camera's violation of Helena. More than this, however, the scene subverts the horror-film convention by which the unsteady I-camera denotes the killer, who will eventually be punished for his viewing habits. For this voyeur is not the killer, nor is he punished within the film text. A brief scene later reveals that the janitor, a small, bald, bespectacled man, is our voyeur; he inhabits a small room high in the institute covered with photographs, at least two of which are of a naked Helena. When the killer is found elsewhere, the scene retrospectively reveals the fallibility not of a character's gaze, but of the extra-diegetic camera. Conventional viewing techniques and the audience's vision are uncovered as defective, impaired and easily manipulated. The film continues to employ visual confusion to mislead characters and audience as to the killer's identity. In thus cinematically exploiting the assumption that vision provides reliable narrative and produces objective views of reality, *Jennifer 8* delivers a critique of normative vision and the will to knowledge. The movie puts us in the position of blind witnesses such as *Red Dragon*'s Reba, but, rather than suggesting touch as fallible and vision as insightful, depicts vision as equally prone to impairment and error.

If *Jennifer 8* challenges reliance on vision by exploiting cinematic conventions in order to deceive, *Blink* undercuts normative visual operation by foregrounding the gaze of the vision-impaired. In *Blink*, unreliable vision is also not credited to the killer but belongs to the victim's reactive gaze: Emma describes her viewing experiences as unpleasant assaults, from which she flees by darkening her apartment and getting drunk. Even at its clearest, her vision is often fabricated out of dreams, memories and expectations. The camera mimics her unclear and hallucinatory vision through blurred, overexposed or darkened images, most extensively in the climactic scene in which Emma confronts the killer, and eventually shoots him dead. *Blink* thus suggests that the unsteady gaze which 'does not see well', rather than designating a pathological killer, characterises experiences of vision generally, and that it is only in the refusal to accept fragmentation and fantasy as necessary elements of vision that the gaze becomes destructive and dis-abling, just as Booker's obsessive effort to re-constitute an ideal and unreal body turns murderous. The concept of disability as a construct designed to shore up illusions of bodily wholeness could not be more clear.

A brief comment about two further films indicates the pertinence of a disability approach to horror films more broadly. The British–French film *Afraid of the Dark* (1991), directed by Mark Peploe, deals overtly with the serial stalking and murder of blind women in a town inhabited by Lucas (Ben Keyworth), whose mother is blind. After a few scenes which use framing and convention to mislead and confuse viewers, the film reveals the killings to be a figment of Lucas's imagination. In reality, Lucas's mother is not blind, and it is Lucas himself who faces imminent blindness. The film presents assaultive voyeurism as an act deriving from male anxiety over an impending loss of sight: Lucas's approaching blindness inspires in him visions of disability as a passive and victimised feminine position, and he recuperates his masculinity through acts of voyeurism. The film emphasises the mediated and constructed nature of disability by providing its viewers with deceptive and partial perspective. However, disability is also pathologised: Lucas's impaired vision is implicated as the cause of his violent behaviour when he attacks a neighbour's dog and then absconds with his baby sister. When his sight is ultimately saved, we are left uncertain whether Lucas is truly cured – in which case his blindness is pathological, symptomatising or causing his morbid behaviour – or is no longer vision-impaired, but remains pathological, in which case disability is severed from the assaultive vision that he practices. Despite this ambivalence, the film, even more explicitly than those above, presents blind female victims as constructs of gazers who pretend to objective, masterful and accurate vision, but whose visions are in fact traversed by inconsistency, fantasy and impairment.

However, horror films do not have to be overtly 'about' disability in order to employ these strategies of pathologisation of visibility and impairment of vision. To take just one example related to the films discussed here, *The Silence of the Lambs* (1991), directed by Jonathan Demme, foregrounds and problematises a masculinised detective gaze throughout, validating the ability of Clarice (Jodie Foster) to 'see' differently. In the dramatic conclusion, Clarice is temporarily blinded, trapped in a darkened room while killer Jame Gumb (Ted Levine) views her through night-vision goggles; from this blinded position Clarice shoots and kills Gumb. The restoration of Clarice's sight and the flooding of light into the basement affirm a visually orientated world-view, but the film's dynamics of sight and blindness still enable a brief validation of 'impaired' vision as less destructive than the gaze which aspires to assaultive and masterful vision.

All of these films thus stage the challenge to social concepts of normalcy enacted by disability rights protests and legislation in the late 1980s and early 1990s. But, like the newspaper reports of blind rape victims and serial rapists who seek to blind, the films exhibit a persisting ambivalence about the far-reaching implications such re-visions of normalcy have for our visually dominated systems of knowledge. Moreover, in an increasingly visual and media-dominated world, and in confirmation of the RNIB survey's testimony of blind people's exclusion from contemporary media, these films have no way of communicating their 'cultural politics of blindness' to blind people. This alone suggests that horror films, like Dolarhyde's audience of corpses with mirrors for eyes, reflect the seeing culture's own crises about vision and disability, and that their most radical contribution is in *revealing* the use of disability to throw into relief our culture's solipsistic and self-serving vision of itself.[34]

Thanks to Matt Basso and Ian Conrich for suggestions and insights during the writing of this article.

Notes

1. Lennard Davis, *Enforcing Normalcy: Disability, Deafness, and the Body*, New York: Verso 1995, p. 183, n76.
2. For a discussion of this scene, and the woman and monster's mutual realisation of their patriarchally defined freakishness, see Linda Williams, 'When the Woman Looks', in Barry Keith Grant, ed., *The Dread of Difference: Gender and the Horror Film*, Austin: University of Texas Press, 1996, pp. 15–34. Also on the dynamic of gazes in classic film, see Ellen Draper, 'Zombie Women When the Gaze Is Male', *Wide Angle*, vol. 10, no. 3, 1988, pp. 52–63; and Rhona Berenstein, *Attack of the Leading Ladies: Gender, Sexuality, and Spectatorship in Classic Horror Cinema*, New York: Columbia University Press, 1996, esp. pp. 88–119.
3. Davis, p. 129. For more on the disability politics of classic American horror, see Angela Marie Smith, *'Hideous Progeny': Eugenics, Disability, and Classic Horror Cinema*, unpublished Ph.D. thesis, University of Minnesota, 2002.
4. Carol J. Clover, *Men, Women, and Chain Saws: Gender in the Modern Horror Film*, Princeton: Princeton University Press, 1992, pp. 185–6.
5. Ibid., p. 187.
6. Ibid., p. 209.
7. Ibid., pp. 191–2.
8. Rosemarie Garland Thomson, *Extraordinary Bodies: Figuring Physical Disability in American Culture and Literature*, New York: Columbia University Press, 1997, p. 23.

9.   Michael Oliver, *The Politics of Disablement: A Sociological Approach*, New York: St. Martin's Press, 1990, p. 11.

10. Ibid., p. 8.

11. Deviant characters are still, however, often marked with physical difference, either overtly (Freddy Krueger), implicitly (the mask-wearing Jason, Michael Myers, Leatherface), or through dis-abling actions (slashers and serial killers).

12. Justin Dart, 'Empowerment of Persons With Disabilities', address to the 1992 Annual Convention of the NFB, repr. in *The Braille Monitor Publication of the National Federation of the Blind*, September 1991, <http://www.nfb.org/bm/bm91/brlm9109.htm>.

13. Joseph Shapiro, *No Pity: People with Disabilities Forging a New Civil Rights Movement*, New York: Times Books, 1993, p. 37.

14. Ian Bruce, Aubrey McKennel, and Errol Walker, *Blind and Partially Sighted Adults in Britain: The RNIB Survey Vol. 1*, London: HMSO, 1991. Available at <http://www.rnib.org.uk/xpedio/groups/public/documents/visugate/public_survviadu.hcsp>.

15. British and American examples of horror-thrillers featuring blindness prior to the late twentieth-century period include *Blind Man's Bluff* (1935), *Dark Eyes of London* (1939), *Eyes in the Night* (1942), *Dead Man's Eyes* (1944), *Union Station* (1950), *On Dangerous Ground* (1951), *Witness in the Dark* (1959), *Wait Until Dark* (1967) and *Blind Terror* (1971).

16. Susan Crutchfield, 'Touching Scenes and Finishing Touches: Blindness in the Slasher Film', in Christopher Sharrett, ed., *Mythologies of Violence in Postmodern Media*, Detroit: Wayne State University Press, 1999, p. 278.

17. In addition to the films under discussion here, blind women are endangered by serial killers in contemporary films such as low-budget horrors like the British *Unmasked, Part 25* (1988), and the American *Silent Night, Deadly Night III: Better Watch Out!* (1989), and psycho-thrillers such as *Blind Fear* (1988) and *Alligator Eyes* (1990). More recent horror films featuring blind *male* characters include *Blind Obsession* (2001) about a blinded cop stalked by two sisters. The concept of blindness as a feminising trait (noted below) is also explored delicately in the Australian drama *Proof* (1992), where a blind man (Hugo Weaving) is menaced by his female housekeeper.

18. Martin F. Norden, *The Cinema of Isolation: A History of Physical Disability in the Movies*, New Brunswick: Rutgers University Press, 1994, pp. 33–8.

19. Ibid., p. 131.

20. Ibid., p. 257.

21. Michael E. Monbeck, *The Meaning of Blindness: Attitudes Toward Blindness and Blind People*, Bloomington: Indiana University Press, 1973, p. 143. Other salient considerations of blindness' cultural and philosophical meanings include Moshe Barasch, *Blindness: The History of a Mental Image in Western Thought*, London and New York: Routledge, 2001; Georgina Kleege, *Sight Unseen*, New Haven, Connecticut: Yale University Press, 1999; and Rod Michalko, *The Mystery of the Eye and the Shadow of Blindness*, Toronto: University of Toronto Press, 1998.

22. Marja Mills, 'Blind Woman Picks Rape Suspect in Lineup', *Chicago Tribune*, 15 January 1990, p. 2C.

23. 'Bar Ends for the Blind in Judiciary', *The Guardian*, 4 February 1991, p. 7; Saundra Torry, 'D.C. Ban on Blind Jurors Raises Question of Rights', *Washington Post*, 19 March 1991, p. B1.

24. James Barron, 'Suspect is Held in Fatal Attack and 3 Others', *New York Times*, 7 August 1989, p. B4; Ronald Sullivan, 'Awaiting Sentence', *New York Times*, 2 November 1991, p. 27. In November 1991, Reyes was sentenced to 33 years to life in prison. In 2002, he confessed – and DNA evidence confirmed – his identity as the 1989 rapist of a Central Park jogger, a crime for which several youths had been wrongfully imprisoned.

25. Crutchfield, p. 282, 284. While Crutchfield mentions as examples *Wait Until Dark, See No Evil, Manhunter, Afraid of the Dark, Jennifer 8* and *Blink*, she examines only *Peeping Tom* and *Proof*, presenting the latter as a drama which copies and critiques slasher-genre themes.

26. Crutchfield, p. 276.

27. A dramatic film exploring this theme, based on a true story, is *At First Sight* (1997); for an analysis see Naomi Schor, 'Blindness as Metaphor', *differences: A Journal of Feminist Cultural Studies*, vol. 11, no. 2, 1999, pp. 76–105. Hong Kong horror film *Gin gwai* (*The Eye*, 2002), and its US remake *The Eye* (2007), explores very similar territory to *Blink*, depicting a young woman whose sight is returned through a corneal transplant, and who inherits the visions of death experienced by her organ donor.

28. The conclusion's radical potential is undercut by the fact that Emma is not 'really' blind and looks set to continue her life as a sighted person.

29. Dennis Giles, 'Conditions of Pleasure in Horror Cinema', in Barry Keith Grant, ed., *Planks of Reason: Essays on the Horror Film*, Metuchen, New Jersey: Scarecrow Press, 1984, pp. 41.

30. Ibid., pp. 42–3.

31. Ibid., p. 44.

32. Ibid., p. 45.

33. As this description suggests, and as other scholars have noted, the role of music in cueing our responses to horror film must not be overlooked and requires further analysis.

34. Susan Crutchfield raises – and, I believe, too quickly counters – this point in discussing blindness in science-fiction films, noting that "their idealisation of blindness leaves these films open to accusations that they are merely metaphorising disability, essentialising the experience of blindness in order to construct a compelling mythology of sighted culture's fears". Crutchfield, 'The Noble Ruined Body: Blindness and Visual Prosthetics in Three Science Fiction Films', in Anthony Enns and Christopher R. Smits, eds, *Screening Disability: Essays on Cinema and Disability*, Lanham, Maryland: University Press of America, 2001, p. 148.

Contributors

Stacey Abbott is Senior Lecturer in Film Studies at Roehampton University. She is the author of *Celluloid Vampires* (2007), and *Angel* (2009) for the TV Milestones series of books. She is the editor of *Reading Angel: The TV Spin-Off with a Soul* (2005), co-editor of *Investigating Alias: Secrets and Spies* (2007), *Falling in Love Again: The Romantic Comedy in Contemporary Cinema* (2009), and *The Cult TV Book* (forthcoming). She has contributed to *The Horror Film: Creating and Marketing Fear* (2005), *Vampires: Myths and Metaphors of Enduring Evil* (2006), *New Zealand Filmmakers* (2007), and *The Routledge Companion to Science Fiction* (2009).

Linda Badley is Professor of English at Middle Tennessee State University. She is the author of *Film, Horror, and the Body Fantastic* (1995), and *Writing Horror and the Body: The Fiction of Stephen King, Clive Barker, and Anne Rice* (1996). She is a co-editor of *Traditions in World Cinema* (2006), and a contributor to the collections *Fantasy Girls: Gender in the New Universe of Science Fiction and Fantasy Television* (2000), *Horror Film and Psychoanalysis: Freud's Worst Nightmare* (2004), and *Caligari's Heirs: The German Cinema of Fear after 1945* (2007).

Mick Broderick is Associate Professor in Media Analysis and Research Coordinator in the School of Media, Communications, and Culture at Murdoch University, in Australia. He is Deputy Director of the National Academy of Screen & Sound (NASS), co-founding editor of *IM: Interactive Media*, and an editorial board member of *ScreenWorks*. He is the author of *Nuclear Movies* (1988), and *Entertaining Armageddon: On Representing the Unthinkable* (forthcoming), and editor of *Hibakusha Cinema: Hiroshima, Nagasaki, and the Nuclear Image in Japanese Film* (1996). He has contributed to the journal *Post Script* and to collections such as *Leaving Springfield: The Simpsons and the Possibility of Oppositional Culture* (2003).

Brigid Cherry lectures at St Mary's University College. She is the author of
Horror (2009), and is a contributor to the collections *Identifying Hollywood
Audiences: Cultural Identity and the Movies* (1999), *British Horror Cinema*
(2001), *Film and Cultural Theory* (2006), *Monstrous Adaptations: Generic
and Thematic Mutations in Horror Film* (2007*)*, and *European Nightmares:
European Horror Cinema Since 1945* (forthcoming). Her work has also
appeared in the journals *Film International*, and *Participations: Journal of
Audience & Reception Studies.*

Ian Conrich is the founding Director of the Centre for New Zealand
Studies, Birkbeck, University of London. He is Editor of the *CNZS
Bulletin of New Zealand Studies*, an Editor of the *Journal of British Cinema
and Television*, an Associate Editor of *Film and Philosophy*, and a Guest
Editor of the *Harvard Review*, *Asian Cinema*, *Post Script*, and *Studies in
Travel Writing*. He is the author of *New Zealand Film – A Guide* (published
in Polish, 2008), *Studies in New Zealand Cinema* (2009), and *New Zealand
Cinema* (forthcoming), and editor or co-editor of eleven books, including
The Cinema of John Carpenter: The Technique of Terror (2004), *Film's Musical
Moments* (2006), and *Contemporary New Zealand Cinema* (2008). He has
contributed to more than 50 books and journals, and his work has been
translated into French, Danish, Polish, Hungarian, and Hebrew, with his
work on the horror genre appearing in collections such as *Trash Aesthetics:
Popular Culture and its Audience* (1997), *The British Cinema Book* (1997),
The Modern Fantastic: The Films of David Cronenberg (2000), *The Horror
Film Reader* (2001), *British Horror Cinema* (2001), *Cauchemars Américains:
Fantastique et Horreur dans le Cinéma Moderne* (2003), *The Horror Film*
(2004), *Contemporary American Independent Film: From the Margins to the
Mainstream* (2004), *Horror International* (2005), *Japanese Horror Cinema*
(2005), *George A. Romero un cinema crépusculaire* (2008), *Seventies British
Cinema* (2008), *The Handbook of the Gothic* (2009), and *Companion to the
Gothic* (forthcoming).

Joan Hawkins is an Associate Professor in the Department of
Communication and Culture at Indiana University. She is the author
of *Cutting Edge: Art-Horror and the Horrific Avant-Garde* (2000), and
a contributor to collections such as *Freakery: Cultural Spectacles of the
Extraordinary Body* (1996), *The Horror Film Reader* (2000), *Defining Cult
Movies: The Cultural Politics of Oppositional Taste* (2003), *The Cinema of
Todd Haynes: All that Heaven Allows* (2007), and *The Cult Film Reader*
(2008).

Matt Hills is Reader in Media and Cultural Studies at Cardiff University. He is the author of *Fan Cultures* (2002), *The Pleasures of Horror* (2005), and *How to do Things with Cultural Theory* (2005). He has been a contributor to the collections *Movie Blockbusters* (2003), *Contemporary Hollywood Stardom* (2003), *Horror Film and Psychoanalysis: Freud's Worst Nightmare* (2004), *The Television Studies Reader* (2004), *The Contemporary Television Series* (2005), *The Lord of the Rings: Popular Culture in Global Context* (2006), *Sleaze Artists: Cinema at the Margins of Taste, Style, and Politics* (2007), *Fandom: Identities and Communities in a Mediated World* (2007), and *The Cult Film Reader* (2008). His work has also appeared in the journals *New Review of Film and Television Studies*, *International Journal of Communication*, *The Velvet Light Trap*, *Social Semiotics*, *Science Fiction Studies*, and the *European Journal of Cultural Studies*.

Ernest Mathijs is Associate Professor of Film Studies at the University of British Columbia. He is the author of *The Cinema of David Cronenberg: From Baron Blood to Cultural Hero* (2008), editor of *The Lord of the Rings: Popular Culture in Global Context* (2006), and *The Cinema of the Low Countries* (2004), and co-editor of *The Cult Film Reader* (2007), *Watching the Lord of the Rings: Tolkien's World Audiences* (2007), *From Hobbits to Hollywood: Essays on Peter Jackson's Lord of the Rings* (2006), and *Big Brother International: Format, Critics, and Publics* (2004). His work has appeared in journals such as *Screen*, *Film International*, *Cinema Journal*, *Social Semiotics*, and *Television and New Media*.

Jay McRoy is Associate Professor and Chair of the Department of English at University of Wisconsin-Parkside. He is the author of *Nightmare Japan: Contemporary Japanese Horror Film* (2008), editor of *Japanese Horror Cinema* (2005), and co-editor of *Monstrous Adaptations: Generic and Thematic Mutations in Horror Film* (2007). He is a member of the editorial board of *Paradoxa*, and his work has appeared in the collections *The Horror Film: Creating and Marketing Fear* (2004), *New Punk Cinema* (2005), *Traditions in World Cinema* (2006), and *Caligari's Heirs: The German Cinema of Fear after 1945* (2007).

Tamao Nakahara is based in San Francisco. Her PhD from University of California, Berkeley, is titled *Bawdy Tales and Veils: The Exploitation of Sex in Post-War Italian Cinema (1949–1979)*. She has contributed to collections such as *Alternative Europe: Eurotrash and Exploitation Cinema Since 1945* (2004).

Angela Ndalianis is Associate Professor in Cinema and Cultural Studies at the University of Melbourne. She is the author of *Neo-Baroque Aesthetics and Contemporary Entertainment* (2004), and *Spectopolis: Theme Park Cultures* (forthcoming), co-editor of *Stars in Our Eyes: The Star Phenomenon in the Contemporary Era* (2002), and *Super/Heroes: From Hercules to Superman* (2007), and editor of *The Contemporary Comic Book Superhero* (2009). She has contributed to the collections *Meta-Morphing: Visual Transformation and the Culture of Quick Change* (2000), *Rethinking Media Change: The Aesthetics of Transition* (2003), *Hop on Pop: The Politics and Pleasures of Popular Cultures* (2003), *The Contemporary Television Series* (2005), *Screen Consciousness: Technology, Cinema, Mind and World* (2006), and *The Essential Cult TV Reader* (forthcoming).

Julian Petley is Professor of Film and Television at Brunel University. He is a Principal Editor of the *Journal of British Cinema and Television*, an editorial board member of *British Journalism Review*, and *Vertigo*, and he has been a Guest Editor of *Index on Censorship*. He is the co-author of *Culture Wars: The Media and the British Left* (2005), and co-editor of *Ill Effects: The Media Violence Debate* (1997, 2001), and *British Horror Cinema* (2001). He has contributed to *The BFI Companion to Horror* (1996), *Agent of Challenge and Defiance: The Films of Ken Loach* (1997), *The Body's Perilous Pleasures: Dangerous Desires and Contemporary Culture* (1999), *Unruly Pleasures: The Cult Film and its Critics* (2000), *Criminal Visions: Media Representations of Crime and Justice* (2003), and *Monstrous Adaptations: Generic and Thematic Mutations in Horror Film* (2007).

Jeffrey Sconce is an Associate Professor in the Department of Radio, Television, and Film at Northwestern University. He is the author of *Haunted Media: Electronic Presence from Telegraphy to Television* (2000), and editor of *Sleaze Artists: Cinema at the Margins of Taste, Style, and Politics* (2007). He has contributed to collections such as *Film Theory Goes to the Movies: Cultural Analysis of Contemporary Film* (1992), *Defining Cult Movies: The Cultural Politics of Oppositional Taste* (2003), *Technological Visions: The Hopes and Fears that Shape New Technologies* (2004), *Contemporary American Cinema* (2006), and *Fandom: Identities and Communities in a Mediated World* (2007).

Angela Marie Smith is Assistant Professor of English at the University of Utah. She has written for the journals *College Literature*, and *Post Script*, and contributed to the collections *The Novel and the American Left: Critical Essays on Depression-Era Fiction* (2004), *Eugenics and American Mass Culture in the Thirties* (2004), and *Contemporary New Zealand Cinema* (2008).

Estella Tincknell is Reader in Media and Cultural Studies at the University of the West of England. She is the joint author of *The Practice of Cultural Studies* (2004), and author of *Mediating the Family: Gender, Culture and Representation* (2005), and *Angels, Demons and Voices: Textual Uncertainties and the Films of Jane Campion* (forthcoming). She has contributed to *p.o.v.*, *Feminist Media Studies*, *Gender and Education*, *Journal of Sociology of Education*, *Journal of European Cultural Studies*, *Journal of Popular Film and Television*, and is on the editorial board of *Body and Society*. She is the co-editor of *Film's Musical Moments* (2006), and has contributed to *New Zealand – A Pastoral Paradise?* (2000), *Lost Highways: The Road Movie Book* (2000), *Reality Television: A Reader* (2003), and *New Zealand Filmmakers* (2007).

Index